Brand Valuation

AF695572

In the new economy where value drivers are shifting from tangible to intangible resources, brands are the most familiar asset. They are well known by consumers, perceived as a critical component of enterprise value, and often motivate large mergers and acquisitions. Yet brands are a complex intangible asset, and their valuation is a difficult task requiring a variety of expertise: legal, economic, financial, sector-specific, and marketing.

Using rigorous methodologies, an analysis of the world of the new economy, and an inquiry into the limits of modern valuation technics, this book offers empirical and theoretical background to the key issue of brand valuation. It provides answers to the many questions that arise when attempting to value a brand: How to understand the origin of brand value? How to assess its value objectively? Why valuations of some brands by consulting firms differ so widely? How to understand that some brands are valued at millions of euros when the companies that own them are losing money?

Brand Valuation explains the economics and finance factors explaining the value and volatility of brands and presents the most commonly used methodologies to value brands, such as the cost methods, the excess earnings approach, the relief-from-royalty method, or the excess revenue approach. The methodologies covered are illustrated with numerous examples, allowing the reader to grasp the advantages and limits of each valuation technique. The book presents the relevant context of brand valuation, including the applicable existing accounting and valuation standards and also discusses the models developed by consulting firms.

Luc Paugam is an Associate Professor at ESSEC Business School, France.

Paul André is a Professor at HEC Lausanne at the University of Lausanne, Switzerland.

Henri Philippe is a Partner at Accuracy in Paris, a corporate finance consulting firm, and teaches finance at the Université Paris-Dauphine, HEC Paris, and École Nationale des Ponts et Chaussées, France.

Roula Harfouche is a Fellow of the Institute of Chartered Accountants in England and Wales and a Partner at Accuracy London, UK.

Routledge Studies in Accounting

For a full list of titles in this series, please visit www.routledge.com

9 **Law, Corporate Governance, and Accounting: European Perspectives**
Edited by Victoria Krivogorsky

10 **Management Accounting Research in Practice**
Lessons Learned from an Interventionist Approach
Petri Suomala and Jouni Lyly-Yrjänäinen

11 **Solvency in Financial Accounting**
Julie Margret

12 **Accounting and Order**
Mahmoud Ezzamel

13 **Accounting and Business Economics**
Insights from National Traditions
Edited by Yuri Biondi and Stefano Zambon

14 **The Nature of Accounting Regulation**
Ian Dennis

15 **International Classification of Financial Reporting, Third Edition**
Chris Nobes

16 **Fraud in Financial Statements**
Julie E. Margret and
Geoffrey Peck

17 **Auditing Theory**
Ian Dennis

18 **Brand Valuation**
Luc Paugam, Paul André, Henri Philippe, and Roula Harfouche

Brand Valuation

Luc Paugam, Paul André,
Henri Philippe, and
Roula Harfouche

Routledge
Taylor & Francis Group
LONDON AND NEW YORK

First published 2016
by Routledge

2 Park Square, Milton Park, Abingdon, Oxfordshire OX14 4RN
711 Third Avenue, New York, NY 10017

Routledge is an imprint of the Taylor & Francis Group, an informa business

First issued in paperback 2018

Copyright © 2016 Taylor & Francis

The right of Luc Paugam, Paul André, Henri Philippe, and Roula Harfouche to be identified as authors of this work has been asserted by them in accordance with sections 77 and 78 of the Copyright, Designs and Patents Act 1988.

All rights reserved. No part of this book may be reprinted or reproduced or utilised in any form or by any electronic, mechanical, or other means, now known or hereafter invented, including photocopying and recording, or in any information storage or retrieval system, without permission in writing from the publishers.

Notice:
Product or corporate names may be trademarks or registered trademarks, and are used only for identification and explanation without intent to infringe.

Library of Congress Cataloging-in-Publication Data
Names: Paugam, Luc, author.
Title: Brand valuation / by Luc Paugam, Paul Andrâe, Henri Philippe, and Roula Harfouche.
Description: New York : Routledge, 2016. | Series: Routledge studies in accounting ; 18 | Includes bibliographical references and index.
Identifiers: LCCN 2016000105 | ISBN 9781138933828 (hardback : alk. paper) | ISBN 9781315677347 (ebook)
Subjects: LCSH: Brand name products—Valuation. | Intangible property—Valuation. | Brand loyalty. | Branding (Marketing)
Classification: LCC HD69.B7 P39 2016 | DDC 657/.7—dc23
LC record available at http://lccn.loc.gov/2016000105

ISBN: 978-1-138-93382-8 (hbk)
ISBN: 978-1-138-61689-9 (pbk)

Typeset in Sabon
by Apex CoVantage, LLC

Contents

Tables and Figures

Tables

Figures

Acknowledgments

This book is based on a translation by John Selman of a book originally published in French in 2014 entitled "Évaluation financière de la marque" (Economica) by Henri Philippe, Luc Paugam, and Delphine Aguilar. The authors acknowledge the financial support of the ESSEC Financial Reporting Centre.

About the Authors

Paul André, PhD, CPA-CA is a Professor at HEC Lausanne. He has been a Professor at ESSEC, University of Edinburgh, HEC Montreal, UQAM, and the University of Ottawa. Paul teaches Financial Statement Analysis and Business Valuation in various programs. His research has focused on financial reporting quality, intangibles, corporate governance, and mergers and acquisitions (M&A).

Roula Harfouche holds an MSc from the LSE and a bachelor's degree from EDHEC Business School. She is a Fellow of the Institute of Chartered Accountants in England and Wales and a Partner at Accuracy London. She has 16 years of experience in business, share, and IP valuations, particularly in dispute contexts.

Luc Paugam, PhD, CFA is Associate Professor at ESSEC Business School. Luc teaches financial accounting and corporate finance in various programs. His research interests focus on issues surrounding financial reporting of intangible assets (goodwill, brands), M&A, and audit. He is a Member of the advocacy group of CFA Society France.

Henri Philippe holds a PhD from the Université Paris-Dauphine, an MBA from Wake Forest University, and is a graduate of ESC Bordeaux. He is a Partner at Accuracy in Paris, a corporate finance consulting firm. He teaches finance at the Université Paris-Dauphine, HEC Paris, and École Nationale des Ponts et Chaussées.

Introduction

After the Second World War, global economic development benefited greatly from the reduction of trade barriers, allowing developed economies to purchase less sophisticated goods and services from developing countries and to concentrate on innovative economic sectors. Progress made in ground and air transport, communications, and medicine resulted in socio-economic development unprecedented in world history. Between 1000 and 1820, GDP per head grew by 50%, and between 1820 and 1950, it grew eightfold. By way of comparison, in a little more than 60 years, between 1950 and 2012, worldwide production increased 16 fold, while the world population was only multiplied by 2.7![1]

Certain economists (e.g., Nakamura, 2004, 2008) explain this explosion by pointing out that, since the 1990s, growth of developed economies has been driven by new forces. In fact, consumer spending changed profoundly during the decade: education and research, medical care, corporate services and social expenses in the wider sense have gradually become key sectors for "developed" economies (In 2006, they made up 33% of US GDP.).

As a consequence of this emergence of new economic sectors, investment in intangible assets since the end of the 1990s (expenditure on research and development, acquisition or creation of software, marketing and organisational change) has reached the same level as that in tangible assets (approximately 10% of US GDP, whereas such investment accounted for approximately 4% of US GDP in 1977). Thus the productive system of modern economies has become generally intensive in intangible assets.[2]

The advent of "intangibility" results from the combination of two major economic forces. The first is the intensification of competition, stimulated by trade globalisation and the deregulation of key economic sectors (e.g., telecommunications, electricity, transport, and financial services). The second force stems from advances in media and information technology, with the emblematic appearance of the Internet. Theorists of "endogenous" economic growth, such as Romer (1990) and Lucas (2002), when explaining the origin of technical progress, recognise the importance of intangible economic assets in the growth process. Intangible assets are synergetic and non-competitive (their use by one individual does not reduce their use by others), have a high initial cost of production and very low marginal costs, and their utilisation can be increasingly protected (e.g., by patents or various means of legal protection).

Newly listed companies illustrate perfectly this shift that occurred in developed economies. Academic research has established that the most recent cohort of initial public offering (IPO) companies (new-list companies) have exhibited progressively higher risks than older IPO companies (e.g., Fama and French, 2004). Companies such as Facebook, which went public in 2012, Twitter (2013), or Criteo (2013), all listed on the NASDAQ stock exchange, are good examples of the recent wave of IPOs. Recent IPO companies tend to show lower profitability, lower survival rates, and higher stock returns and earnings volatility than companies listed prior to 1970. Several arguments have been provided to explain this phenomenon: increasing risk appetite of IPO investors (Brown and Kapadia, 2007) or the fact that companies list their shares at an earlier stage of their life cycle, i.e., before they can demonstrate steady profitability (Ritter and Welch, 2002). More recently, Srivastava and Tse (2015) provided compelling evidence that more recent cohorts of IPO companies adopt and retain operating innovations based on intangible-intensive businesses that lead to higher risks. Since the 1970s, traditional business models based on physical assets have become less distinct and a lesser source of competitive advantage (Zingales, 2000). Thus more recent IPO companies starting their operations are more likely to offer innovative products and customer-centric services and less likely to compete by being cheaper manufacturers of products rapidly becoming commodities. Innovation and the provision of customer-centric services require more intangible inputs such as R&D, information technology, databases, and expert human capital than the manufacture of goods. As a result, future economic benefits from intangible-intensive business models lead to increasing idiosyncratic risks (Comin and Philippon, 2005).

Because of the importance of intangible assets in the economic performance of businesses and thus economies as a whole, it is necessary to measure their value. The most successful companies increasingly need to control their creation of intangible assets. Today, brands or trademarks are probably the intangible assets best known to the general public. As consumers, we experience their influence on our economic decisions every day. Yet a brand is not merely a reference for the consumer; it fulfils numerous functions within a company, for example, by federating employees and ultimately increasing the value of the company's human capital. For many companies, it is also one of their essential assets, the value of which must be estimated to understand the value of the company as a whole.

A brand is a complex intangible asset, and its valuation remains a challenging exercise requiring the use of advanced legal, economic, financial, sectorial, and marketing knowledge. In this context, certain economic players, in particular consulting firms, regularly produce rankings of the value of major international brands. Some standard-setters, for example, the International

Valuation Standards Council (IVSC), the International Organization for Standardization (ISO) or the Association Française de Normalisation (AFNOR) propose methods for valuing intangible assets, including brands. At the same time, we can only be surprised by the volatility of these values.

Overall, the issue of brand value raises numerous questions. How can we understand a brand? Is it even feasible to (seriously) estimate the value of a brand from a financial point of view? How can a brand have value? What should we make of the rankings of brand values that certain firms produce on a regular basis? Are they objective? Are the proposed valuation standards appropriate? How and when should we apply them? How can we understand why certain brands are valued at millions of euros, while their underlying operations make losses? More fundamentally, is today's manager sufficiently well equipped to understand the economic nature of brands and to benefit from the economic environment in which brands now play a major role?

Faced with this flurry of questions, this book aims to provide the knowledge and methods necessary to estimate the value of brands. Applying rigour of method, it aims to shed light on the theoretical and practical problems involved in the valuation of brands. The methods and models of valuation presented are each discussed in turn; their strengths and weaknesses are highlighted and practical illustrations are provided.

This book is therefore intended for a wide audience: financial analysts assessing the impact of brands on the value of companies they follow, managers and those preparing financial statements needing to satisfy the growing fair-value reporting requirements promoted by recent accounting changes, financial auditors needing to analyse and constructively challenge the choices of those preparing financial statements, tax authorities assessing transfer pricing issues involving brands, students wishing to pursue a career in corporate finance or hoping to understand the financial implications of brand value, lawyers involved with protecting brand value, and, finally, managers wishing to control the development and utilisation of the value derived from brands.

Chapter 1, "What Is a Brand?", focuses on defining brands, trademarks, trade names, and other elements associated with marketing-related intangible assets. It explains the nature of a brand and its functions and, in particular, describes its temporal and geographical properties. The economics of intangibles, of which brands are a part, is also analysed. The reader will therefore understand why brands are such complex assets to value. Chapter 2, "Brand Value", explains the origins of brand value, introduces the fundamental principles involved in brand valuation, and provides an initial glimpse of intrinsic brand valuation models. These first two chapters define brands and the many issues associated with them (economic, marketing, and legal) and introduce the key financial concepts required for their valuation.

Chapter 3, "Brands and Accounting Standards", describes recent developments in the financial reporting of intangible assets and brands. Indeed, much of the financial information necessary for brand valuation is to be found in financial reporting. Thus international standards (International Financial Reporting Standards or IFRS and International Accounting Standards or IAS) as well as UK accounting standards relating to brands are explained in this chapter. The rules for reporting intangible assets (initial recognition on the balance sheet and subsequent value monitoring) and their consistency with respect to brands are analysed.

The five chapters that follow are devoted to approaches and specific methods of brand valuation. First, three distinct intrinsic valuation methodologies are developed: the "Excess Earnings Method" (Chapter 4), the "Revenue Premium Method" (Chapter 5), and the "Relief-From-Royalty Method" (Chapter 6)—which is based on a mix of intrinsic and market approaches. Next, the "Market-Based Approach" (Chapter 7) and the "Cost-Based Approach" (Chapter 8) are presented. All these methods are illustrated and discussed. These methods are currently the principal references for brand valuation.

In Chapter 9, "Brands and Valuation Standards", the standards put forward by international organisations, such as the IVSC or ISO, or national ones such as AFNOR, are discussed in detail. This chapter explains the needs for standard-setting in respect to brand valuation, as well as the main methodological references available today.

Using the methods presented in Chapters 4 to 8, Chapter 10, "*Ad Hoc* Valuation Models", discusses the specific approaches adopted by a number of international consulting firms (e.g., Interbrand, BrandEconomics, and BrandFinance) in their annual brand league tables. This chapter will allow the reader to compare the advantages and disadvantages of each of these models and to place them in the broader context of the consistent set of methods defined in Chapters 4 to 8.

Beyond purely methodological aspects, the last chapter, "Volatility of Brand Values", analyses a brand's economic characteristics and discusses the impact of synergistic phenomena, network effects, non-exclusivity, and intangible asset risk on the value of brands. At the end of Chapter 11, the reader will understand why a brand is an asset with a necessarily volatile value. We also provide food for thought on how to improve brand valuation models.

This book is the result of more than 15 years' professional experience acquired in various contexts and countries in the field of financial consulting, brand valuation, academic research on intangible assets, their characteristics and their valuation, and, finally, teaching valuation and financial reporting in various academic institutions, including the École Nationale des Ponts et Chaussées, ESSEC Business School, HEC Paris, and Université Paris-Dauphine. This book aims to harness this varied experience, expertise, and skill set to satisfy the expectations and requirements of managers, consultants, lawyers, academics, and students with respect to brand valuation.

Notes

1. See Maddison (2007) and the macroeconomic statistics of the IMF and the World Bank. See also: The IP Commission Report (2013) "The Report of the Commission on the Theft of American Intellectual Property", p. 17 available at: http://www.ipcommission.org/ (accessed 26 December 2015).
2. These may be defined as non-financial assets, sources of future benefits but without physical substance.

References

Brown G. and Kapadia N. (2007), "Firm-Specific Risk and Equity Market Development" *Journal of Financial Economics,* Vol. 84, pp. 358–388.

Comin D. and Philippon T. (2005), "The Rise in Firm-Level Volatility: Causes and Consequences" *NBER Macroeconomic Annual*, Vol. 20, pp. 167–201.

Commission on the Theft of American Intellectual Property (The) (2013), *The IP Commission Report—The Report of the Commission on the Theft of American Intellectual Property*, The National Bureau of Asian Research, May.

Fama E.F. and French K.R. (2004), "New Lists: Fundamentals and Survival Rates" *Journal of Financial Economics*, Vol. 73, pp. 229–269.

Lucas R.E. (2002), *Lectures on Economic Growth*, Harvard University Press, Cambridge, MA.

Maddison A. (2007), *The World Economy: A Millennial Perspective/Historical Statistics*, OECD, Paris.

Nakamura L. (2004), "A Trillion Dollars a Year in Intangible Investment and the New Economy" *Federal Reserve Bank of Philadelphia's Paper, in* Hand J.R.M. et Lev B., *Intangible Assets: Values, Measures, and Risks*, Oxford University Press, Oxford, UK, pp. 19–47.

Nakamura L. (2008), "Intangible Assets and National Income Accounting", *Working paper* No 08–23, Research Department, Federal Reserve Bank of Philadelphia.

Ritter J.R. and Welch I. (2002), "A Review of IPO Activity, Pricing, and Allocations" *Journal of Finance*, Vol. 57, pp. 1795–1828.

Romer P.M. (1990), "Endogenous Technical Change" *Journal of Political Economy,* Vol. 98 (5), pp. 71–102.

Srivastava A. and Tse S.Y. (2015), "Why Are Successive Cohorts of Listed Firms Persistently Riskier" *Working paper.*

Zingales L. (2000), "In Search of New Foundations" *Journal of Finance*, Vol. 55, pp. 1623–1653.

1 What Is a Brand?

Brands are at the heart of corporate life. They are of course of interest to those outside of companies, to consumers, and are also increasingly of interest to financial analysts who monitor companies and to banks that finance their business. Inside a company, a brand is an asset that unites employees, used mainly by the marketing and communication departments, but also of interest to strategic, financial, legal, and accounting management.

In addition to the numerous parties for whom brands are important, brands raise a wide range of issues, and there is uncertainty surrounding how to define them and what makes them valuable for a company. Before examining how brand value is created in the next chapter, we first explore exactly what constitutes a brand.[1]

The objective of this chapter is to show that a brand is a complex asset and therefore particularly challenging to value. This complexity is due to a number of factors. Section 1 explains the differences between a brand and other legal terms (such as trademark) and demonstrates that a brand gives its owner legal rights and is in this respect an asset of the company which may, under certain conditions, be *recognised* on its balance sheet. Nonetheless, a brand is a very specific asset to which the entire company has access but that may have many uses, which will vary from one brand to another (Section 2). Section 3 illustrates a second level of complexity: the scope of a brand can never be clearly defined because it evolves over time. Finally, Section 4 reminds us that a brand is an intangible asset that obeys the rules of the economy of intangibles, the overriding principles of which directly impact brand value.

1. A Brand Is a Right and an Asset

There is sometimes confusion as to what constitutes a brand. It is therefore important to define what we refer to as a "brand" and how it differs from other associated terms such as "trademark", "trade name" or even "service mark".

Trademarks consist of legally protected visual elements such as names, colours, shapes, words, or symbols used to differentiate a good or a service and fuel consumer demand. A trademark, or a trade name, is generally considered to be a bundle of legally defined property rights that can be defended in court. In the United States, a trademark is a *brand name* that has been registered with the US Patent and Trademark Office. To be recognised as such, a trademark must perform a distinguishing function to allow the source of goods or services to be identified. Registration of a *brand name* as a trademark affords the owner of that trademark legal recourse if someone else uses that name.

From an economic standpoint, a brand is a wider concept and consists of a set of attributes that are attached to a particular identity and are perceived to be associated with future economic benefits for the entity that controls the brand. A brand is not limited to a trademark but also refers to formulas, recipes, or trade dress and can be seen as a consistent pool of interrelated assets. The term "trademark" has a legal origin, whereas the term "brand" is used in marketing and finance to designate a larger bundle, usually consisting of a trademark associated with other intellectual property rights (Haigh and Knowles, 2004). The term "brand" is relevant to business decision makers, whereas the use of the term "trademark" is relevant in court. From a valuation perspective, we will use the term "brand" to refer to this pool of assets and to refer to its valuation as a whole.

A brand is therefore a collection of markers or signs providing visual, auditory, or even olfactory identification of goods or services. A brand may appear as a word, an expression, an acronym, a series of numbers, a slogan, a visual symbol, a colour, a melody, or a form. This list is long and not exhaustive. Think of the famous Nike "swoosh", the stylised "*M*" of McDonald's, and the signature sound of BMW in its TV advertisements. Each one is a perfectly distinctive brand marker. Moreover, most brands use a combination of these markers to ensure they are clearly differentiated, for example, a word written in a particular graphic style combined with a specific colour. Yet a brand is not limited to the single sign that conveys it: by virtue of this sign, it is an expression of an identity. For the consumer, a brand expresses the identity of the products and services provided by the company, indeed the identity of the company itself. For example, the "apple" logo of Apple Inc. has become synonymous with technological products with streamlined design and refined ergonomics.

1.1. A Brand Is a Right . . .

If these signs have a monetary value, it is because the brand represents a bundle of rights. According to the World Intellectual Property Organization (WIPO), "A trademark is a distinctive sign that identifies certain goods or services as those produced or provided by a specific person or enterprise".[2] As defined in the US Trademark Act of 1946 (the Lanham Act), a trademark is "any word, name, symbol or device or any combination thereof [used by someone to] identify and distinguish his goods, including a unique product, from those manufactured or sold by others and to indicate the source of the goods". Legally, therefore, a trademark constitutes a company's exclusive right to utilise a particular sign to designate its products or services and to authorise a third party to use this sign in return for payment. It is precisely because this right is exclusive and, therefore, it can be assigned or licensed, that it has a monetary value.

This right is generally acquired through registration of the *brand name* in a national brand registry. The registration of *trademarks* in the United Kingdom is achieved through the UK Intellectual Property Office and lasts ten years, after which it must be renewed to preserve the owner's rights. Various forms (signs) may be registered: for example, a name, a colour or a combination of colours, a slogan, a piece of music, or a smell. Registering a brand guarantees that it cannot be used by another entity without its owner's agreement.

Registration of a Smell Trademark

Unconventional trademark forms such as sounds, touches, or smells open opportunities to reach consumers differently and therefore offer economic potential to businesses. Smells are strongly associated with memory and can trigger instantaneous consumer responses. In the United Kingdom, in order to achieve smell mark registration, the smell must meet the requirement of "graphical representation" and must not result from the nature of the good itself. For example, an application by Chanel to register its well-known No. 5 fragrance as a smell mark in the United Kingdom was unsuccessful, as the scent of the perfume was indistinguishable from the product. However, some smell mark descriptions have been successfully registered, such as the smell of the Sumitomo Rubber Co, a global tyre and rubber company based in Japan, which applied to register "a floral fragrance/smell reminiscent of roses as applied to tyres."

In certain countries, such as the United States, for example, it is not necessary to register a brand to obtain exclusive use of it: a company that can demonstrate an extended usage of certain signs to designate its products obtains the exclusive of use of these signs. Registered brand names are identifiable by the symbol ® (*registered*), and the initials ™ (*trademark*) indicate a commercial brand that is not necessarily registered. However, this is not the case in the United Kingdom or other countries such as France, where only registered brands enjoy legal protection. However, intellectual property rights are not always respected.

Risks Associated with Intellectual Property in the United States

A report published in 2013 by the Commission on the Theft of American Intellectual Property estimates the total impact of intellectual property theft suffered by the United States at more than $300 billion a year, i.e., approximately the annual level of American exports to Asia. This figure includes not only loss suffered from brand infringement but also from infringement of patents, trade secrets, and copyrights. This estimate is approximate, because the effects are complex and may be direct or indirect, making the exact amount difficult to quantify: loss of earnings in certain sectors (sales, jobs, and additional legal expenses), loss of tax revenue for the United States and additional administrative expenditure to enforce existing laws, problems of quality, confusion in the minds of consumers, and a drag on economic growth due to reduced motivation to add value through creation and innovation.

In the particular case of brand infringement, the principal source of loss is counterfeiting. This can affect all types of products: shoes, mobile phones, medication, computers, cigarettes, cosmetic products, household appliances, automobile parts, etc. The report refers to the particular case of an "Apple store", which opened completely illegally in 2011 in the Chinese city of Kunming (a city of six million inhabitants). The store bore all the distinctive signs of the Apple brand, from the wooden tables to the staff's T-shirts. The employees themselves thought they were working for the California company, which was simply unaware of the existence of the store. Counterfeiting also affects celebrities. For instance, according to the *Wall Street Journal*, there were in 2015 nine trademarks registered under the name Taylor Swift in China, three of which are owned by individuals other than Ms. Swift. Unauthorised Taylor Swift products include fake perfume and pirated autographed guitars. In China, the right to a trademark is based on who files first, regardless of other factors such as celebrity (Burkitt and Abkowitz, 2015).

When a consumer purchases a counterfeit product, the true owner of the brand foregoes the revenue from the sale. This reasoning potentially overestimates the loss of revenue, because the consumers who purchase counterfeit products, often at low prices and in locations suggesting that they are not authentic, would not necessarily all purchase these products at their true price. Nonetheless, online sales platforms such as eBay, Craigslist, or Amazon now potentially provide widespread access to counterfeit products and may induce buyers to think that the genuine article is simply being sold off cheaply. The indirect costs for manufacturers can also be significant, because counterfeit products often do not meet quality standards and requirements, which can harm the brand.

The Commission's report emphasises the important role played by China in intellectual property theft. The report cites a 2009 survey showing that 37.7% of the US companies surveyed attributed theft of intellectual property to the Chinese market.

1.2. . . . That Can Be an Asset for the Company

A brand is a right for the company. It can therefore be considered an "asset" in financial terms. Logically, this asset could be shown in the company's accounts. A brand constitutes part of the company's wealth and, accordingly, could be "recognised" as such on its balance sheet.

However, a brand is different from other assets, and accounting standards require a certain number of criteria to be met before it can be recognised on a company's balance sheet, as for any physical asset. Accounting standard-setters have laid down many conditions for the recognition of brands in a company's accounts. Brands are in fact intangible assets with characteristics that are hard to reconcile with the traditional accounting principles of prudence and verifiability. Thus it is difficult to distinguish the value of a brand from that of the company's other assets (its technology and its know-how, for example—branded medicines are a good case in point).

This is a common difficulty for most intangible assets (brands, know-how, patents, and intellectual property). As a result, accounting standard-setters have defined a number of criteria which must be met for it to be appropriate to recognise intangible assets on a company's balance sheet. For example, under IFRS a brand is an asset subject to the provisions of IAS 38 "Intangible Assets", which outlines the accounting treatment of intangible assets. According to this standard, an intangible asset must meet three conditions: (i) it must be "identifiable", (ii) it must be "controlled" by the company, and (iii) it must represent a "source of future economic benefits". An asset is considered identifiable if it can be separated or divided from the entity and can be transferred; licensed, rented, or sold individually or together with related assets; or arises from contractual or other legal rights (IAS 38.12). A company controls an asset if it has access to the future economic benefits derived from this asset and has the means to restrict access by third parties to these future benefits. Finally, future economic benefits associated with an intangible asset do not only consist of future revenue generated by this asset, but may also reflect future cost savings that this asset may generate.

However, meeting these criteria is not sufficient to be able to recognise a brand in a company's financial statements. Under IAS 38, two more conditions must be met to be able to capitalise an intangible asset on the balance sheet: first, it must be probable that the expected future economic benefits attributable to the asset will flow to the entity that is entering the asset in its accounts (and not to a third party) and, second, the cost of the asset must be reliably measurable. For many brands, this last requirement is often difficult to satisfy.

There are two possible cases:

- The brand is developed internally. The expenses linked to its creation are difficult to separate from the total amounts spent on developing the business as a whole. For a brand generated internally, the only costs directly attributable to the brand and consequently recorded on the balance sheet are generally those of its registration as a legal property right. These costs are minor and not representative of the economic value of the brand. That is why the accounting value recorded on the balance sheet is usually much lower than the value of an internally developed brand.

- The brand is acquired (separately or through a business combination). In this case, the cost of the brand is easier to estimate. In the case of mergers or acquisitions of companies, IFRS 3 "Business Combinations" requires the buyer to allocate the purchase price to the various assets acquired and liabilities assumed. This allocation is done on the basis of their *fair values*.[3] In this context, the brand is generally considered a significant acquired intangible asset and is therefore valued independently so that it may be recorded at its fair value on the buyer's balance sheet.[4]

As we have seen, IAS 38 makes a distinction between the criteria for the existence of an intangible asset and the criteria under which it may be recognised for accounting purposes. Thus under international accounting standards, brands created internally exist (obviously), but can rarely be recognised on the company's balance sheet. Nevertheless, these brands, which are not recognised in the companies' financial statements because their development costs are not sufficiently measurable or separable from other costs, may possess considerable economic value and constitute strategic intangible assets for the company. Moreover, other companies may be willing to pay considerable sums to acquire these brands, which would then be recorded on the buyer's balance sheet.

For accounting purposes, only one type of brand (those acquired) is generally recorded on companies' balance sheets. But it is very often brands developed internally that have the highest value. Thus the Coca-Cola, Apple, McDonald's, or Harley Davidson brands do not appear on the balance sheets of these four groups; only brands acquired over the years are recognised in financial statements.

To illustrate this, Table 1.1 shows the fixed assets of the company Barbara Bui. This company, listed on Euronext Paris, operates in the world of ready-to-wear women's luxury clothing and accessories. In the company's annual report, management explains that it protects its brands in the various countries in which it operates (the group generated 53% of its revenues outside France in 2014). However, although a strong brand is a key value driver in the luxury industry, the consolidated balance sheet of Barbara Bui includes no brands.

Nonetheless, financial reports indirectly enable outsiders to know the level of investment companies make in their brands through their marketing expenses, which can often be seen in the accounts (although some highly

Table 1.1 Details of fixed assets on the balance sheet of Barbara Bui (2013–2014)

Thousands of Euros		*2014*	*2013*
Goodwill		–	–
Intangible assets (net values)		626	1,254
	including brands	–	–
	including leasehold rights	*556*	*1,152*
	including software	*70*	*102*
Tangible assets		3,428	4,029
Financial assets		1,071	1,084
Total		**5,125**	**6,367**

Source: Barbara Bui annual report, 2014.

Table 1.2 Top-ten S&P 500 firms by advertising expense in 2014

Rank	*Company Name*	*Advertising Expense ($ million)*
1	Procter & Gamble Co	9,236
2	Ford Motor Co	4,300
3	Coca-Cola Co	3,499
4	Amazon.com Inc.	3,300
5	AT&T Inc.	3,272
6	Pfizer Inc.	3,100
7	Google Inc.	3,004
8	Estée Lauder Co	2,840
9	Walt Disney Co	2,800
10	Johnson & Johnson	2,600

Source: Compustat.

valuable brands can be created with limited marketing expenses). Table 1.2 ranks the top-ten S&P 500 companies (the 500 companies with the largest market capitalisations in the United States) by their level of advertising expense.

Procter & Gamble dedicates, by far, the largest budget to marketing and advertising, with an annual advertising expense for 2014 of more than $9 billion. Ford Motor Co, the second company by advertising expense spent "only" $4.3 billion for advertising in 2014. Not surprisingly, all the companies in this ranking are well known by consumers and own global brands.

In order to obtain a more systematic view of advertising budgets, Table 1.3 shows advertising expenses of the S&P 500 companies grouped by sector over the period 2004 to 2014. To make the comparisons meaningful, advertising expenses are shown as percentages of operating profits

Table 1.3 Advertising expenses by sector (Global Industry Classification Standards)—S&P 500 companies from 2004 to 2014

		Mean	*Median*	*Standard Deviation*
Energy	*As % of EBIT*	0.04%	0.00%	0.23%
	As % of TA	0.00%	0.00%	0.01%
	As % of Capex	0.03%	0.00%	0.24%
Materials	*As % of EBIT*	1.72%	0.00%	5.82%
	As % of TA	0.25%	0.00%	0.94%
	As % of Capex	8.87%	0.00%	33.20%
Industrials (e.g., Capital Goods, Transportation)	*As % of EBIT*	2.58%	0.00%	6.90%
	As % of TA	0.32%	0.00%	0.82%
	As % of Capex	8.85%	0.00%	22.69%
Consumer Discretionary (e.g., Automobiles, Consumer Durables)	*As % of EBIT*	29.04%	17.68%	52.95%
	As % of TA	4.21%	2.34%	5.94%
	As % of Capex	136.33%	48.52%	281.22%
Consumer Staples (e.g., Food & Staples Retailing, Household & Personal Products)	*As % of EBIT*	9.17%	24.19%	411.29%
	As % of TA	5.33%	2.92%	7.75%
	As % of Capex	153.52%	87.50%	214.30%
Health Care (e.g., Pharmaceuticals, Biotechnology & Life Sciences)	*As % of EBIT*	2.19%	0.00%	6.05%
	As % of TA	0.32%	0.00%	0.84%
	As % of Capex	17.63%	0.00%	46.78%
Financials (e.g., Banks, Insurance, Real Estate)	*As % of EBIT*	0.65%	0.00%	21.65%
	As % of TA	0.10%	0.04%	0.28%
	As % of Capex	32.93%	13.34%	52.32%
Information Technology (e.g., Software & Services, Technology Hardware & Equipment)	*As % of EBIT*	5.93%	0.55%	52.44%
	As % of TA	0.82%	0.11%	1.44%
	As % of Capex	28.41%	3.98%	75.41%
Telecommunication Services	*As % of EBIT*	18.78%	10.25%	1092.19%
	As % of TA	1.05%	1.05%	0.90%
	As % of Capex	15.49%	14.72%	17.25%
Utilities	*As % of EBIT*	0.00%	0.00%	0.00%
	As % of TA	0.00%	0.00%	0.00%
	As % of Capex	0.00%	0.00%	0.00%

TA = Total Assets, EBIT = Earnings Before Interest and Tax, Capex = Capital Expenditure (this represents funds used for additions to property, plant, and equipment, excluding amounts arising from acquisitions).

Source: Compustat.

(EBIT), total assets (TA), and capital expenditure on tangible fixed assets, such as property, plant, and equipment (Capex).

Certain economic sectors include companies that invest massively in advertising: on average, advertising expenditure accounts for 29% of the

Consumer Discretionary sector EBIT, 19% of the Telecommunication Services sector EBIT and 9% of the Consumer Staples sector EBIT. The Information Technology and Telecoms sectors also spend relatively large sums on advertising. In contrast, the Utilities, Energy, Industrials, Materials, and Financials sectors spend less than 5% of their EBIT on advertising. Companies in business-to-business sectors (e.g., Industrials, Materials) generally rely less on a strong brand than companies in business-to-consumer sectors (e.g., Consumer Discretionary or Consumer Staples).

It is also striking to observe that in some sectors, average annual advertising expenses exceed capital expenditure on tangible fixed assets. Companies in the Consumer Discretionary and Consumer Staples sectors spend on average 136.3% and 153.5%, respectively, of Capex on advertising alone. This shows that their business models rely more intensively on the value of intangible assets than on plant and equipment.

Table 1.4 shows the relationship between marketing expenditure as a percentage of total assets, operational performance (return on total assets), future sales growth, and future market performance (market return).

Table 1.4 splits S&P 500 companies into ten groups of equal size (deciles) based on the level of their marketing expenditure. We can draw two conclusions from the table:

- There is a positive relationship between the level of marketing expenditure and the operating performance of the companies (ROA) in the same year: the more a business spends on advertising, the more profitable it tends to be and vice versa (although caution is required, because correlation does not necessarily imply causality).

Table 1.4 Relationship between advertising expenditure, operational performance, sales growth, and market return (for S&P 500 companies with positive advertising expenditure from 2004 to 2014)

Deciles	*Ad (% TA)*	ROA_t	ΔROA_{t+1}	$\Delta Sales_{t+1}$	$Return_{t+1}$
1	0.06%	2.60%	-4.69%	1.87%	9.05%
2	0.13%	6.15%	-1.85%	4.61%	5.05%
3	0.41%	13.28%	0.49%	6.45%	11.82%
4	0.77%	13.21%	-1.23%	5.97%	11.28%
5	1.36%	12.17%	-0.68%	5.30%	8.99%
6	1.95%	14.44%	1.67%	5.78%	11.82%
7	2.64%	12.29%	-0.65%	5.24%	4.49%
8	3.72%	13.79%	-0.91%	5.83%	10.75%
9	5.82%	15.12%	-3.19%	3.50%	4.93%
10	11.49%	20.59%	0.37%	7.68%	11.34%

Ad (% TA) = advertising expenditure as a percentage of total assets, ROA = EBIT over total assets, ΔROA_{t+1} = annual change in ROA in year t + 1, $\Delta Sales_{t+1}$ = sales growth in year t + 1, and $Return_{t+1}$ = market return in year t + 1. Table 1.4 reports the median for each decile.

Source: Compustat.

- Companies with the lowest advertising expense levels tend to have the lowest future sales growth (+1.9%), whereas those with the highest advertising expense levels tend to have the strongest future sales growth (+7.7%). However, the link between the level of advertising expenditure and future operational (ΔROA_{t+1}) and financial performance ($Return_{t+1}$) is not direct. There is, therefore, no clear correlation between the level of advertising expenditure and future performance.

Both legal and accounting standards specify cases where a brand may be treated as an asset in accounting terms—that is, a part of corporate assets that may be acquired or sold. However, legal and accounting standards are silent on how brands generate "future economic benefits" or "cost savings". Therefore, understanding the different functions of a brand is essential to identifying the source of brand value.

2. An Asset with Multiple Uses

2.1. For Consumers

When making economic decisions, consumers depart from the rational decision-making models described by neoclassical economic theory and follow heuristics. Human beings do not process information about the price and properties of dozens of apparently similar products, such as shampoo or detergent. Instead, they rely on mental shortcuts to increase the efficiency of their decision-making process. Nobel laureate Herbert Simon coined the term "bounded rationality", which is the idea that when individuals make decisions, their rationality is limited by the information they have, the cognitive limitations of their minds, and the time available to make the decision (e.g., Simon, 1997). Herbert Simon argued that in real situations, people make decisions on the basis of heuristics, or mental shortcuts, rather than rule-based optimisation methods. Brands facilitate these mental shortcuts.

However, the importance of brands to consumers is not limited to speeding up decision making. One way brands influence consumers is through their "personalities". According to consumer behaviour research, brands, like people, have a personality, i.e., a set of associated human characteristics. For instance, Absolut Vodka could be described as a cool, hip, contemporary 25-year-old. Conversely, Stolichnaya could be described as an intellectual, conservative, older man (Aaker, 1997). Brand personality allows consumers to express their own self and ideal self or specific dimensions of the self (e.g., Belk, 1988; Malhotra, 1988; Kleine *et al.*, 1993). Research suggests that the greater the similarities between the actual or projected (ideal) self and those that characterise a brand, the greater the preference for the brand (Sirgy, 1982; Malhotra, 1988). Aaker (1997) suggests five reliable dimensions to measure brand personality:

- Sincerity: genuine, kind, family-oriented, thoughtful;
- Excitement: carefree, spirited, youthful;
- Competence: successful, accomplished, influential, a leader;
- Sophistication: elegant, prestigious, pretentious; and
- Ruggedness: rough, tough, outdoors, athletic.

Generally, from the consumer's perspective, a brand serves a number of functions which depend on the product or service category. Kapferer (2012) focuses on eight:

1. Identification: a brand allows consumers to identify products quickly. A brand is a means for consumers to differentiate between products that might otherwise be difficult to distinguish (brands of detergent or tyres);
2. Practicality: a brand allows consumers to remember their past choices and thus simplifies their future decisions;
3. Guarantee: a brand offers a certain assurance as to the quality of the product or service provided;
4. Optimisation: a brand allows consumers to identify the best product within a category;
5. Personalisation ("badge"): by using a brand's products, consumers may feel they enhance their image, acquire status, and believe they are asserting their personalities or membership in a specific group;
6. Playfulness ("hedonistic excitement"): a brand is a source of pleasure for the consumer because it is attractive and offers experimental rewards;
7. Continuity: the relationship of familiarity and intimacy of consumption of a particular brand over the long term creates satisfaction;
8. Ethical: a brand potentially creates satisfaction linked to the responsible behaviour of the brand in relation with society (corporate social responsibility, citizenship, sustainability). For instance, the coffee brand Malongo promotes high ethical behaviour. The company claims, "Our unique quality culture is the basis for our values: preservation of the roasted coffee, respect for the men and women growing the plants, plus customer satisfaction".[5]

According to Kapferer (2012), the first two functions are mechanical and relate to the definition of the brand, i.e., a recognised marker in order to facilitate consumer choice. The next three functions reduce the perceived risk of the product or service. The last three functions are associated with a pleasure dimension. Therefore, a brand is indispensable for consumers and serves a number of functions. Consequently, consumers agree to pay a higher price to purchase a branded product. A brand is also a source of many other economic advantages, in particular for the company owning it.

2.2. For Companies

A brand allows a company to distinguish itself in the marketplace or differentiate its products from those of its competitors. A company's brand portfolio allows it to convey an attractive image of its products or services in order to influence consumer behaviour and encourage consumers to choose its products or services over those of its competitors.

With the help of its brands, a company addresses potential consumers concerning its products/services, the identity of which are expressed in the brand. Depending on the market that a product serves, a brand targets specific categories of consumers who can be defined by geographical, social, economic, gender, age, or professional sector criteria. The strategic positioning of a brand aims to convey an appealing image of the product to target consumers. It is all about establishing a clear position that is sufficiently narrow that consumers can recognise themselves in it, but sufficiently broad so as not to exclude too large a part of the potential consumers of the product, and, above all, perfectly adapted to the product or service characteristics. In particular, depending on their positioning, brands may convey an image of quality, prestige, innovation, tradition, responsibility, or enjoyment.

Regardless of its positioning, a brand must enable the company that owns it to differentiate itself from the competition in order to win consumer preference. This is not only a matter of presenting the virtues of the brand itself, but also of differentiating the product from what is currently on offer: to demonstrate its superiority so it is seen as higher quality, more prestigious, less expensive, younger, multipurpose, or more environmentally friendly. The aim of a brand is to bolster corporate revenue by increasing sales volumes or sales prices and sometimes both.

For a company, a brand is also a means of creating customer loyalty. It guarantees consumers specific and stable product features and, in particular, real or perceived quality. Gaining consumer loyalty involves both a certain continuity of the brand's positioning and a capacity to change as the world changes and customer behaviour evolves. It is almost always cheaper for a company to keep existing customers loyal than to attract new ones. This explains the long-term importance of brand strategy. Developing loyalty is especially vital for recurrent purchases, such as food products, for which consumers do not study the market before each purchase but rather head unthinkingly towards their usual products. In this respect, the brand brings a promise of continuity and even allows a company to save on costs (of acquiring new customers or maintaining its current customer portfolio).

Financially, it is possible to measure the effects of a brand when it increases sales prices or sales volumes. Measurement is more challenging when a brand has a defensive function and allows a company to preserve its customer portfolio or to maintain it at a lower cost. A brand is also a complex asset because its analysis involves two other critical factors: a brand evolves in space (brand scope is not limited), and its economic properties fluctuate over time with its life cycle.

3. An Asset That Evolves in Space and Time

3.1. Brand Scope

A brand represents the identity of the business and/or that of its products. Thus a consumer buys a "Porsche", which designates both the brand of the manufacturer and that of the product sold. Sometimes a company's different product lines are identified by distinct brands, with the company also possessing its own "umbrella" brand. For example, Unilever distributes Amora, Carte d'Or, Dove, and Lipton products, amongst others. The scope of a brand is therefore variable.

Several different types of brands need therefore to be identified according to their scope and how they are used. Dubois *et al.* (2013) distinguish six categories of brands according to their scope:

- The product-brand: the name of the brand is associated with a single product. Badoit and Nutella are examples of brand-products. In its most extreme form, the brand and the product may become inseparable when the product only exists under a single brand name and, having no generic name, can only be designated by the name of the brand (e.g., Kleenex or Hoover). We refer to it as a "branduct".
- The range-brand: the brand brings together a collection of homogeneous products. The image of the brand or of one of the products in the range then extends to the others. This allows all the products to benefit from the image of the key products of the brand, but it also represents a risk for the entire range in the case of a single product's failure. Nivea (skincare) or Amora (sauces) are range-brands.
- The line-brand: the brand includes a collection of products for homogeneous consumers. The Abercrombie & Fitch ready-to-wear group states "we want to market to cool, good-looking people".
- The umbrella brand: a single brand includes different products for diverse consumers. Thus Philips brings together different household electrical products for healthcare, consumer lifestyle and lighting, etc. The umbrella brand can be the *mother-brand* when associated with product-brands.
- The guarantee-brand: in conjunction with another brand, the guarantee-brand offers additional security and authenticity. Danone is such a security-brand for Danette.
- The designer label: this indicates an original creation which is not associated with a product but with specific know-how or style. Designer labels exist in the luxury sector, for example, Yves-Saint-Laurent and Louis Vuitton.

Companies currently tend to reduce the size of their brand portfolios so that their product ranges gain in clarity and secondary products benefit from the brand image of their flagship products. In the long term, this reduction also limits the costs of maintaining numerous brands, although in the short term, rebranding requires investment. Thus, in 2012, the Accor group realigned its hotel brands around the Ibis brand, henceforth available in several ranges: with the brands' Etap Hotel and All Seasons disappearing in favour of the new labels Ibis Budget and Ibis Style. The large retailer Carrefour followed a similar path a few years earlier when it replaced its Champion brand with Carrefour Market.

This variable scope makes brand value analysis complicated. The future economic benefits attributable to the umbrella brand must be distinguished from those attributable to the product-brand. Similarly, it may be complex to allocate to each of these brand types the possible cost savings resulting from a stable customer portfolio.

As well as the impact they have on value, marketing issues also influence the level of complexity of brand valuation. In particular, the wider the scope of a brand, the more difficult its valuation proves to be. It is possible to value a brand-product based on cash flows from sales of the product. This proves more complicated when valuing an umbrella brand and even more so in the case of a guarantee-brand, for which it is difficult to distinguish the contribution of the brand-product from that of the guarantee-brand. For example, is the price premium observed for a Danette chocolate dessert compared with the price of a no-brand chocolate dessert attributable to the Danette brand or to the guarantee-brand Danone? More generally, when valuing a brand, what scope should be used to value this brand? Its current scope or all the territories that the brand might address? In most cases, the context of the valuation provides the answers to these questions. For example, in a transaction, the buyer will probably only be ready to pay for the current brand scope, but he will also be interested in how the brand will be able to develop under its control.

The shifting scope of brands creates another difficulty. Brand valuation is based on a methodology (a technique) initially developed for traditional financial assets, such as shares or bonds, which may be bought or sold on the market. The possibility of selling a brand, however, decreases as its scope widens. Thus, whereas a brand-product can easily be sold (together with its business), the sale of an umbrella brand, although theoretically possible, remains highly unlikely. As for a designer label, it cannot be sold in isolation because it is embedded in specific know-how. It cannot therefore easily be valued by applying methods used to value a conventional financial asset.

3.2. The Life Cycle of a Brand

The economic scope of a brand evolves in space, but its strength and vitality also fluctuate over time. The brand life cycle from Dubois *et al.* (2013), reproduced in Figure 1.1, can be used to analyse these fluctuations over time.

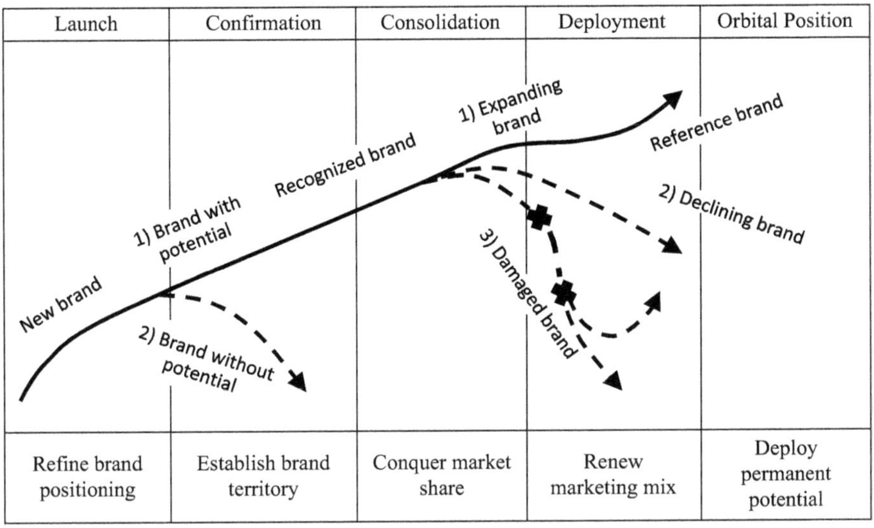

Figure 1.1 The brand life cycle.

Source: Dubois *et al.* (2013).

A brand's life cycle begins with its launch. In this first phase, the company defines the brand's strategic positioning and differentiates it from what the market currently offers. For example, the launch of the car brand Dacia by Renault in the early 2000s aimed to position it as a low-cost vehicle, simple and reliable.

Once introduced into the market in the second phase, the brand must confirm its staying power despite changes in fashion and natural novelty appeal. This means protecting ground already gained. If the brand lacks the potential to last and expand, it will rapidly decline and probably disappear. If it has real potential, its influence could grow substantially.

In the third phase, referred to as consolidation, the brand will seek to expand its territory and gain market share by attracting a larger customer base. Thus Renault increased the number of Dacia car models by introducing the small Logan saloon in 2004, followed by the compact Sandero in 2007, the Duster SUV in 2010, and the Dokker leisure activity vehicle (LAV) in 2012.

The fourth phase, deployment, implies developing the brand by renewing and extending its range of products or services. This is a crucial phase, because it can give the brand solid market prestige or, in the case of failure, lead to its disappearance. Successful deployment will allow the brand to hold a larger position in the market. If, however, extending the range blurs the clarity of the brand's positioning, the brand will decline, losing its power of differentiation for the consumer. Blockbuster, the brand owned by the American-based provider of home movie and video game rental services Blockbuster LLC, is an example of failure to adapt the services covered by the brand to a fast-changing market environment. The company filed for bankruptcy in 2010, unable to face the competition of companies such as Redbox or Netflix. Inappropriate strategic choices by management may also harm the brand. The Nokia mobile phone brand suffered due to untimely strategic choices by management, who missed the smartphone revolution at the beginning of this century. Growth through acquisition may also lead to brand portfolio reorganisation. For example, after American Match.com acquired the European online dating site Meetic in 2011, it did not use the Match.com brand in France because it was less well known in the country than Meetic.

The fifth and final phase, described as the orbital position, sees the brand reach the status of reference-brands, of icons, which enjoy considerable and positive renown among a large consumer segment. Its acquired strength allows constant renewal without loss of visibility. The brand now forms part of the collective cultural heritage of consumers. Certain brands, although no longer used commercially, may even retain their influence. This is the case of the Pan Am brand, created by airline company Pan American World Airways in 1930. The airline went bankrupt in 1991, but the brand is still well known and was purchased by another airline company in 1992 and by a railway company in 1998.

A brand's life cycle has a particular effect on the probable economic life of the brand. As we will see later, there is a direct correlation between a brand's value and its useful economic life. Most brands do not live forever. A brand's useful economic life depends on where it is in its life cycle. To illustrate this, Table 1.5 shows possible brand life expectancies at different points in the life cycle.

Table 1.5 shows the importance of brands' life cycles to their economic value. The figures given are only suggestions. The characteristics of each brand must be analysed in detail before assessing its probable economic life expectancy.

The life cycle of a brand makes value analysis somewhat complicated: a brand in its launch phase cannot be treated in the same way as a brand in orbital position. Choosing the most appropriate valuation method also depends upon where the brand is in its life cycle. Obviously it would be meaningless to use reproduction cost (see Chapter 8) for a century-old brand. On the other hand, projected cash flows based on forecast information cannot be used for a young brand with uncertain development potential. Once again, it is vital to know the context in which the brand is being valued.

Table 1.5 Brand life cycle and probable life expectancy (LE)

Launch	*Confirmation*	*Consolidation*	*Deployment*	*Orbital Position*
LE < 2–5 years	[2–5 years] < LE < [8–10 years]	[8–10 years] < LE < [20–25 years]	LE > [20–25 years]	LE = Indefinite

Life Expectancies Used in Accounting Brand Valuations

The audit firm Ernst & Young (2007) published a study of brand valuations carried out in 61 business combinations of companies listed on the SBF 120 index of the Paris Stock Exchange that took place in 2006. Half the brands were considered to have a finite lifespan, and the average lifespan for brand valuation was assumed to be just over six years.

Smith and Richey (2013) carried out a similar study on American companies. Their results are shown in Table 1.6.

Table 1.6 Lifespans used in accounting valuations of brands in the United States

	Trade Name	*Brand Name*	*Trademark*
Software and associated services	[0.2–15 years]	[4–10]	[1–30]
Other services	[1–15]		[1.5—indefinite]
Electronics	[3.5–8]		[3–10]
Medical	[5–23]	[10–12]	[8—indefinite]
Telecom equipment	[3.7—indefinite]		[1.5–23]
Laboratory equipment	[1–20]	[8]	[10]
Management and public relations	[5–10]	[10]	[1—indefinite]
Healthcare	[10–37]		[5–20]
IT and hardware	[2.5–4.5]	[5]	[4.9–16]
Average (excluding indefinite lifespans)	**[3.5–16.6]**	**[7.4–9]**	**[4–18.2]**

Note: There is in fact a difference between the distinctive elements describing a brand which can be protected (*trade name*, *trademark*) and the general set of characteristics valued by the customer (*brand*).

Source: Smith and Richey (2013).

4. An Economy of Intangibles

A brand is an extremely complex asset; its financial impact for a company is not always easy to identify. A brand may affect a company's business model in many ways: it enables the company to sell more and at higher prices, and it can also sometimes generate cost savings. This first level of complexity is exacerbated by the fact that a brand shifts in space (its scope) and in time (its life cycle).

In order to understand these complexities, it is essential to examine how the economy of intangibles in general operates. This presentation will shed a new light on the difficulties of brand valuation and suggest ways to overcome them.

Knowing how brands work does not explain how they create value for a company differently than other assets. To understand this, we must view a brand as an intangible asset. We review and discuss in this section several arguments developed by Lev (2001) regarding the specificities of intangible assets versus tangible assets. Of course, cost-benefit analysis can be applied to intangible assets as well as to other assets, but what makes them different is the specific relationship between costs and benefits in their case. This results from five characteristics that have an impact on the value of any intangible asset. Two of these characteristics have a positive impact, three a negative one.

4.1. *Absence of Conflict in Intangible Resources*

The use of intangible assets is never exclusive, contrary to physical tangible assets. For example, a factory line dedicated to manufacturing a certain product cannot be used to manufacture something else at the same time. Tangible assets and human and financial resources are all subject to the same restriction; they can only be used for one thing at a time. At best, a factory can manufacture several products on a single production line, but not simultaneously. In the same way an employee (or a robot) can be polyvalent but cannot do everything at once. This means that an "opportunity cost" arises when such resources are put to a particular use: the possibility of using them for something else is foregone. There is therefore a conflict between the different ways in which a resource can be used. The rarer and more expensive the resource, the greater the conflict.

A brand, however, can be everywhere at once. It can be put to various uses in different places at the same time. Using a brand on television does not prevent a company from promoting the brand in other media in the same instant. In this respect, the opportunity cost of intangible assets is generally non-existent or insignificant at most.

The zero opportunity cost of intangible assets generally goes hand in hand with virtually inexistent marginal deployment costs. These assets often require massive initial investment to create them (*sunk costs*), but their marginal cost thereafter is low or non-existent. The cost of manufacturing a drug is therefore totally disproportionate to the cost of developing it. Similarly, putting a brand on a yoghourt pot implies no additional production cost; the most significant cost was already incurred when the brand was created and launched.

In addition, intangible assets sometimes benefit from favourable scale effects. The value of a tangible asset often decreases over time after the initial investment, and further investment is needed to replace the ageing asset. Due to the number of Ford Model T's produced, their selling price decreased to the satisfaction of customers who could—at last—buy a car. For some intangible assets, however, any further expense after the initial investment may have a cumulative effect and increase exponentially the value of that investment. Expenditure on R&D, training, and advertising are cumulative: any new expenditure can amplify the impact of previous expenditure. The strategic repositioning of a brand towards new products can promote and enhance awareness of existing products.

With no conflict in their use, virtually no utilisation costs, and favourable scale effects, the only limit to the development of an intangible asset is the size of its market.

4.2. The Network Effect

The value that can be placed on intangible assets depends in many cases on the role they play in the network economy. This type of economy works on a simple principle: the value of a network increases as its size increases. What is the point of having a telephone if no one else has one? It becomes more worthwhile as the number of users grows, until it becomes imperative to have one.

In this type of economy, success breeds success, and a company which manages to dominate a network will become more successful and more dominant as the network expands. This is due not so much to first mover advantage as to the ability to define and impose a standard (on customers, regulators, or competitors). VHS, PCs, and credit cards are prime examples.

Within these networks, "tipping points" can be observed, whereby a sometimes minor advantage can create a swing of the customer network towards a company's solution or product. In this case, it is noticeable that, because the costs of switching products can be high (e.g., training costs, costs of translating archives), small advantages can make all the difference, and technically superior products may not be able to make their mark due to the switching costs for customers being prohibitive.

The existence and importance of physical networks (telecom infrastructure, for example) cannot be denied, but intangible assets are just as crucial. It is often these assets that lie at the centre of networks (technology, brands, patents). Intangible assets also often enable ecosystems to develop around physical networks. The various ecosystems around mobile phones come to mind, first and foremost apps and iTunes, which have developed tremendously due to the iPhone.

4.3. Managerial Inefficiency

Several factors limit the development of these economic models based on intangibles. The first, already referred to earlier, is the size of the underlying markets. A second is the difficulty of managing intangible assets. It is easy to determine the utilisation rate of a machine, a tool, or a factory, but the question is more complicated where human resources are concerned and meaningless in the case of brands.

The information systems and management tools normally used by managers to run their operations are not adapted for managing intangible assets. They are actually designed to control physical assets with the aim of optimising the use of more or less scarce resources. In the economy of intangibles, these tools and systems, which underpin accounting and management control systems, become irrelevant and poorly suited to managing intangible assets.

Given the absence of specific tools and performance indicators for managing intangible assets, managers have great difficulty operating these assets on a day-to-day basis with traditional methods. It is therefore not surprising to conclude that existing models should be rethought for intangible assets to be managed effectively.

4.4. Non-exclusivity and Vague Property Rights

The absence of conflict in the use of intangible assets has a drawback. As we have seen, physical assets typically have strictly defined functions, and their property rights are not open to doubt. Intangible assets, on the other hand, do not have exclusive use: they can be (and generally are) used for several things at the same time. Moreover, it is not easy to identify how certain intangible assets are used or what impact they may have. For example, training received by an employee from his company forms part of his intellectual capital, which he puts to use every day in his work. He will take this intellectual capital with him if he leaves the company. It therefore enhances his value in the employment market and, ironically, makes him more likely to leave. The company promotes its employees' personal development and in so doing makes it easier for them to leave the company.

The question arises as to ownership of certain intangible assets. Ownership is (almost always) clear for physical assets: it is obvious who is using a machine or a piece of tooling at a given moment. Ownership is much trickier to define for certain intangible assets. Note, for example, how difficult it is for countries to tax intangible assets and the business they generate.

This phenomenon applies to most intangible assets and is referred to in relevant literature as "spillover", whereby certain players appropriate the benefits of these assets without owning them. An obvious example is technological innovation that falls into the public domain after several years or can suffer from counterfeiting or reverse engineering. When an innovative product is launched, it is therefore up to the brand to educate consumers on the use and technical features of the product. But copies then appear which have taken advantage of this information and learnt from the mistakes of the market entrant. A good example is the Apple iPod, which was not the first to the market but which succeeded brilliantly in creating an ecosystem around its brand and around another intangible asset: the iTunes system. More recently, Apple, which is not the first entrant in the market of streaming music for a fixed subscription payment, is competing against more established companies such as Spotify.

This question can be analysed in terms of "asset specificity" (as used by Williamson, 1983): assets (tangible and intangible) may be designed for a more or less specific use and are more or less redeployable by a third party. In this sense, all intangible assets are not easily redeployable. As an example, if a brand is launched and fails, it is difficult and costly to turn back. A brand is thus an asset that can be considered very "specific." Similarly, a failure or an error in communication can be expensive. Thus Abercrombie & Fitch, the ready-to-wear brand for adolescents, suffered a severe setback in 2013 as the result of an aggressive advertising campaign that was perceived by some stakeholders as offensive.

4.5. High-Risk Intangible Assets

In general, intangible assets are considered to be higher-risk assets than physical or financial assets. Lev (2001) demonstrates this based on the fact that intangible assets are at the heart of every creative or innovative process. Several finance studies have shown corroborative evidence of this phenomenon (Srivastava and Tse, 2015). In fact, many empirical studies clearly demonstrate a significant link between innovation and risk. This correlation is due to the low success rate of innovative projects: a few succeed, the vast majority fails.

The comparison with innovation is also important here, because innovation has a life cycle akin to that of brands described previously. At their outset, innovative projects rely on intangibles (e.g., technology, concept, patents, and brands). As development gets underway, the share of tangible assets increases and overall project risk falls. Because the physical assets called into play (e.g., plant and machinery) typically have a resale value, the overall risk of the project diminishes gradually; if the project fails, these physical assets can at least be sold in secondary markets.

We therefore intuitively tend to think of intangible assets as high-risk assets, because the total investment, or *sunk costs*, can be lost in case of failure. Total loss is less common in the case of tangible assets that can often be sold on a secondary market. In general, the more an asset is "specific", the more difficult it is to sell to a third party and the more risky it is. Conversely, later on, developed intangible assets can actually protect their holders against negative events and reduce the company's risk profile. In adverse economic circumstances, exploiting a strong brand can mitigate negative consequences for the firm. For instance, during the global financial crisis, Hermès focused on its core strategy rather than on reducing prices: produce expensive but high quality classic items with a very long useful life.

Consumers are willing to buy one special and timeless item supported by a strong brand, even during a recession.

This generalisation concerning risks inherent to intangible assets must be qualified in respect of brands. It is, of course, true that certain intangible assets can be considered very specific and thus not easily redeployable, and they may be at the heart of risky innovative projects. This is not, however, the case for all intangible assets, some of which may be unspecific and easily redeployable in mature and therefore low-risk businesses. This is especially true for brands. Despite the airline going bankrupt, the Pan Am brand was thus able to be sold by its owner.

4.6. Assets Without an Organised Market

In general, tangible assets are hardly or not at all specific, and they can be traded in fairly organised and competitive markets. This is not the case for intangible assets, which cannot be traded on organised markets.

However, intangible assets are not compatible with trading on an organised market, because it is difficult to establish contracts suitable for such assets. Assets traded on organised markets are those for which "complete" contracts can be easily established. A contract is said to be complete when the parties to the contract can specify in advance all their actions under the contract. A complete contract can therefore be written for a real estate asset (sale or lease agreement). Everything that can happen during the life of the asset can be foreseen (e.g., how future charges are allocated, whether the property can be sublet). In the case of an intangible asset (know-how or technology, for example), it is often impracticable or impossible to imagine all possible future events and therefore to establish a contract properly setting out future rights and obligations in respect to the asset. Who could have imagined that Caterpillar, a well-known brand of construction equipment and machinery, could one day become a brand of ready-to-wear clothing? Franchise agreements demonstrate, however, that it is nevertheless possible to draw up effective contracts relating to intangible assets whilst limiting their scope.

Consequently most intangible assets are not traded in organised markets, which are ill-equipped to deal with such incomplete contracts. This absence of organised trading has an important consequence: the absence of reliable information on the value of these assets and their level of risk.

Conclusion

In this first chapter, we have sought to define the nature of a brand, to explain its role for a company and consumers, to show how and where it appears in the accounts, and to understand its multiple facets. Brands are at the heart of strategic, legal, accounting, and economic issues. Brand valuation requires a good command of all these subjects and an understanding of how the various aspects of a brand interact with each other. Due to the complexity of brand valuation, a valuer needs more than ever to embrace the managerial, economic, legal, accounting, and financial dimensions of a brand. The next chapter deals with the origins of brand value.

Non-Financial Measurement of Brand Performance

The aim of a brand is to convey to consumers a positive and attractive image of companies to encourage consumers to buy the companies' products and services. As a result, brand efficiency is usually measured from the viewpoint of the consumer rather than that of the financier.

The first indicator is the degree of *brand recognition*: this is the ability of a consumer to recognise a brand from its logo, slogan, or a description of its features or certain of its characteristics. Recognising the brand does not necessarily mean being able to link it to the related product.

Brand awareness measures how present the brand is in the mind of the consumer. It implies not only recognising the brand but being able to identify the corresponding product. There are different levels of brand awareness. Awareness is "aided" if a consumer recognises a brand from a list given to him or her; it is "unaided" if the consumer names a brand when asked what brands he or she knows for a given product or sector. Awareness is known as "top of mind" when a brand name is the first one given spontaneously by the consumer.

Brands can be described as more or less strong depending on how well known they are by consumers. However, being known is not enough; for a brand to fulfil its role of promoting a product, it must be perceived positively and in a manner consistent with the product's market position. Brand image is the way a brand is perceived by present and potential consumers and the characteristics they associate with it: a good or poor quality product, good or poor value for money, a masculine or feminine product, classic or quirky, for young or older people, etc. Companies obviously try to develop a positive brand image and one which is appropriate to the targeted market segment.

There are many indicators to measure brand performance. By way of example, Figure 1.2 shows brand awareness for sporting goods brands in the United States.[6]

In addition to brand awareness, the characteristics of a brand referred to earlier can also be measured.

Is this a really satisfactory way to assess brand performance? This is the consumers' viewpoint, which potentially neglects the impact of the brand on the company. With a valuation, we turn the tables: how does the brand benefit the company? Brand value gives a different vision of brand performance.

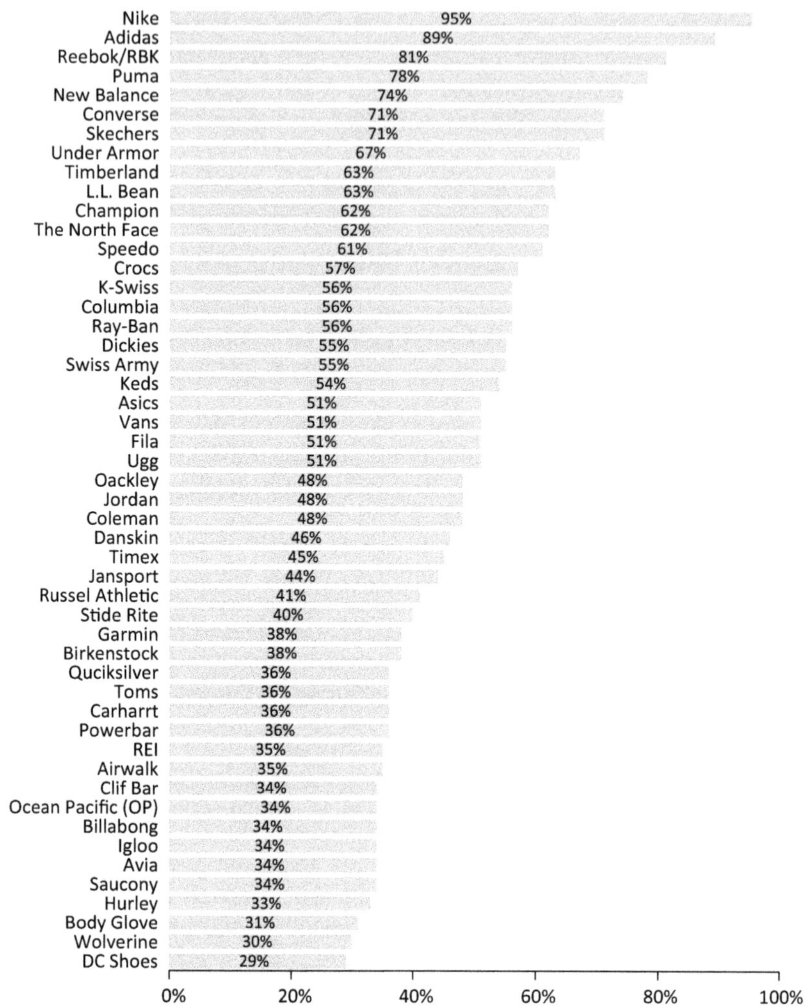

Figure 1.2 Sporting goods brands ranked by brand awareness amongst US consumers in 2014.

The percentage shows the brand awareness for the top-50 brands amongst US consumers. Source: www.statista.com (accessed 26 December 2015).

Notes

1. See also Kapferer (2007, 2012).
2. WIPO Publication No. 848(E), *Guidelines on Developing Intellectual Property Policy for Universities and R&D Institutions in African Countries.*
3. Fair value is the "price that would be received for selling an asset or paid to transfer a liability during a transaction arranged between market participants at the measurement date" (IFRS 13).

4. Accounting standards applicable to brands, and the registration and evolution of the value of brands on companies' balance sheets, will be further discussed in Chapter 3.
5. http://www.malongo.com/uk/company/malongoinjustafewwords-presentation.php?page=139 (accessed 26 December 2015).
6. http://www.statista.com/statistics/305790/brand-awareness-top-50-sporting-goods-brands-united-states/ (accessed 26 December 2015).

References

Aaker J. (1997), "Dimensions of Brand Personality" *Journal of Marketing Research*, Vol. 34, pp. 347–356.

Belk R.W. (1988) "Possessions and the Extended Self" *Journal of Consumer Research*, Vol. 2 (September), pp. 139–168.

Burkitt L. and Abkowitz A. (2015), "Taylor Swift Hits Fakes in China" *The Wall Street Journal*, Thursday July 23, p. 17.

Commission on the Theft of American Intellectual Property (The) (2013), *The IP Commission Report—The Report of the Commission on the Theft of American Intellectual Property*, The National Bureau of Asian Research, May.

Dubois P-L. Jolibert A. Gavard-Perret M-L. and Fournier, C. (2013), *Le Marketing, Fondements et Pratique*, 5th edition, Economica, Paris.

Ernst & Young (2007), *PPA: quels impacts sur vos résultats futurs? Analyse des acquisitions du SBF 120* Ernst & Young, Paris La Défense.

Haigh D. and Knowles J. (2004), "How to Define Your Brand and Determine Its Value?" *Marketing Management* Vol. 13 (3), pp. 22–28.

IASB (2004), *International Financial Reporting Standards (IFRS) No. 3: Business Combinations,* IASC Foundation Publications Department, London.

IASB (2008), *International Accounting Standards (IAS) No. 38: Intangible Assets,* IASC Foundation Publications Department, London.

IASB (2011), *International Financial Reporting Standards (IFRS) No. 13: Fair Value Measurements,* IASC Foundation Publications Department, London.

Kapferer J.N. (2007), *Les marques, capital de l'entreprise: Créer et développer des marques fortes*, 4th edition, Eyrolles, Paris.

Kapferer J.N. (2012), *The New Strategic Brand Management: Advanced Insights and Strategic Thinking,* 5th edition, Kogan Page, Croydon, UK.

Kleine R.E. Kleine S. and Kernan J.B. (1993), "Mundane Consumption and the Self: A Social-Identity Perspective" *Journal of Consumer Psychology* Vol. 2 (3), pp. 209–235.

Lev B. (2001), *Intangibles: Management, Measurement, and Reporting,* Brookings Institution Press, Washington DC.

Malhotra N. K. (1988), "Self Concept and Product Choice: An Integrated Perspective" *Journal of Economic Psychology,* Vol. 9, pp. 1–28.

Simon H. (1997), *Administrative Behavior: A Study of Decision-Making Processes in Administrative Organization,* 4th edition, The Free Press, New York.

Sirgy J. (1982), "Self-Concept in Consumer Behavior: A Critical Review" *Journal of Consumer Research*, Vol. 9 (December), pp. 287–300.

Smith G.V. and Richey S.M. (2013), *Trademark Valuation*, 2nd edition, John Wiley & Sons, New York.

Srivastava A. and Tse S.Y. (2015), "Why Are Successive Cohorts of Listed Firms Persistently Riskier" *Working paper.*

Williamson O.E. (1983), "Organization Form, Residual Claimants, and Corporate Control" *Journal of Law and Economics*, Vol. 26 (2), pp. 351–366.

World Intellectual Property Organization (WIPO) Publication No. 848(E) (2005), *Guidelines on Developing Intellectual Property Policy for Universities and R&D Institutions in African Countries,* World Intellectual Property Organization, Geneva, Switzerland.

2 Brand Value

> If you attempt to assess intrinsic value, it all relates to cash flow. The only reason to put cash into any kind of investment now is that you expect to take cash out—not by selling it to somebody else, that's just a game of who beats who—but by the asset itself . . .
>
> Warren Buffet, Berkshire Hathaway Annual Meeting, 1997[1]

Valuation consists of estimating a value, i.e., a theoretical price, at which well-informed and consenting market participants would accept to exchange an economic asset. Neoclassical economic theory assumes that individuals are rational and make choices with the aim of best satisfying their preferences. Investors collate and analyse available information to conduct monetary exchanges in the market and thereby increase their satisfaction ("utility" in economic terminology). The price arrived at is the expression of this available information on which market participants build their expectations.

An asset is worth what it will earn for its owner, and its value is therefore equivalent to the present value[2] of the expected future economic benefits deriving from it. This is a fundamental idea for any valuer and was explained by Fisher (1930):

> [t]he value of any property, or right to wealth, is its value as a source of income and is found by discounting that expected income. [. . .] The principle is, of course, not confined to bonds. It applies in any market to all property and wealth—stocks, land, buildings, machinery, or anything whatsoever.

The logic is relatively straightforward. An asset (including a brand), is worth what it will earn, but a major issue remains: the real "value" of an asset can never be measured. All that can be measured is the price at which an asset is exchanged in transactions that have taken place. Samuelson (1983) explained moreover that "no one has ever seen the right price or right value on land or on sea. They exist only on economists' bookshelves." The aim of valuation is therefore to assess the price at which an asset can potentially be exchanged based on the most reasonable (probable) expectations of future income, as if the asset were traded on an organised market.

This principle works reasonably well when applied to a uniform group of assets frequently traded in the market, such as shares or bonds. This type of market, with its virtually continuous transactions, provides access at any time to operators' expectations of the future economic benefits of the traded assets. Valuation models can thus be regularly recalibrated. This is, however, not the case for brands which are unique and rarely traded on organised markets.

The valuation method that derives most directly from the idea of "intrinsic" or "fundamental" valuation is termed the discounted cash flow (DCF) method. It implies assessing the future economic risks and benefits which may be obtained from owning and operating an economic asset. It is this approach, referred to by Warren Buffet earlier, which this chapter introduces, because brands are seldom traded at public prices. Where such transactions do exist, however, the "potential price" calculated by the valuer can be compared with the expectations of other economic agents. The main task of the valuer will therefore be to collate and understand the information relevant to the valuation of a brand. The quality of his work will depend largely on how realistic the assessment of the economic risks and benefits based on that information is.

Chapter 1 explained why brands are a particular type of asset. As we have seen, this has important consequences when valuing them. At least three characteristics of brands can in fact be distinguished:

- Brands are idiosyncratic. By definition, the aim of a brand is to differentiate a product or a service from the product or service of competitors. It is therefore difficult to compare one brand with another. Each brand has to be analysed in depth and caution should be exercised when comparing different brands.
- Brands have a high degree of synergy with other assets. Having a brand will enhance the profitability of industrial equipment, distribution channels, or technologies and *vice versa*. The Intel Inside brand thus increases the value of the technology of the processors it promotes. It is extremely difficult to isolate the economic benefits associated with a brand from the economic benefits associated with other assets. A brand is "intertwined" in a given set of assets, and the value of the whole is greater than the sum of the value of the individual constituent parts. Brands are rarely sold alone, but more often exchanged as part of a set of assets (for example, with a distribution channel, with one or a number of technologies, or a manufacturing process). What would the Coca-Cola brand be worth without its famous recipe?
- Brands have a complex risk profile. The probability that the initial investment in a brand will be lost is high. For every well-known and

hugely successful brand, there are numerous unsung failures where the investment failed to bring the hoped for renown. The value of a brand varies considerably over time and can fluctuate exponentially during certain periods of its life cycle. Its initial value is low because probability of failure is high. On the other hand, once the brand has become established, the risk diminishes significantly and the value of the brand increases sharply. There remains always, however, a risk that even a well-established brand can disappear. Certain events can result in a brand disappearing (for example, the Enron financial scandal destroyed the Arthur Andersen brand held by the accounting firm of the same name). More typically, brands age and need to be maintained periodically (for example, by redesigning a company logo or repositioning a brand in order to refresh it). As a consequence, the way the future economic benefits associated with a brand are spread out in time is strongly affected by its life cycle. At its creation, the future economic benefits of a brand are a long way off and risky (uncertain). Once the brand is established, the economic rewards it brings will be high compared with the initial investment.

As we have seen, a central issue which the valuer needs to take into account in order to address these questions is the context in which the valuation is being carried out. It is essential to determine for whom the brand is being valued and with what objective. Expectations of the future cash flows deriving from the brand and the associated risks will vary according to the context and the economic agent for whom the brand is valued. The brand owner will have different expectations from a potential buyer who will wish to reposition the brand and use his own distribution channels to operate it. It is vital that the context of the valuation be understood before any valuation is undertaken.

Section 1 introduces, with the aid of a simple case study, the basic notions of intrinsic or fundamental valuation using the discounted cash flow method. These notions will be examined in greater detail in Chapters 4 to 8. Section 2 contains an overview of the different types of valuation approaches and methods, and Section 3 contains a discussion of the various contexts in which brand valuation takes place.

1. Valuing a Brand

Valuation basically uses two elements: first, an estimation of the future economic benefits associated with an asset and, second, an assessment of the degree of uncertainty or risk that surrounds those benefits. Let us consider the imaginary case of Fashion 22, a company that manufactures ready-to-wear sportswear. The company owns a factory and its balance sheet is shown in Table 2.1.

Table 2.1 Balance sheet of Fashion 22 at 31/12/20×4

Fixed assets Plant Machinery	20	**Equity**	80
Working capital (WC) Stock Trade debtors Trade creditors	60	**Net debt**	0
Capital employed	80	**Invested capital**	80

The sportswear market does not require any particular know-how or technology. However, the use of a brand in this sector considerably improves expected financial performance. Let us assume that after several years of marketing investment, Fashion 22 has a brand. This brand was developed internally and is not recognised on the balance sheet. To keep things simple, let us also assume that the sportswear market has zero growth; in other words, we can say that Fashion 22 and its competitors share a market the size of which does not change.[3]

Before estimating the value of the Fashion 22 brand, we shall first estimate the value of the company as a whole. Second, we shall examine the relationship between the value of the brand and the value of the company, which will enable us to understand the links between the two values.

As we explained in the introduction to this chapter, valuation models are based on discounting the future benefits derived from an asset. The value of "Fashion 22" is therefore equal to the sum of the future free cash flows that the company will generate (cash flows from operations minus investments in operating working capital and non-current operating assets or free cash flows to be distributed to lenders and shareholders). This can be formally expressed by equation (1):

$$V_t = \sum_{\tau=1}^{\infty} \frac{E_t\left[F_{t+\tau}\right]}{(1+k)^{\tau}}, \qquad (1)$$

where V_t = value of the company at date t;
$F_{t+\tau}$ = free cash flows generated in year $t + \tau$;
$E_t[.]$ = expectation operator (mathematical);
k = discount rate, a function of the increasing uncertainty of future cash flows $F_{t+\tau}$.

Equation (1) is considerably simplified if we assume that the free cash flows $F_{t+\tau}$ have a constant growth rate designated as g (Fashion 22's market has zero growth rate, therefore, g = 0). By applying the formula of the sum of the terms of a geometric sequence with a common ratio (1+g)/(1+k) (with k > g) we can simplify equation (1) and express it as follows:

$$V_t = \sum_{\tau=1}^{\infty} \frac{E_t\left[F_{t+\tau}\right]}{(1+k)^{\tau}} = \sum_{\tau=1}^{\infty} \frac{F_t \times (1+g)^{\tau}}{(1+k)^{\tau}} = \frac{F_t \times (1+g)}{(k-g)} = \frac{F_t}{k}, \quad (2)$$

where F_t = free cash flows in year t.

To value Fashion 22, we must therefore determine the free cash flows generated by the company (F_t). The income statement of the company is shown in Table 2.2.

Let us assume that the company's working capital requirement is stable and that each year capital expenditure is roughly equivalent to depreciation. This means that the company maintains its production facilities without increasing capacity. Both these assumptions are consistent with an assumption of zero growth. The free cash flows generated by the company in year 20X4 (see Table 2.3) can then be calculated from the net operating profit after tax (NOPAT), the same as net profit in the earlier example, because Fashion 22 has no debt.

Because the free cash flows F_t are known (F_t = 8), and g is assumed to equal zero, we only need to know the appropriate discount rate in order to calculate the value of Fashion 22. The discount rate is an increasing function of two elements: (1) the uncertainty (risk) of future cash flows and (2) the time value of money, i.e., the risk-free rate. Risk (element (1)) corresponds

Table 2.2 Income statement of Fashion 22 for year 20×4

Revenue	1,000
Cost of sales	(800)
Gross profit	**200**
Operating expenses	(150)
Depreciation	(38)
Operating profit	**12**
Finance costs	–
Taxation	(4)
Net profit	8

Table 2.3 Cash flows generated by Fashion 22 for year 20×4

NOPAT	8
Depreciation	38
Capital expenditure	(38)
Variation in working capital	–
Free cash flows	8

in finance to the uncertainty of future flows.[4] The discount rate is also called the cost of capital and reflects the rate of return that a financial investor would require to finance a business with an equivalent risk. This financial investor is deemed to hold a diversified portfolio of assets and to require a return only on the part of the risk he cannot eliminate by diversification (Markowitz, 1952). The box that follows sets out some important concepts underlying the notion of cost of capital.[5]

Cost of Capital

Capital providers who finance risky businesses require a higher rate of return than they do for a risk-free business, as risky assets offer a higher degree of uncertainty.

This rate of return is also called the cost of capital. It consists of two parts:

- the time value of money, i.e., the interest rate for riskless assets;
- an economic risk premium: "the price of risk".

Cost of Capital = *Time Value of Money* + *Economic Risk Premium*

If the company has no debt, the only capital providers are the shareholders, and the cost of capital is strictly the same as the cost of equity.

Cost of Equity = *Cost of Capital* if *Debt* = 0

If the company has debt, the inherent riskiness of its assets is unchanged. The economic risk premium and thus the cost of capital do not change. The risk borne by the shareholders, however, increases, because debt is senior to equity, and there is a possibility that the company may not be able to repay its debt. It is therefore logical that the shareholders demand a higher return (the "financial risk premium") in addition to the two elements previously referred to.

Cost of Equity = *Cost of Capital* + *Financial Risk Premium* if *Debt* > 0

In our example, let us assume that Fashion 22's cost of capital is 10%. This is the return required by a provider of capital investing in the company. It is based solely on economic risk, because the company is debt free (see Table 2.1).

Applying equation (2), the value of Fashion 22 is equal to

$$V_t = \frac{F_t \times (1+g)}{(k-g)} = \frac{8 \times (1+0\%)}{(10\% - 0\%)} = 80\,. \qquad (3)$$

The value of the company is 80. This value is the same as the book value of the capital employed, which excludes its brand from the assets recogniserecognized on its balance sheet. The company's intrinsic value is therefore equal to its book value. What is more surprising in this first example is that the brand owned by Fashion 22 adds no value to the company. We shall see that this conclusion is logical given the assumptions made concerning the company's economic performance.

To understand the relationship between the value of a company and that of its brand, it is helpful to refer to the concept of economic rate of return, often referred to as ROCE (*return on capital employed*).[6] The economic rate of return reflects the return earned by a business. It corresponds to the ratio between net operating profit after tax and capital employed. The performance of a business over a year (net operating profit after tax) is compared to the amount of capital necessary to fund that performance (capital employed).

In our example, Fashion 22 yields a rate of return of 10% (= 8 / 80), i.e., a profitability strictly identical to its cost of capital. The return *obtained* by investors is identical to that *required*. The economic profit, in other words, profit remaining after remunerating all factors of production (book capital employed), is zero.

In our example, the existence of a brand does not enhance the operational performance of the company (for example, by allowing the market to command higher prices) and therefore in all logic does not enable the company to earn excess or super profits. The market value of the capital employed is thus the same as its accounting value. As a result, the brand, which has no impact on the company's financial performance, has no value from a financial point of view.

Let us now assume that Fashion 22 differentiates itself from its competitors due to its brand. The brand means it can charge higher prices than its competitors. This price difference results in higher revenues than previously (+ 3%), but also in higher costs, as Fashion 22 must maintain its brand name through advertising campaigns (12 per year). Fashion 22's income statement is therefore modified as shown in Table 2.4.

Table 2.4 Income statement of Fashion 22 for year 20×4 with the effects of the brand

Revenue	1,030
Cost of sales	(800)
Gross profit	**230**
Operating expenses	(150)
Marketing expenses	(12)
Depreciation	(38)
Operating profit	**30**
Finance costs	–
Taxation	(10)
Net profit	**20**

Table 2.5 Estimated cash flows of Fashion 22 and incremental brand-related cash flows

	Fashion 22	*Brand*
Revenue	1,030	30
Cost of sales	(800)	
Gross profit	**230**	
Operating expenses	(150)	
Marketing expenses	(12)	(12)
Depreciation	(38)	
Operating profit	**30**	**18**
Taxation	(10)	(6)
NOPAT	**20**	**12**
Depreciation	38	–
Capital expenditure	(38)	–
Working capital variation	–	–
Free cash flows	**20**	**12**

What is the value of the company and the brand after taking account of the economic effects of the brand? To answer this question, we must identify the incremental cash flows generated by the brand after deducting the additional costs it created (see Table 2.5).

In this second example, the brand enables additional cash flows to be generated each year, which we shall assume to be constant at 12. The value of Fashion 22 can be determined by applying equation (2):

$$V_t = \frac{F_t \times (1+g)}{(k-g)} = \frac{20 \times (1+0\%)}{(10\% - 0\%)} = 200\,. \tag{4}$$

The value of the brand can thus be calculated as the difference between the value of the company, including the effect of the brand on the cash flows and the value without that effect, i.e., 200 – 80 = 120 (see equations (3) and (4)).

Alternatively, the value of the brand can be derived directly from the cash flows attributable to it (right-hand column of Table 2.5):

$$V_t = \frac{F_t \times (1+g)}{(k-g)} = \frac{12 \times (1+0\%)}{(10\% - 0\%)} = 120\,. \tag{5}$$

Fashion 22 earns a return of 25% (= 20 / 80) after taking the net benefits of the brand into account, whilst the rate of return is only 10% (= 8 / 80) if the economic effect of the brand is ignored. Under these new assumptions, the company yields a rate of return in excess of that required by its capital providers (10%) thanks to its brand. The brand enhances Fashion 22's economic performance and therefore has a certain value for the company.

When the company yields a rate of return equivalent to its cost of capital (ROCE = cost of capital), the value of its brand is zero. In other words, if the return earned by the company is the same as that required by its investors, the brand has no value. Where the expected rate of return is higher than the rate required by its investors (ROCE > cost of capital), the economic profit is positive, and the value of the company is greater than its book value. In the second instance, the Fashion 22 brand enables the company to yield a return in excess of that required by its investors. The value of the brand is the expression of these "excess earnings".[7,8]

In the real world, valuing a brand is more complex for several reasons.

- Estimated future cash flows must be based on in-depth economic analysis. Future performance depends on the level of expected competition, the "power" of the brand, the role played by the brand in the company's business model, and the efficiency of the company that owns the brand. In practice, projections will cover two periods. The first period includes a forecast for the coming three to five years in the business plan; the second period includes a projection of normalised cash flows that are sustainable in the long term. Several scenarios can be developed depending on how reliable the estimates are, for example, a best-case, a worst-case, and a medium-case scenario.
- The risk surrounding the cash flows also requires close examination. Thought must be given to the nature of the risk and statistical comparisons of different business models may often be necessary in order to choose the most appropriate discount rate or range of rates. The Capital Asset Pricing Model (CAPM) is generally used to determine the economic risk premium.[9]
- It is difficult to estimate the incremental revenue and costs directly attributable to a brand; the excess profits generated by a business do not generally relate to the brand alone. Other intangible assets not recognised in financial statements can also contribute to all or part of the excess earnings. The employees' know-how (human capital) and the company's organisational capital or its technologies can also produce excess earnings. The company's business model must be analysed and understood in order to allocate the excess earnings to the various intangible assets that generate them, so as to include in the brand valuation only the excess earnings attributable to the brand.

All methods described as fundamental or intrinsic valuation methods are based on the underlying principles of valuation we have described earlier. The way these methods are applied may vary considerably depending upon the set of simplifying assumptions used in each case. The next section provides an introduction to the different types of brand valuation approaches and methods.

2. Main Approaches to Brand Valuation

There are four main types of brand valuation approaches:

- **Fundamental (intrinsic) approach.** This stems directly from the definition given by Irving Fisher earlier. It is also called the income approach. We shall rule out this method of directly valuing future cash flows derived from a brand (*discounted cash flows*), because in most cases, it is in fact impossible to isolate the cash flows attributable solely to a brand. The valuation of the Fashion 22 brand shown earlier is based on an incremental profit or excess earnings method discussed in more detail in Chapter 4. The intrinsic approach also includes the *revenue premium* method, which estimates the value of a brand based on the additional number of units sold (volume) or the price *mark-up* that can be achieved when compared with an unbranded product or service. These methods are presented in Chapter 5.
- **Market approach.** This approach is based on using market data from comparable brands or actual transactions in brands to calculate implicit multiples of revenues, EBIT, or EBITDA.[10] It is also called relative or comparables valuation. Comparable brands or acquisitions of brands show the expectations of other market players. The multiples are then applied to similar financial indicators (value drivers) related to the brand being valued. A comparable multiple is calculated by dividing the market value (price paid) for the brand by an indicator such as historical or future revenues or a contribution to profit. In practice, however, it is challenging to apply these methods because brands are rarely traded separately. The approach is also relatively difficult to apply because it is complex to isolate revenue or contribution attributable solely to a brand. This method, described in Chapter 7, can be seen as a benchmark approach rather than a valuation method per se.
- **Mixed approach.** The main example of a mixed approach method is the relief-from-royalty method, which lies between the intrinsic and market approaches. It is based on the principle that if a business did not own a brand, it would have to license it from a third party and pay royalties. Because the company owns the brand, it is therefore *relieved* from paying royalties. It consists of analysing royalty rates charged for the right to use other brands. Ideally, the brands used should be highly similar to the brand being valued. The precise legal nature of the comparable royalty agreements needs to be examined; for example, the geographical area covered, the exact nature of the products under licence, and legal restrictions. To this end, the valuer proceeds by analogy with royalty agreements relative to other brands. The future hypothetical royalty payments which are saved because the brand is owned

are then discounted to arrive at the value of the brand. This method is discussed in Chapter 6.

- **Cost-based approach.** This approach consists of valuing a brand based on costs historically incurred to develop it (historical costs method) or the expenditure necessary to replace it with an identical or similar brand (reproduction costs method). These methods are presented and discussed in Chapter 8.

Figure 2.1 maps the different types of valuation methods discussed earlier. This mapping presents a *continuum* of approaches as a function of the quality of the forecast information available. At one end of the spectrum, the intrinsic valuation approach requires reliable and relatively detailed information. At the other end of the spectrum, the cost-based approach pays little or no attention to forecast information.

Valuation is typically performed using one main valuation method based on one of the possible approaches. The value obtained is then cross-checked against values obtained using other valuation methods, depending on available information. A valuer can apply an intrinsic approach such as the excess earnings method and confirm the results by applying the relief-from-royalty method. Cost-based methods of valuation are normally considered, in theory, the least relevant, as they are not based on the concept of expected future cash flows. They often provide a minimum or floor value.

The following section introduces the various contexts in which brand valuations can be needed.

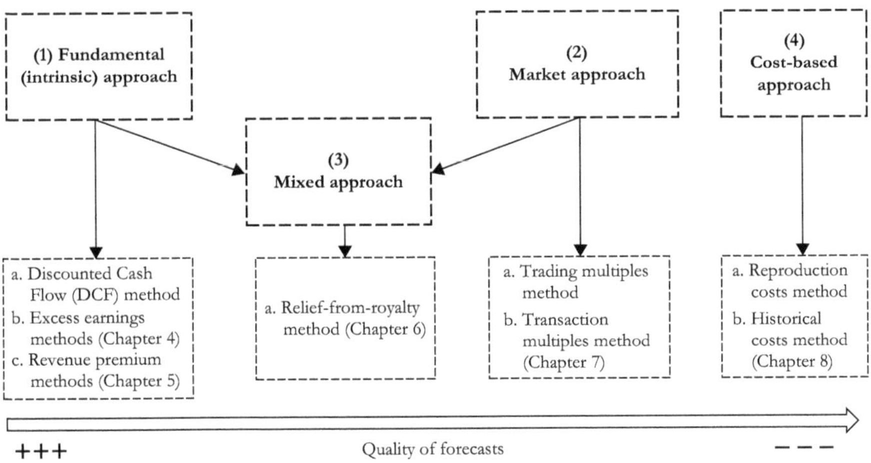

Figure 2.1 Mapping of the different brand valuation methods.

3. The Contexts in Which Brand Valuations Are Performed

In Chapter 1, we highlighted the importance of the context in which the valuation is carried out and especially the definition of the scope of the brand to be valued. There are a number of circumstances in the life of companies where it is necessary to value a brand.

- Transactions require valuations. The sale or purchase of a brand means a valuation is needed. In practice, this case rarely arises, because brands are seldom sold alone. In most cases, they are sold along with other tangible assets such as production capacity and/or other intangible assets such as the business, know-how, or technologies. In this context, valuing the brand can prove complicated, as it is only one part of the transaction.
- Since 2005, there has been an increasing need to value brands for financial reporting purposes. The introduction of IFRS has completely changed corporate financial reporting, the role of auditors, and the day-to-day life of financial analysts. Amongst the many changes entailed by these standards, accounting for intangible assets, and brands in particular, has changed considerably. This change is the result of a set of financial reporting standards that require intangible assets to be recognised at their *fair value*. Chapter 3 describes in detail the accounting rules relating to brands. Brand valuation is now at the forefront of international accounting standards.
- Brands are also valued for legal and tax reasons. Brands and intangible assets in general have become a key success factor in many economic sectors. As a result, brands can be the subject of legal transactions with possibly significant tax consequences. It has become frequent for groups to gather their portfolio of brands in a single entity typically based in a country with an attractive legal and fiscal regime. The role of these *ad hoc* companies is to protect the brands they hold. They are remunerated by royalties paid by the group companies that use the brands to generate revenue. In these cases, valuing the brands is essential to ensure that the royalties paid to the brand-holding company are fair, or on arm's length terms, given the market value of the brands held. Tax authorities in most countries pay close attention to transfer pricing issues, which has given rise to standards or codes of best practice for brand valuation. These valuation standards are dealt with in Chapter 9.
- Brand valuation is also needed for internal reporting purposes. In Chapter 1, we explained that controls and information systems are weak with regards to intangible assets. Yet it is crucial for management to regularly value the brands on which the company's business model depends. If brand value is known, the value created by the company can be measured and managed in light of the financial and human

resources necessary to develop the brand (for example, marketing costs spent on advertising campaigns). In addition, companies often manage brand portfolios and need to know and monitor the value of each brand to determine how to allocate scarce resources (financial, human, and managerial).

Conclusion

In this chapter, we have introduced, with the aid of a simple case study, the basic notions of intrinsic or fundamental valuation using the discounted cash flow method. We then presented an overview of the different types of valuation approaches and methods and followed with a discussion of the various contexts in which brand valuation takes place. Valuation methods will be examined in greater detail in Chapters 4 to 8. Before doing so, we discuss brand accounting in the next chapter.

Notes

1. http://www.buffettfaq.com/ (accessed 26 December 2015).
2. "Present value" takes the uncertainty of future cash flows and the time value of money into account.
3. This assumption will be relaxed at a later stage.
4. In mathematics, this corresponds to the variance of these flows; in other words, it corresponds to the second moment of their distribution.
5. See Appendix 1. For a detailed theoretical and empirical study on the cost of capital, which is beyond the scope of this book, see Pratt and Grabowski (2010).
6. Sometimes called Return on Invested Capital (ROIC) or Return on Net Operating Assets (RNOA).
7. Also referred to as *excess return* or *excess profit*. Alternatively called super profits, abnormal profits, residual profits, or economic value added (EVA).
8. This approach is set out in Chapter 4.
9. See Appendix 1.
10. Earnings Before Interest, Tax, Depreciation, and Amortisation.

References

Fisher I. (1930), *The Theory of Interest*, Macmillan, New York.

Markowitz H. (1952), "Portfolio Selection" *Journal of Finance*, Vol. 7 (1), pp. 77–91.

Pratt S.R. and Grabowski R. (2010), *Cost of Capital: Applications and Examples*, 4th edition, Wiley, Hoboken, New Jersey.

Samuelson P.A. (1983), *Paul Samuelson and Modern Economic Theory*, E.G. Brown and R.M. Solow eds., McGraw-Hill, New York.

3 Brands and Accounting Standards

The aim of financial *reporting*[1] is to provide relevant information for present and future investors and creditors of companies.[2] This position is held by the international (International Accounting Standards Board), UK (Financial Reporting Council), and US (Financial Accounting Standards Board) regulators who are at the forefront of international accounting discussions. In this chapter, we shall see how this objective relates to the accounting treatment of intangible assets and brands in particular.

Intangible assets—human capital, patents, software, customer relationships, organisational capital, and brands—create value for shareholders and confer a decisive competitive advantage on the companies owning them. Certain authors estimate that the value of these assets represents more than half the market capitalisation of quoted companies (Lev, 2004). Companies have been investing massively in intangible assets for several decades. In the 1990s, the amount spent each year on intangibles in the United States was at least a trillion dollars (Nakamura, 2004). Because accounting is an age-old information system whose treatment of intangible assets has varied little, these changes have led to financial statements becoming less relevant. This discrepancy between corporate economic reality, rich in intangibles, and the limited way these are recorded in the accounts, results today in a disconnection between *book values* and *market values*, as shown by the decrease in the *book-to-market ratio* (Lev, 2003).

The rules of brand recognition have been, and still are, stringent for those preparing financial statements. Brands may be capitalised only in a limited number of cases, and the allowable valuation methods are mainly based on historical costs (see Sections 2 and 3). Yet the principles of relevance and *true and fair representation* prescribed by the majority of national and international accounting standards should call for intangible assets to be more widely recognised. However, in most cases, these principles conflict with the principles of prudence and of the verifiability of financial information. Even now, one of the main issues with accounting systems is that they are unable to recognise the fair value of brands developed internally.

Given the absence of complete accounting information as to the market value of intangible assets, and especially brands, readers of financial statements have to make their own estimates. Problems arise if these estimates systematically result in an erroneous assessment of the value of intangible assets. Overvaluation leads to speculative bubbles, such as the dot-com boom of the early 2000s. Undervaluation leads to investors in intangible-intensive companies requiring rates of return that are excessive given the level of risk. The direct consequence of systematic undervaluation of intangibles is an excessive cost of capital, which leads, therefore, to continuous underinvestment in intangible assets. This undervaluation has macroeconomic implications, as it can damage the long-term growth potential of companies and economies as a whole.

Because intangibles represent an increasingly significant part of corporate value, the accounting standard-setters have been encouraged to widen considerably the list of identifiable intangible assets (for example, brands, patents, contractual and noncontractual customer relationships, customer lists, broadcasting rights, mandates, concessions, databases, and order backlogs) so long as they are controlled (or are separable) or arise from contractual rights and can be measured reliably.

This chapter describes the main accounting rules governing the recognition of brands in international standards (IFRS) and UK GAAP. Section 1 explains the rules for initial recognition of brands under IFRS. Section 2 analyses the rules for monitoring their value under IFRS. Section 3 explains how UK accounting standards in relation to intangible assets have evolved over the past 30 years and the standards currently applicable. Finally, Section 4 concludes the chapter with an analysis of the level of intangible assets recognised in the accounts of FTSE 100 companies.

1. Initial Recognition of Brands Under IFRS

As stated at the beginning of this chapter, under the "Conceptual Framework for Financial Reporting" (IASB, 2001), the main objective of IFRS is to provide financial information useful to existing and potential investors, lenders, and other creditors in making decisions about providing resources to entities.

Let us first remember how the international standard-setters define an asset. An asset is

> a resource controlled by the entity as a result of past events and from which future economic benefits are expected to flow to the entity [. . .]. The future economic benefit embodied in an asset is the potential to contribute, directly or indirectly, to the flow of cash or cash equivalents to the entity.
>
> (IASB, 2001)

The two essential elements of this definition are control (which may not mean legal ownership) and future economic benefits.[3] A brand clearly meets this requirement because it provides future economic benefits for its holder: higher margins, higher volumes due to product recognition, royalties if licensed, cash if sold, etc.[4]

Measuring the future economic benefits of intangible assets is difficult due to their nature. Intangible assets are cumulative, synergistic, and often inseparable from other tangible and intangible assets (Basu and Waymire, 2008). Standard-setters have, however, made a certain effort to allow recognition of the value of some intangible assets in recent years, more specifically following business combinations.

The main rules covering the accounting treatment of brands are to be found in IAS 38 "Intangible Assets" and IFRS 3 "Business Combinations".

- IAS 38 was first issued on 31 March 2004 and was revised in 2008. The revised version was adopted by the European Union (EU) in European Regulation No 1126/2008. This standard outlines the principles to be applied to brands acquired separately or in a business combination or developed internally.
- IFRS 3 was published on 31 March 2004 and also revised in 2008. It was adopted by the EU on 3 June 2009 in European Regulation No 495/2009. This standard deals more specifically with the accounting to be applied to brands acquired during a business combination and, in particular, the identification and valuation of brands during the process of *purchase price allocation*.

Specific rules on the valuation of intangible assets are also contained in IAS 36 "Impairment of Assets", including monitoring the value of brands, and in IFRS 5 "Non-Current Assets Held for Sale and Discontinued Operations", which describes how to treat assets and, in particular, brands, which management intends to sell. We quote the latest versions of the relevant IFRS/IAS in the rest of this chapter.

1.1. General Principles

IFRS includes a number of recommendations concerning brands, dealing with how to define them and to account for them.

1.1.1. Accounting Definition of Brands

Under IFRS, an item and, in particular, a brand is defined as an intangible asset if it satisfies three conditions. It must be (i) identifiable, (ii) controlled by the entity, and (iii) expected to generate future economic benefits. IAS 38 also states that "If an item within the scope of this Standard does not meet the definition of an intangible asset, expenditure to acquire it or to generate it internally is recognised as an expense when it is incurred" (IAS 38.10).

In other words, if these conditions are not met, the expenses incurred are written off immediately.

An intangible asset is identifiable if it

> is separable, i.e. is capable of being separated or divided from the entity and sold, transferred, licensed, rented or exchanged, either individually or together with a related contract, identifiable asset or liability regardless of whether the entity intends to do so; or arises from contractual or other legal rights, regardless of whether those rights are transferable or separable from the entity or from other rights and obligations.
>
> (IAS 38.12)

The idea behind this condition is to distinguish an intangible asset from goodwill acquired or internally generated. It is easier for a brand, which entails legal rights and can be licensed, to meet the aforementioned conditions than certain other intangible assets, such as customer relationships.

An entity controls the asset if "the entity has the power to obtain the future economic benefits flowing from the underlying resource and to restrict the access of others to those benefits" (IAS 38.13). A company can protect its brand by using various legal tools available. Registering a trademark prevents competitors from using it. For instance, in the United Kingdom, a brand registered with the Intellectual Property Office can be used exclusively by the registering company for ten years. This monopoly period can be prolonged indefinitely, and the company can take legal action against anyone imitating or using the trademark. European Union protection can be obtained by applying for a Community Trade Mark (CTM) through the Office for Harmonization in the Internal Market (OHIM) based in Spain.

The condition of economic benefits is quite clear for a brand, as these normally represent revenues from the sale of products using the brand. The standard recognises other types of future economic benefits, for example, cost savings, which apply more frequently to production processes.

1.1.2. Accounting for Brands

To capitalise a brand on the balance sheet, the entity must demonstrate that it meets the three aforementioned intangible asset definition criteria and the criterion for recognition, which requires the following two conditions to be met (IAS 38.21):

a) "it is probable that the expected future economic benefits that are attributable to the asset will flow to the entity" and
b) "the cost of the asset can be measured reliably".

Condition a) must be satisfied using reasonable forecast information consistent with economic conditions. The valuer must give greater weight to external evidence (IAS 38.23). Condition b) implies that a direct link must be established between expenditure incurred and the brand.

A brand must be measured initially at cost (IAS 38.24), whether it was developed internally or acquired externally or as part of a business combination. What the balance sheet carrying the value of a brand tells us about its value is very different if the "cost" represents expenditure incurred directly on the internal development of the brand (legal costs only) or if it is the price paid for the brand on the market or in a business combination (in principle, the market value of the brand). Three situations must therefore be dealt with: brands developed internally, brands acquired separately, and brands acquired as part of a business combination.

1.2. Brands Developed Internally

In theory, when a brand satisfies the three criteria for definition as an intangible asset, the directly related costs can be recognised on the balance sheet. In practice, these criteria prove to be extremely strict, as the standard stipulates that "Expenditure on internally generated brands, mastheads, publishing titles, customer lists and items similar in substance cannot be distinguished from the cost of developing the business as a whole. Therefore, such items are not recognised as intangible assets" (IAS 38.64). Only fees to register a legal right can be capitalised, because they are directly attributable to the brand. The standard states in effect that whilst legal registration fees can be capitalised (IAS 38.66), other expenditures must be written off immediately. The standard-setters justify this position as follows: "the cost of generating an intangible asset internally cannot be distinguished from the cost of maintaining or enhancing the entity's internally generated goodwill or of running day-to-day operations" (IAS 38.51).

Applying the condition that directly attributable costs must be reliably measurable means that internally developed brands are very prudently valued on company balance sheets, but it also means that book values are disconnected from market values. The stance taken by IFRS here seems to be contradictory with the overall objective of producing financial information useful for decision making by investors. This valuation seems to go against the principle of fair value prescribed for numerous other assets (e.g., employee benefits under IFRS 2 and IAS 19). An alternative accounting solution could perhaps be found. IAS 38 classifies, for example, R&D expenditure into two phases: a research phase and a development phase (IAS 38.52). Under IFRS, as well as under UK GAAP, expenditure incurred in the development phase can in certain conditions be capitalised[5] (e.g., after the technical and commercial feasibility of the asset for sale or use have been established). Such a two-phased approach could perhaps be considered in the future for brands for the purpose of supplying more useful information to users.

1.3. Brands Acquired Separately

A brand is simplest to value when it is acquired on its own, but unfortunately this happens rarely. Brands are usually linked to a set of complementary assets, such as a trademark, a trade name, a formula, a process, a technology, or even a particular recipe. The sale of a "pure" brand is therefore rare, because a transaction usually covers a group of assets, a division, or an entire company. In a separate acquisition, "the price an entity pays to acquire separately an intangible asset will reflect expectations about the probability that the expected future economic benefits embodied in the asset will flow to the entity" (IAS 38.25). The type of costs directly attributable to a brand acquired separately are similar to those for a tangible asset i.e., "(a) its purchase price, including import duties and non-refundable purchase taxes, after deducting trade discounts and rebates; and (b) any directly attributable cost of preparing the asset for its intended use " (IAS 38.27).

For the user, the price paid represents the fair value of the asset at the date of purchase and is therefore relevant for the reader of the financial statements. The further we move away from the transaction date, however, the less useful this measurement becomes.

1.4. Acquisition as Part of a Business Combination

A company is sometimes acquired with the sole aim of purchasing the brand it has developed, and this explains the price paid. There are well-known examples of such acquisitions: that of Cadbury by Kraft in 2009 for £10.2 billion or the sale of the Jaguar and Land Rover brands by Ford to Tata Motors in 2008 for more than £1 billion.

The treatment of brands acquired in business combinations is a major topic in accounting standards, as evidenced by the frequent revisions of the standards. In the United States, APB 16 and SFAS 38 were replaced by SFAS 141 in 2001, which was amended in 2007. Internationally, IFRS 3 replaced IAS 22 in 2004 and was revised in 2008.

Under the latest version of IFRS 3, business combinations are to be accounted for by using the acquisition method (IFRS 3.4), whereby "[a]s of the acquisition date, the acquirer shall recognise, separately from goodwill, the identifiable assets acquired, the liabilities assumed and any non-controlling interest in the acquiree" (IFRS 3.10).

The possibilities of recognising a brand are greater when a brand is acquired in a business combination than when it is developed internally. IAS 38 stipulates that "the probability recognition criterion in paragraph 21(a) [i.e., the probability of future economic benefits] is always considered to be satisfied for separately acquired intangible assets" (IAS 38.25). In the case of a business combination, "an acquirer recognises at the acquisition date, separately from goodwill, an intangible asset of the acquiree, irrespective of whether the asset had been recognised by the acquiree before the business combination" (IAS 38.34).

The position of the IASB with regards to brands acquired in business combinations has changed over the past years. Previously, there was doubt as to the reliability of the measurement of brand value and the possibility of recognising it on the balance sheet, but the amended version of IAS 38 (2008) considers that the value of brands so acquired can always be reliably measured. The standard states: "[w]hen, for the estimates used to measure an intangible asset's fair value, there is a range of possible outcomes with different probabilities, that uncertainty enters into the measurement of the asset's fair value" (IAS 38.35). Rather than demonstrating the impossibility of reliably measuring fair value, the uncertainty surrounding future economic benefits must be factored into the brand's fair value, for example, by using a higher discount rate rather than including the value in residual goodwill.

The 2008 amendment to the standard reinforced the procedure for identifying intangible assets and separating them from acquired goodwill. Because brands sometimes cannot be disassociated from other tangible and intangible assets, IAS 38 distinguishes between different types of brands acquired alongside other assets in a business combination. The standard makes a distinction between "brand" in the normal marketing sense, and pure "brand name" in the legal sense. The term "brand" is typically used "to refer to a group of complementary assets such as a trademark (or service mark) and its related trade name, formulas, recipes and technological expertise" (IAS 38.37), whilst "brand name" refers to a trade name. The accounting treatment depends on whether the fair values of these items can be assessed separately or not. Thus, "The acquirer may recognise a group of complementary intangible assets as a single asset provided the individual assets have similar useful lives." (IAS 38.37). If the individual fair values can be assessed, the acquirer may also recognise them separately.

For purchase price allocation purposes, identifiable brands are therefore distinguished from goodwill, which is "an asset representing the future economic benefits arising from other assets acquired in a business combination that are not individually identified and separately recognised" (IAS 38.11). If a brand cannot be identified, the goodwill, calculated as the difference between the purchase price and the value of the net assets identified, will mechanically be greater. Goodwill is effectively the difference between the consideration transferred (plus any non-controlling interest in the acquiree or previously held equity interest in the acquiree) and the net fair value of identified acquired assets and liabilities assumed (IFRS 3.32).

This zero-sum equation, including intangible assets and goodwill, is a real issue when preparing financial statements after an acquisition. Because the value of these two categories of assets is subsequently dealt with differently, the initial purchase price allocation may be carried out by management with the aim of protecting the future results of the company. There is a balancing act between the desire to limit the number of separately identifiable assets, which are subject to future systematic amortisation, and the amount of purchased goodwill (or brands with an indefinite useful life), which is not amortised (charged to the profit and loss account) but which will be subject to annual impairment tests (see Section 2.2).[6] Indeed, the useful life of brands can be indefinite, and their future value is monitored similarly (but not identically) to purchased goodwill (unlike goodwill, brand impairment losses can be reversed under IFRS). An influencing factor will be the possibility of goodwill or brand impairment losses due to poor performance post-acquisition. Recently in practice, however, brand life has tended to be considered finite, making things more complicated for the preparer of financial statements.

2. Monitoring Brand Value: Revaluation, Amortisation, and Brand Impairment Tests Under IFRS

The previous section dealt with the initial recognition of brands, for example, upon their acquisition by a company. This section describes how accounting standards require the value of brands to be monitored and, in particular, the fact that the revaluation of intangible assets cannot apply to brands, the amortisation of brands when applicable, and, finally, impairment testing of brands.

2.1. The Revaluation Method: Not Applicable to Brands

IAS 38 allows two possible valuation models of intangible assets after initial recognition: (1) the cost model and (2) the revaluation model. Under the first model, "[a]fter initial recognition, an intangible asset shall be carried at its cost less any accumulated amortisation and any accumulated impairment losses" (IAS 38.74). If a company chooses to apply the revaluation model to its intangible assets, "[a]fter initial recognition, an intangible asset shall be carried at a revalued amount, being its fair value at the date of the revaluation less any subsequent accumulated amortisation and any subsequent accumulated impairment losses" (IAS 38.75). It would therefore seem possible to measure at their fair value brands initially recognised at cost, thereby enhancing the quality of information shown in the accounts. The standard states, however, that for the purpose of revaluations, "fair value shall be measured by reference to an active market" (IAS 38.75). An active market is defined as a market in which all of the following conditions exist: (i) the items traded are homogeneous, (ii) willing buyers and sellers can normally be found at any time, and (iii) prices are available to the public (IAS 36.6).[7]

This definition clearly means that the revaluation model cannot apply to brands because in general, "an active market cannot exist for brands, newspaper mastheads, [. . .] because each such asset is unique" (IAS 38.78). The specific nature of brands means the revaluation model cannot be applied to them; transactions involving brands (sale or licensing) do not form an active market. Such transactions are extremely specific, and prices are rarely disclosed to the public.

2.2. *Amortisation of Brands*

Brands are often thought to have an indefinite useful life because there is no foreseeable end to the period over which the holding entity expects to receive future economic benefits from them. But the useful life of a brand can also be considered finite. The most obvious examples are to be found in the events sector and sports in particular. We can give as examples organisers of sporting events: FIFA tried to protect brands such as *World Cup 2006 Germany* or *World Cup USA 94*. Even if these types of brands can be legally protected, which today seems dubious,[8] they clearly have a finite useful life, that of the sporting event itself.

The depreciable amount of a brand with a finite useful life must be allocated on a systematic basis over its useful life (IAS 38.97). The amortisation method must reflect the expected pattern of consumption of the expected future economic benefits of the brand.

If the brand's useful life is deemed indefinite, its value must be tested at least annually. This is referred to as an impairment test.

2.3. *Impairment Testing of Brands*

IAS 36 sets out the procedures to follow to ensure that the carrying value of an asset on the balance sheet does not exceed the future economic benefits to flow from this asset. In practice, this is for an entity "to ensure that its assets are carried at no more than their recoverable amount" (IAS 36.1). The way the standard applies is summarised in Figure 3.1, which shows in the form of a decision tree the procedures to apply in an impairment test.

Impairment tests under IAS 36 must be conducted in two cases: (1) where there is indication that an asset is impaired (IAS 36.9) and (2) at least once annually for an intangible asset with an indefinite useful life or an intangible asset not yet available for use (IAS 36.10). This procedure must normally be followed for brands with an indefinite useful life.

Impairment tests can be of major importance for brands acquired separately or in a business combination, as their net book value represents their fair value at initial recognition. This fair value reflects management expectations based on forecast economic information. However, the net book value of internally developed brands represents only their legal registration costs, leading to an underestimation of the brands' fair value. In that case, the impairment test is therefore less sensitive, because the recoverable value is generally much higher than book value.

Indications of loss of value can be internal or external. Examples of an external indication of loss of value of a brand might be an increase in the expected

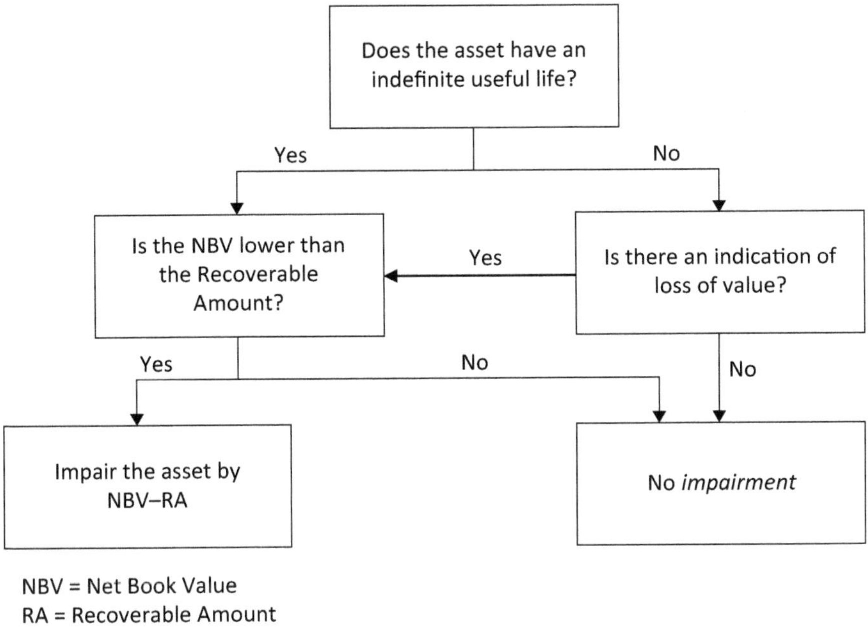

Figure 3.1 Decision tree for an impairment test under IAS 36.

rate of return during the reporting period, which would lead to an increase in the discount rate applied to future cash flows or a negative change in the technological, market, economic, or legal environment of the entity (IAS 36.12). Notable examples of internal indications are cash flows that are disappointing compared to the business plan or a higher than budgeted level of cash required to maintain the value of the brand. Another example is the discontinuation of a brand, which results in total impairment; for example, the withdrawal and replacement of several brands exploited by France Telecom (now Orange SA) in 2005, which led to the full impairment of the Equant and Amena brands.

Impairment losses must be recognised immediately in the profit and loss account. Impairment losses for brands can be reversed. This is not the case for goodwill, where an impairment loss cannot be reversed.

The recoverable amount of an asset (or a cash-generating unit[9]) is defined as the higher of 1) its fair value less costs to sell and 2) its value in use (IAS 36.18). It is not always necessary to determine both of these values as long as either of them exceeds the asset's carrying amount.

2.3.1. Fair Value Less Costs to Sell: What This Means for Brands

Fair value less costs to sell is defined as "the amount obtainable from the sale of an asset or cash-generating unit in an arm's length transaction between knowledgeable, willing parties, less the costs of disposal" (IAS 36.6). IAS 36 further states that

> the best evidence of an asset's fair value less costs to sell is a price in a binding sale agreement in an arm's length transaction, adjusted for incremental costs that would be directly attributable to the disposal of the asset.
>
> (IAS 36.25)

Therefore, the selling price of a brand is the best indication of its fair value. The standard states that if this information is not available, prices of recent transactions in an active market may be used. No such market exists, however, for brands in general, so the financial statements should be prepared using

> the best information available to reflect the amount that an entity could obtain, at the end of the reporting period, from the disposal of the asset in an arm's length transaction between knowledgeable, willing parties, after deducting the costs of disposal.
>
> (IAS 36.27)

In practice, this implies applying a market approach using comparable transaction multiples. This is usually challenging because, as already explained, sales of brands are few and far between.

2.3.2. *Estimating the Recoverable Amount of a Brand Using Value in Use*

Although fair value less costs to sell can be considered the external reference of the value of a brand, the lack of market information and the specific nature of brands make using a fair-value approach complicated. In practice, impairment tests for brands are based on estimates of value in use. This is assessed internally by a company and equates to the recoverable value of the future economic benefits stemming from the brand.

IAS 36 requires that the calculation of an asset's value in use reflects

a) "an estimate of the future cash flows the entity expects to derive from the asset;
b) expectations about possible variations in the amount or timing of those future cash flows;
c) the time value of money, represented by the current market risk-free rate of interest;
d) the price for bearing the uncertainty inherent in the asset; and
e) other factors, such as illiquidity, that market participants would reflect in pricing the future cash flows the entity expects to derive from the asset" (IAS 36.30).

This approach involves discounting the future cash flows deriving from the brand, as does the relief-from-royalty method explained in Chapter 6. The standard states that brand risk, such as the volatility of expected cash flows (item b), the price of risk (item d), and other risk factors (item e) must be reflected either in the cash flows or in the discount rate used (IAS 36.32). In practice, it is important to ensure consistency between cash flow projections and the discount rate applied to those cash flows.

The cash inflows and outflows attributable to a brand must be based on a business plan using reasonable assumptions as to the future level of business in normal conditions. Therefore, "In using information from financial budgets/forecasts, an entity considers whether the information reflects reasonable and supportable assumptions and represents management's best estimate of the set of economic conditions that will exist over the remaining useful life of the asset" (IAS 36.38). This means using reasonable assumptions concerning competition and market trends (for example, forecast sales growth and long-term growth rate beyond the business plan period).

2.3.3. *Valuation Principles Addressed by Impairment Testing Procedures*

IAS 36 contains an appendix which addresses several valuation aspects, in particular the identification of cash flows and the choice of discount rate.[10]

2.3.3.1. ESTIMATING CASH FLOWS

IAS 36 describes two methods of forecasting cash flows. The first is referred to as "traditional approach", the second as "expected cash flow approach". This latter approach (in the mathematical sense of "expected") computes likely cash flows by taking into account the probabilities of possible cash flows and the timing of those cash flows.

Table 3.1 shows an example of cash flow projections when the cash flows are uncertain.

The traditional approach takes account only of the most probable amount i.e., the amount with the highest probability; in other words, that would be 100 in our example. The amount in year n + 1 is then discounted at a rate

Table 3.1 Uncertainty as to the amounts of expected cash flows generated by a brand in year n + 1

	Cash Flow in Year n + 1	*Probability*
Cash flow value		
Worst case	50	30%
Average case	100	60%
Best case	150	10%

reflecting the potential uncertainty of the cash flow forecast to obtain its net present value. According to IAS 36,

> the traditional approach assumes that a single discount rate convention can incorporate all the expectations about the future cash flows and the appropriate risk premium. Therefore, the traditional approach places most of the emphasis on selection of the discount rate.
>
> (IAS 36.A4)

The expected cash flow approach "uses all expectations about possible cash flows instead of the single most likely cash flow" (IAS 36.A7). The expected cash flow for n + 1 is, therefore, 90 (= 50 × 30% + 100 × 60% + 150 × 10%). The standard explains that "the expected cash flow approach differs from the traditional approach by focusing on direct analysis of the cash flows in question and on more explicit statements of the assumptions used in the measurement" (IAS 36.A7).

The expected cash flow approach can also accommodate uncertainties about the timing of the cash flows. The difference in this respect between the traditional and the expected cash flow approach is shown in Table 3.2.

With the traditional approach, the best estimate of the present value of the cash flows generated by the brand is 88.5 (= $100/1.063^2$). The present value in the expected cash flow approach is slightly higher at 88.6 (= 25% × 100/1.061 + 50% × $100/1.063^2$ + 25% × $100/1.064^3$). The uncertainty as to the timing of the cash flows can be factored into the brand value using the expected cash flow approach, but not the traditional approach.

2.3.3.2. CHOOSING THE DISCOUNT RATE

The appendix of IAS 36 gives guidance on the choice of the appropriate discount rate. Under the standard and in line with best valuation practices,

> [w]hichever approach an entity adopts for measuring the value in use of an asset, interest rates used to discount cash flows should not reflect

Table 3.2 Uncertainty as to the timing of cash flows generated by a brand in years n + 1 to n + 3

	Cash Flow n + 1	*Cash Flow n + 2*	*Cash Flow n + 3*	*Probability*	*Discount Rate*
Cash flow value					
Scenario 1	100	0	0	25%	6.1%
Scenario 2	0	100	0	50%	6.3%
Scenario 3	0	0	100	25%	6.4%

> risks for which the estimated cash flows have been adjusted. Otherwise, the effect of some assumptions will be double-counted.
>
> (IAS 36.A15)

When a discount rate for an entity is not directly available from the market, it must be estimated using the following: the weighted average cost of capital determined by such techniques as the CAPM (or later versions deriving from the Arbitrage Pricing Theory, such as the Fama-French model or the Pastor-Stambaugh model)[11] and the entity's incremental borrowing rate or other market borrowing rates (IAS 36.A17).

The standard also makes the essential point that

> the discount rate is independent of the entity's capital structure and the way the entity financed the purchase of the asset, because the future cash flows expected to arise from an asset do not depend on the way in which the entity financed the purchase of the asset.
>
> (IAS 36.A19)

This point introduces into the standard the Modigliani and Miller theorem (1958), which demonstrates that asset value is independent of financial structure where certain conditions of market efficiency are met.

Example of Financial Reporting for Brand Impairment

Orange SA is a major player in the European telecoms sector. Its activities include, in particular, fixed and mobile telecommunications, data transmission, Internet access, multimedia, and data management services. The company's operations are split into two divisions: fixed telephony and Internet, and mobile telephony. At the end of 2011, the company had a customer base of 226 million consumers, of which 167.4 million were mobile phone customers and 14.7 million Internet customers. Since 2006, these activities have been carried out under the Orange brand. The brand was acquired after the sale of Orange Plc by Vodafone for approximately €40 billion in 2000 in a business combination finalised during the late 1990s stock market euphoria around new technology stocks. This period was one of disconnection between market values and intrinsic company values, and it was described by Robert Shiller as "irrational exuberance", using the famous quote by Alan Greenspan, chairman of the US Federal Reserve System. France Telecom paid a lot for the Orange brand, which was partially included in the goodwill acquired in the acquisition in 2000. French accounting standards applicable at the time did not require intangible assets to be separated from goodwill. In the years following the acquisition, varying amounts of amortisation were booked, in particular, in 2001, goodwill amortisation of €872 million was allocated to Orange SA.

Further impairment was recorded by France Telecom management as it applied a strategy of using a single brand for its different services from 2006 onwards. France Telecom explained in its 2005 annual report: "[i]n 2005, the impairment on non-current assets included primarily a depreciation of 345 million euros on the Amena brand and a depreciation of 191 million euros on the Equant brand following the decision to replace them with the Orange brand as part of the "NExT" program [. . .] (*Nouvelle Expérience des Télécommunications*—New Experience in Telecommunications) (France Telecom, Financial Report Form 20-F for 2005, p. 161).

With the introduction of IFRS, the company explained: "[u]nder IFRS and US GAAP, intangible assets with indefinite lives are not amortized, but tested for impairment on at least an annual basis." (Form 20-F p. 229). "Intangible assets with an indefinite useful life comprise the Orange and Telekomunikacja trademarks recognized in the Group's consolidated balance sheet" (Form 20-F for 2005, p. F-40).

3. UK Accounting Standards in Relation to Intangible Assets: Evolution in the Last 30 Years and Current Standards

3.1. Legislative Requirements

Financial reporting in the United Kingdom is subject to company law. The main body of law relevant to financial reporting was found in the Companies Act 1985, which was replaced by the Companies Act 2006. The Companies Act 1985 contains little guidance regarding intangible assets. Schedule 4 (balance sheet formats) of the Companies Act 1985 requires separate disclosure of intangible assets listed as 1. development costs; 2. concessions, patents, licences, trademarks, and similar rights and assets; 3. goodwill; and 4. payments on account. Amounts in respect of concessions, patents, licences, trademarks and similar rights and assets shall only be included in a company's balance sheet if either (a) the assets were acquired for valuable consideration and are not required to be shown under goodwill or (b) the assets in question were created by the company itself. The general rule is that the amount to be included in respect of any fixed asset shall be its purchase price or production cost (with special rules for development costs and goodwill). Under the alternative accounting rules, intangible fixed assets, other than goodwill, may be included at their current cost.

There are no specific provisions on intangible assets in the Companies Act 2006. Instead, the relevant accounting provisions are included in "The

Large and Medium-sized Companies and Groups (Accounts and Reports) Regulations 2008" and "The Small Companies and Groups (Accounts and Directors' Report) Regulations 2008". The balance sheet formats in "The Large and Medium-sized Companies and Groups (Accounts and Reports) Regulations 2008" are similar to those in the Companies Act 1985. Amounts in respect of concessions, patents, licences, trademarks and similar rights and assets are to be included in the balance sheet only if the assets were acquired for valuable consideration or were created by the company itself. The amount to be included in respect of any fixed asset must be its purchase price or production cost (with special rules for development costs and goodwill). Also, under the alternative accounting rules, intangible fixed assets other than goodwill may be included at their current cost.

The details of the accounting requirements in respect of the treatment of intangible assets are included in the relevant accounting standards.

3.2. Accounting Standards

Until 1997, the treatment of intangible assets was governed by SSAP 22,[12] "Accounting for Goodwill", issued in 1984. This standard states that assets of an intangible nature can be recognised in financial statements provided they are separable, i.e., they can be identified and sold separately without necessarily disposing of the business as a whole. SSAP 22 states that a recognisable intangible asset must be carried on the balance sheet at its fair value, which is derived from its acquisition cost. Many intangible assets do not arise from a single market transaction, and there is usually uncertainty over the costs of their creation. Fair values for such assets are more difficult to estimate. This explains why accounting standard-setters more readily recognise purchased intangibles rather than non-purchased intangibles.[13]

In December 1997, SAAP 22 was replaced by FRS 10,[14] "Goodwill and Intangible Assets". It defines intangible assets as non-financial fixed assets that are identifiable and are controlled by the reporting entity through custody or legal rights. An identifiable asset is one that can be disposed of separately without disposing of the entity.

Under FRS 10, purchased intangible assets should be capitalised as assets at their cost if purchased separately from a business and at their fair value if purchased as part of a business acquisition. FRS 7, "Fair Values in Acquisition Accounting", requires that where an intangible asset is recognised, its fair value should be based on its replacement cost, which is normally the asset's estimated market value. It also states that it is not possible to determine a market value for unique intangible assets, such as brands, and that replacement cost may be equally difficult to determine directly. However, FRS 7 states that certain techniques for estimating the value of intangible assets indirectly may be used for their initial recognition at the time of purchase. These techniques include multiples of turnover or estimating the present value of the royalties that would be payable to license the asset from a third party. If the value of purchased intangible assets cannot be measured reliably, it should be included within goodwill.

Under FRS 10, internally developed intangible assets should be capitalised only where they have a readily ascertainable market value, i.e., where (a) the asset belongs to a homogeneous population of assets that are equivalent in all material respects and (b) an active market, evidenced by frequent transactions, exists for that population of assets.

Under FRS 10, purchased intangible assets should be amortised over their useful economic life (the period over which the entity expects to derive economic benefits from an asset), which is presumed to be limited and not to exceed 20 years. However, this presumption may be overridden if the intangible asset can be measured continually so that annual impairment reviews can be performed. Where intangible assets are regarded as having indefinite useful economic lives, they should not be amortised but should instead be tested for impairment at the end of each reporting period. Intangible assets with readily ascertainable market values may be revalued in reference to those market values.

The financial reporting standards for the United Kingdom and the Republic of Ireland have been revised for periods beginning on or after 1 January 2015 and have been replaced by FRS 100, "Application of Financial Reporting Requirements", FRS 101, "Reduced Disclosure Framework", and FRS 102, "The Financial Reporting Standard applicable in the UK and Republic of Ireland". These financial reporting standards bring UK GAAP up to date and increase its consistency with IFRS (see the previous section in this chapter). Section 19 of FRS 102, "Business Combinations and Goodwill", replaces FRS 10 with respect to goodwill. Section 18 of FRS 102, "Intangible Assets other than Goodwill", replaces FRS 10 with respect to other intangible assets.

Under FRS 102, an intangible asset is an identifiable, non-monetary asset without physical substance. Such an asset is identifiable when (a) it is separable, i.e., capable of being separated or divided from the entity and sold, transferred, licensed, rented, or exchanged either individually or together with a related contract, asset or liability, or (b) it arises from contractual or other legal rights, regardless of whether those rights are transferable or separable from the entity or from other rights and obligations.

An entity shall recognise an intangible asset as an asset if, and only if: (a) it is probable that the expected future economic benefits that are attributable to the asset will flow to the entity and (b) the cost or value of the asset can be measured reliably. This probability recognition criterion is always considered satisfied for intangible assets that are separately acquired. An intangible asset acquired in a business combination is normally recognised as an asset because its fair value can be measured with sufficient reliability. However, an intangible asset acquired in a business combination is not recognised when it arises from legal or other contractual rights and there is no history or evidence of exchange transactions for the same or similar assets and otherwise estimating fair value would be dependent on immeasurable variables. FRS 102 specifically states that an entity shall recognise expenditure on internally generated brands, logos, publishing titles, customer lists, and items similar in substance as an expense and shall not recognise them as intangible assets. It also has special rules for development costs.

An entity shall measure an intangible asset initially at cost. The cost of a separately acquired intangible asset comprises (a) its purchase price and (b) any directly attributable cost of preparing the asset for its intended use. The cost of an internally generated intangible asset is the sum of expenditure incurred from the date when the intangible asset first meets the recognition criteria and comprises all directly attributable costs necessary to create, produce, and prepare the asset to be capable of operating in the manner intended by management. If an intangible asset is acquired in a business combination, the cost of that intangible asset is its fair value at the acquisition date. Fair value is the amount for which an asset could be exchanged, a liability settled, or an equity instrument granted could be exchanged between knowledgeable, willing parties in an arm's length transaction (Section 2 of FRS 102).

An entity shall allocate the depreciable amount of an intangible asset on a systematic basis over its useful life. According to FRS 102, all intangible assets shall be considered to have a finite useful life. The useful life of an intangible asset that arises from contractual or other legal rights shall not exceed the period of the contractual or other legal rights, but may be shorter depending on the period over which the entity expects to use the asset. If an entity is unable to make a reliable estimate of the useful life of an intangible asset, the life shall not exceed five years.

4. Brands and Accounting Recognition: Practice Among FTSE 100 Companies

This section aims to put in perspective the way in which recognition of intangible assets has evolved since the beginning of the 1990s and to survey the level of intangibles recognised in the 2014 accounts of the largest UK-quoted companies.

Have changes in accounting standards dealing with the recognition of intangibles and in company reporting practices led to more intangible assets being recognised in balance sheets? An accounting approach based on economic substance and fair value prescribed by IFRS has replaced the previous approach based on legal form set out in UK accounting standards. The following paragraphs review how recognition of intangibles has changed among FTSE 100 companies.

4.1. Balance Sheet Recognition of Intangible Assets

If we ignore accounting principles and accept a wide definition of intangibles assets as "all non-monetary assets without physical substance that generate future economic benefits", we cover an extensive range of intangibles. In addition to those assets, which traditionally spring to mind when we talk about intangibles (e.g., brands or patents), this definition encompasses human capital, all unrecognised trademarks, organisational capital (the efficiency of an organisation), customer relationships, and, in general, internally developed goodwill.[15] These types of assets, which for reasons of reliability are not recognised, are nevertheless sources of future economic benefits, and their present value is, under the efficient market hypothesis (Fama, 1970), factored into the market capitalisation of public companies.

If we pursue this logic, the accounting value of a company, or book value, divided by its market capitalisation or market value gives a measure of the percentage of market value that is explained by the accounting system. This ratio also shows the value attributed by the market to unrecognised intangible assets in the broadest sense. Figure 3.2 shows how the median book-to-market ratio of FTSE 100 companies varied between 1990 and 2014.

Between 1990 and 1998, the book-to-market ratio followed a downward trend, as market values increased by more than book values. The median book value of net assets represented almost 57% of market value at the

Figure 3.2 Evolution of the book-to-market ratio of FTSE 100 companies.

Source: Datastream.

end of 1992 compared to 30% at the end of 1998. After the dot-com bubble burst, market values fell by more than book values, which resulted in the ratio increasing until 2004, when it fell because of a faster increase in market values than in book values. In 2007, the subprime crisis triggered a new period of financial crisis with the collapse of Lehman Brothers in September 2008, the instability of the world banking system in 2009, and the European sovereign debt crisis from 2010 onwards. Market values fell significantly while book values continued to grow, resulting in an increase in the book-to-market ratio until 2010, when market values recovered while book values plateaued (in part due to impairment losses).

One stylised fact emerges, however, from this figure. Market perception of the value of non-recognised economic intangible assets (e.g., organisational capital, human capital, internally developed goodwill) is volatile and depends on aversion to risk and on how expectations of future economic benefits vary as the market context evolves.

Figure 3.3 breaks down the book-to-market ratio and shows in parallel the progression of the book value of net assets of FTSE 100 companies since 1990 and that of the FTSE 100 index over the same period.[16]

Apparently both aggregates follow a similar pattern between 1990 and 2007. Nevertheless, two trends can be observed: (1) not surprisingly, variations in market values are larger than variations in book values, and

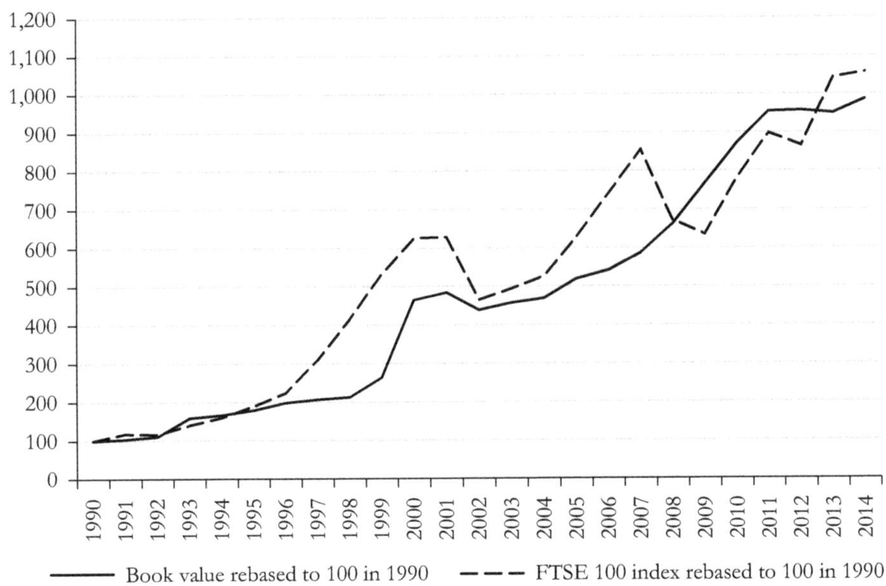

Figure 3.3 Evolution of shareholders' funds and market capitalisation from 1990 to 2014.

Source: Datastream.

(2) market values progress in advance of book values. The first trend is due to earnings smoothing in accounts, and the second is due to earnings conservatism compared with the inherent volatility and anticipation of variations in market values. Between 2007 and 2009, there is a clear disconnect between changes in book values, which continue to increase, and those of market values, which fall. After 2010, book values and market values move more in synch again. This suggests that the economic reality underlying the financial crisis took some time to be reflected in the accounts of quoted companies.

4.2. *Effect of the Introduction of IFRS on Intangible Asset Recognition*

We should note that it is not possible to identify in detail the various types of intangibles recognised in balance sheets using information available in financial databases (e.g., Bloomberg, Compustat, and Thomson Financial Datastream). These databases generally distinguish purchased goodwill from other intangible assets,[17] which include brands but also patents, customer relationships, capitalised developments costs, etc.

Table 3.3 identifies the ten FTSE 100 companies whose intangible assets (excluding purchased goodwill) represented the highest proportion of total assets at the end of 2014.

Reckitt Benckiser (RB) was the company that recognised the most intangibles in its balance sheet at the end of 2014, representing 51.6% of its total assets. The consumer goods company is a producer of health, hygiene, and home products, and it owns a wide portfolio of brands, many of which were acquired as part of business acquisitions; in particular, in 2005, the company acquired the over-the-counter drugs manufacturing business Boots Group, which added the three main brands Nurofen, Strepsils, and

Table 3.3 Recognition of intangible assets by FTSE[18] 100 companies

	Company	*Sector*	*% of total assets*
1	RECKITT BENCKISER GROUP	Consumer goods	51.6%
2	UNILEVER	Consumer goods	46.2%
3	SHIRE	Pharmaceuticals	36.2%
4	ASTRAZENECA	Pharmaceuticals	35.8%
5	DIAGEO	Beverages	29.1%
6	SMITH & NEPHEW	Healthcare	23.9%
7	GLAXOSMITHKLINE	Pharmaceuticals	20.5%
8	EXPERIAN	Support services	20.4%
9	IMPERIAL TOBACCO GROUP	Tobacco	20.3%
10	WEIR GROUP	Industrial Engineering	19.6%

Source: Datastream.

Clearasil. In 2010, RB purchased SSL International and added the brands Durex and Scholl.

Unilever, another global consumer goods company, follows closely with intangible assets making up 46% of its total assets at the end of 2014. Its products include food, beverages, cleaning agents and personal care products, and it owns over 400 brands. A number of these brands were acquired as part of business acquisitions, including Radox, which was purchased as part of the personal care business of Sarah Lee. Unilever also purchased the brands Simple, VO5, Nexxus, and TRESemmé as part of its acquisition of Alberto-Culver, a maker of personal care and household products.

Shire (dual listing on LSE and NASDAQ) and AstraZeneca, two pharmaceutical companies, follow with intangible assets making up around 36% of total assets. These mainly include acquired product rights, technology, development costs, and supply agreements. Smith & Nephew and Glaxo, in healthcare and pharmaceuticals, respectively, are also in the top ten.

The other companies in this top ten operate in different sectors: beverages (Diageo), support services (Experian), tobacco (Imperial Tobacco), and industrial engineering (Weir). Brands make up a significant part of the total assets of Diageo, which owns a large portfolio of beverage brands (e.g., acquired brands include McDowell's No.1 whisky and rum; Old Tavern, Haywards, and Bagpiper whisky; Shui Jing Fang Chinese white spirit; and Ypióca cachaça), and also of Imperial Tobacco (e.g., acquired brands include Fortuna, Gauloises Blondes, and Gitanes).

The introduction of IFRS for public companies, which became mandatory in 2005, has generally resulted in greater recognition of intangible assets in the accounts of FTSE 100 companies.

Figure 3.4 traces the evolution of the average amount of intangible assets (excluding goodwill) as a percentage of total assets for FTSE 100 companies since 2003.

In Figure 3.4, a change can clearly be seen in 2005 when IFRS was introduced. The average percentage of intangible assets increased from 4.7% in 2004 to around 7% from 2008 onwards.

Figure 3.5 presents this information for 2003 to 2014 for each of the five companies that capitalised the most intangible assets at the end of 2014.

Figure 3.5 shows that the impact of the introduction of IFRS was not the same across all companies. They did not all recognise intangible assets at the same time:

- It seems that AstraZeneca and Shire recognised few intangible assets before 2005 and 2007, respectively, and then considerable amounts once IFRS was introduced.
- Reckitt Benckiser, Diageo, and Unilever recognised intangible assets to a large extent before 2005. The share of intangibles recognised by Unilever increased in 2014 compared to prior years.

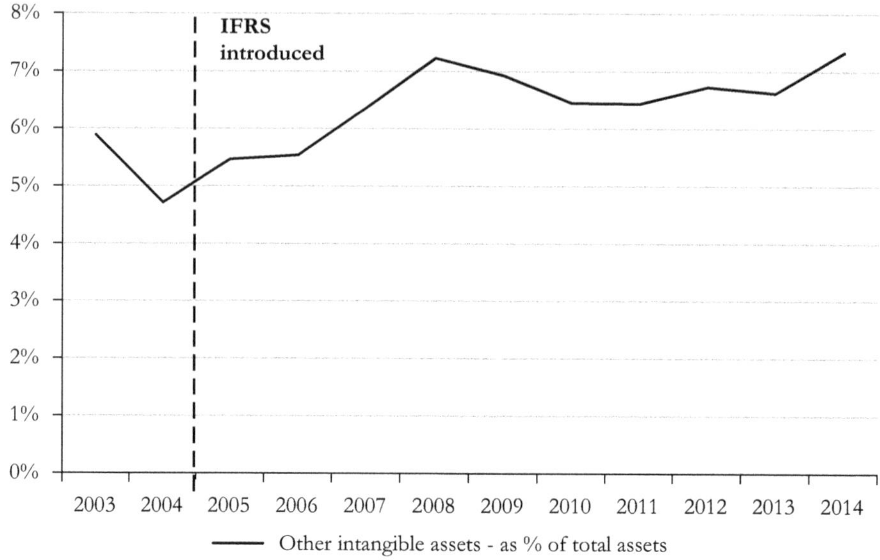

Figure 3.4 Other intangible assets of FTSE 100s as a per cent of total assets (average).

Source: Datastream.

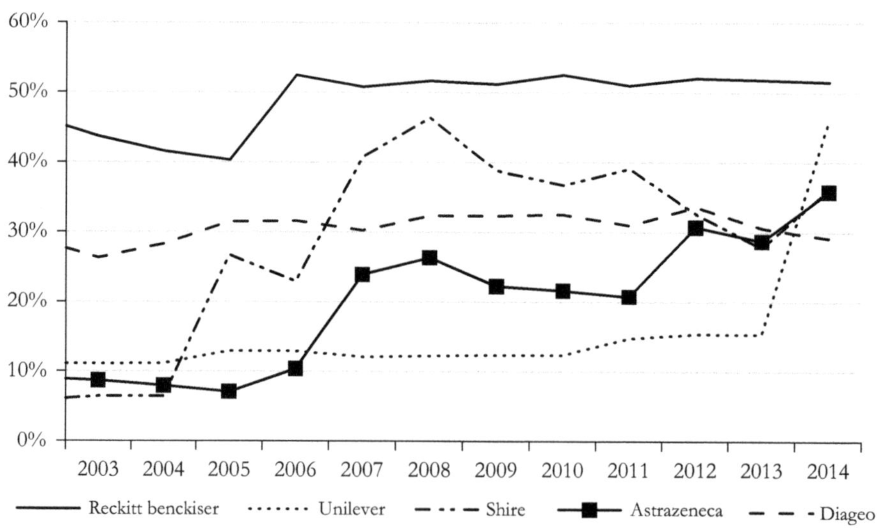

Figure 3.5 Recognition of intangible assets by the five most intangible-intensive companies (as a per cent of total assets).

Source: Datastream.

Conclusion

When we analyse the accounting standards that deal with initial recognition in the balance sheet and monitoring the value of brands, we see that treatment varies according to the method of acquisition. Whilst brands developed internally are recognised at the amount of directly attributable legal costs, brands acquired in business combinations are valued to arrive at their market value. How informative the accounting "value" of a brand is depends on whether it was developed internally or was acquired in a transaction less than six months prior to year-end. The accounting rules laid down by national and international standard-setters are today insufficient for a number of decisions where the market value of brands is needed.

Notes

1. The notion of "reporting" covers financial statements, notes to the financial statements, other information required by accounting standards, and other modes of communication (see, for example, the United States' Financial Accounting Standards Board (FASB) *Statement of Financial Accounting Concept* No 5, 1984).
2. In the United Kingdom, the FRC (Financial Reporting Council) issues Financial Reporting Standards, in particular FRS 3, "Reporting Financial Performance", the objective of which is (paragraph 1): "to aid users in understanding the performance achieved by a reporting entity in a period and to assist them in forming a basis for their assessment of future results and cash flows."
3. For example, under IFRS, leases are treated as assets acquired if certain conditions are met (transfer of risk and future economic benefits), even though legal ownership is not transferred.
4. The May 2015 Exposure Draft for a new Conceptual Framework proposed defining an asset as "a present economic resource controlled by the entity as a result of past events. An economic resource is a right that has a potential to produce economic benefits. Rights that constitute economic resources may be rights established by contract such as intellectual property rights, e.g., registered trademarks, or again rights that give the entity the potential to receive future economic benefits that are not available to all other parties, for example, rights to the economic benefits that may be produced by items such as know-how not in the public domain or by customer or supplier relationships" (IASB, 2015). This new definition will change somewhat the argumentation but should not in practice, we believe, change much in the way brands are recognised in financial statements.
5. IFRS and UK GAAP differ in this instance from US GAAP, which specifically forbids the capitalisation of development costs.
6. On the subject of managing purchase price allocations, see Shalev (2009), Shalev *et al.* (2013), and Paugam *et al.* (2015).
7. IAS 38 gives examples of intangible assets for which an active market exists in certain jurisdictions, including taxi licences, fishing licences, or production quotas, where these assets are freely transferable (IAS 38.78).
8. See Bariteau (2010).
9. "A cash-generating unit is the smallest identifiable group of assets that generates cash inflows that are largely independent of the cash inflows from other assets or group of assets" (IAS 36.6). In practice, the geographical areas or operational divisions of a company often constitute cash-generating units.

10. For a more detailed discussion of the valuation aspects addressed by IFRS and their practical implications, see Ramond *et al.* (2012).
11. Models derived from the *Arbitrage Pricing Theory* include risk factors in addition to the factor of sensitivity to market variation. Based on several econometric studies published in the 1990s, the Fama-French model contains two additional factors: company size (smaller companies are statistically associated with larger returns) and potential expected growth (for companies with lower potential, "value" shares exhibit higher returns than "growth" shares) (Fama and French, 1993, 1996). The Pastor and Stambaugh model (2003) includes a fourth factor explaining the returns required by investors: share liquidity. These models are based on empirical statistical patterns but provide limited theoretical explanation. They are therefore rarely used in practice in corporate finance.
12. Statement of Standard Accounting Practice 22.
13. http://core.ac.uk/download/pdf/76386.pdf.
14. Financial Reporting Standard 10.
15. For a detailed analysis of internally developed goodwill, see Zanoni (2009).
16. The lines show the sum of year-end book values and the sum of year-end market capitalisations of the companies in the FTSE 100 rebased to 100 at the end of 1990.
17. Values for goodwill and other intangible assets are usually only available from 2003 onwards.
18. The Financial Times Stock Exchange (FTSE) 100 is an index that measures the average share prices in the 100 largest, most actively traded companies on the London Stock Exchange (see: http://lexicon.ft.com/Term?term=FTSE-100).

References

Bariteau M.F. (2010), "La marque événementielle, une protection nécessaire contre l'ambush marketing" Master Thesis, Université Paul-Cézanne Aix-Marseille III, Aix-en-Provence, France.

Basu S. and Waymire G. (2008), "Has the Importance of Intangibles Really Grown? And If So, Why?" *Accounting and Business Research*, Vol. 8 (3), pp. 171–190.

Fama E. (1970), "Efficient Capital Markets: A Review of Theory and Empirical Works" *Journal of Finance,* Vol. 25 (2), pp. 383–417.

Fama E.F. and French K.R. (1993), "Common Risk Factors in the Returns on Stocks and Bonds" *Journal of Financial Economics*, Vol. 33 (1), pp. 3–56.

Fama E.F. and French K.R. (1996), "Multifactor Explanations of Asset Pricing Anomalies" *Journal of Finance*, Vol. 51 (1), pp. 55–84.

FASB (1984), *Statement of Financial Accounting Concept No. 5: Recognition and Measurement in Financial Statements of Business Enterprises*, Financial Accounting Standards Board, Norwalk, CT.

FASB (2001), *Statement of Financial Accounting Concepts No. 141: Business Combinations*, Financial Accounting Standards Board, Norwalk, CT.

FASB (2007) *Statement of Financial Accounting Concepts No. 141R: Business Combinations—Revised*, Financial Accounting Standards Board, Norwalk, CT.

IASB (2001), *Conceptual Framework for Financial Reporting 2001 (The IFRS Framework)*, IASC Foundation Publications Department, London.

IASB (2004a), *International Financial Reporting Standards (IFRS) No. 3: Business Combinations,* IASC Foundation Publications Department, London.

IASB (2004b), *International Financial Reporting Standards (IFRS) No. 5: Non-Current Assets Held for Sale and Discontinued Operations,* IASC Foundation Publications Department, London.

IASB (2008a), *International Accounting Standards (IAS) No. 38: Intangible Assets*, IASC Foundation Publications Department, London.

IASB (2008b), *International Financial Reporting Standards (IFRS) No. 3: Business Combinations—Revised*, IASC Foundation Publications Department, London.

IASB (2009), *International Accounting Standards No 36: Impairment of Assets*, IASC Foundation Publications Department, London.

IASB (2015), *Exposure Draft—Conceptual Framework for Financial Reporting*, IASC Foundation Publications Department, London.

Lev B. (2003), "Remarks on the Measurement, Valuation, and Reporting of Intangible Assets" *Federal Reserve Bank of New York, Economic Policy Review*, Vol. 9 (3), pp. 17–22.

Lev B. (2004), "Sharpening the Intangibles Edge" *Harvard Business Review*, June, pp. 109–116.

Modigliani F. and Miller M. (1958), "The Cost of Capital, Corporation Finance and the Theory of Investment" *American Economic Review*, Vol. 48 (3), pp. 261–297.

Nakamura L. (2004), "A Trillion Dollars a Year in Intangible Investment and the New Economy" *Federal Reserve Bank of Philadelphia's Paper*, *in* Hand J.R.M. et Lev B., *Intangible Assets: Values, Measures, and Risks*, Oxford University Press, Oxford, UK, pp. 19–47.

Pastor L. and Stambaugh R.F. (2003), "Liquidity Risk and Expected Stock Returns" *The Journal of Political Economy*, Vol. 111 (3), pp. 642–685.

Paugam L. Astolfi P. and Ramond O. (2015), "Accounting for Business Combinations: Do Purchase Price Allocations Matter?" *Journal of Accounting and Public Policy*, Vol. 34 (4), pp. 362–391.

Ramond O. Paugam L. Casta J.F. and Batsch L. (2012), *Évaluation financière et normes IFRS*, Economica, Paris.

Shalev R. (2009), "The Information Content of Business Combination Disclosure Level" *The Accounting Review*, Vol. 84 (1), pp. 239–270.

Shalev R. Zhang I.X. and Zhang Y. (2013), "CEO Compensation and Fair Value Accounting: Evidence from Purchase Price Allocation" *Journal of Accounting Research*, Vol. 51, pp. 819–854.

Zanoni A.B. (2009), *Accounting for Goodwill*, Taylor & Francis, New York and Abingdon, Oxon.

4 The Excess Earnings Method

> The development of the model shows the relevance of abnormal (or residual) earnings as a variable that influences a firm's value. This accounting-based performance measure is defined by earnings minus a charge for the use of capital [. . .].
>
> Ohlson (1995)

The excess earnings (or profits) method is part of the intrinsic or income approach to valuation. It is based on the forward-looking vision described in Chapter 2 according to which an asset is valued using the specific future cash flows it will generate. It relies, therefore, on discounting forecast cash flows attributable to an asset (*discounted cash flows*).

Using this approach, as we have seen, the value of a company is equivalent to the sum of the discounted expected free cash flows

$$V_t = \sum_{\tau=1}^{\infty} \frac{E_t\left[F_{t+\tau}\right]}{(1+k)^{\tau}}, \tag{1}$$

where V_t = intrinsic value of the company at time t;
$E_t[.]$ = mathematical expectation operator;
k = cost of capital;
F_t = free cash flows generated by company in period t.

The excess earnings method consists of attributing excess earnings to the brand by deducting the contribution of all the other tangible and intangible assets (contributory assets) to a company's total economic earnings. To apply this approach, an overall valuation of the business operating the brand must first be carried out. This can be done using a *discounted cash flows approach* (see Chapter 2) or an *economic profit* (*excess return*) approach. We review the latter here, as the *excess earnings method* derives from this approach.

The excess earnings method is a sophisticated equivalent version of equation (1). To understand its meaning, we need to know where the method came from. Research on valuation carried out by Edwards and Bell (1961), Peasnell (1982), and Ohlson (1995), among others, established formal relationships between intrinsic value, accounting profit, and cost of capital.

First, we begin with the following valuation model, which is based on expected dividend flows that represent free cash flows to shareholders (equity providers) in equation (1):

$$VE_t = \sum_{\tau=1}^{\infty} \frac{E_t\left[DIV_{t+\tau}\right]}{\left(1+k_e\right)^{\tau}}, \tag{2}$$

where VE_t = value of shareholders' equity at time t;
DIV_t = dividends in period t;
k_e = cost of capital required by equity providers.

Next, we need an accounting identity that explains how net equity (*BVE or book value of equity*) varies: accounting profit (*NI or net income*) minus dividends (*DIV*) contributes entirely to the difference in book value between dates *t -1* and *t*. This is known as the *clean surplus relation* assumption, formally expressed as

$$BVE_t = BVE_{t-1} + NI_t - DIV_t. \tag{3}$$

The value of net equity at date *t* is equal to the value of net equity at *t -1* plus net income for the period between *t -1* and *t*, less dividends paid in *t*. By combining equations (2) and (3), we obtain identity (4):

$$VE_t = BVE_t + \sum_{\tau=1}^{\infty} \frac{E_t\left[BVE_{t-1+\tau} + NI_{t+\tau} - DIV_{t+\tau}\right]}{\left(1+k_e\right)^{\tau}}. \tag{4}$$

The notion of excess earnings, or *residual* (or *abnormal*) *earnings,* is defined as follows:

$$NI_t^a = NI_t - k_e \times BVE_{t-1}, \tag{5}$$

where NI_t^a = *Excess, residual* (or *abnormal*) earnings in *t*.

Excess earnings represent earnings which are in excess of the remuneration expected by (equity) investors, i.e., the return required by capital providers[1] who have regard to the level of risk. Equation (5) can be rewritten by highlighting the ROE (*Return on Equity* = NI_t/BVE_{t-1}):

$$NI_t^a = \left(ROE_t - k_e\right) \times BVE_{t-1}. \tag{5bis}$$

The basic valuation equation (equation (4)) can thus be reformulated as follows:

$$VE_t = BVE_t + \sum_{\tau=1}^{\infty} \frac{E_t\left[ROE_{t+\tau} - k_e\right] \times BVE_{t-1+\tau}}{\left(1+k_e\right)^{\tau}}. \qquad (6)$$

Equation (6) is important because it highlights the impact of expected performance compared with the minimum return on net equity required by shareholders (cost of equity, k_e). If expected performance (ROE) is equivalent to required performance (k_e), then the market value of equity will be the same as book value of equity. However, the market value of equity capital will be higher than book value of equity when the expected rate of return is greater than the cost of capital and vice versa. In formal terms, equation (6) results in the following equalities and inequalities:

$$\begin{aligned} VE_t = BVE_t &\Leftrightarrow ROE = k_e \\ VE_t > BVE_t &\Leftrightarrow ROE > k_e \\ VE_t < BVE_t &\Leftrightarrow ROE < k_e. \end{aligned} \qquad (7)$$

Without financial debt, the book value of equity (BVE) is also equal to the capital employed (CE). Further, net income (NI) is equal to net operating profit after tax ($NOPAT$), because there are no finance costs. Thus the notion of excess earnings, or *residual (or abnormal) earnings*, can also be defined for a company relying on equity and debt financing as follows:[2]

$$NOPAT_t^a = NOPAT_t - k \times CE_{t-1}, \qquad (5')$$

where $NOPAT_t^a$ = *Excess, residual* (or *abnormal*) operating earnings in t;
k = Cost of capital for suppliers of funds (shareholders and debt-holders).

In this case, excess operating earnings represent earnings which are in excess of the remuneration expected by all providers of funds, k, i.e., the return required by capital providers having regard to the level of risk of the capital employed, also called the weighted average cost of capital of WACC (see Appendix 1). Equation (5') can be rewritten by highlighting the ROCE (*return on capital Employed* = $NOPAT_t/CE_{t-1}$)

$$NOPAT_t^a = \left(ROCE_t - k\right) \times CE_{t-1}. \qquad (5'bis)$$

The basic valuation equation can thus be reformulated as

$$V_t = CE_t + \sum_{\tau=1}^{\infty} \frac{E_t\left[ROCE_{t+\tau} - k\right] \times CE_{t-1+\tau}}{\left(1+k\right)^{\tau}}. \qquad (6')$$

Equation (6'), like equation (6), is important because it highlights again the impact of expected performance compared with the minimum return, but in this case, return on capital employed as required by all suppliers of funds (cost of capital, k). If expected performance ($ROCE$) is equivalent to required performance (k), then the market value of capital employed will be the same as book value of capital employed. However, the market value of capital employed will be higher than book value when the expected rate of return is greater than the cost of capital and vice versa. In formal terms, equation (6') results in the following equalities and inequalities:

$$\begin{aligned} V_t = CE_t &\Leftrightarrow ROCE = k, \\ V_t > CE_t &\Leftrightarrow ROCE > k, \\ V_t < CE_t &\Leftrightarrow ROCE < k. \end{aligned} \tag{7}$$

Brands are highly synergistic assets which make it easier for companies that use them to outperform economically.[3] They enable excess profits to be earned. In effect, they lead to "monopoly rents", because they differentiate goods and services from those of competitors. The value of a brand is then seen as those excess profits earned by a highly profitable business. Valuations using this method involve identifying excess profits and forecasting them. This approach was applied in a simplified form in Chapter 2.

Before presenting the main principles of the method, it is worth noting that it has several variants. The EVA-MVA[4] method is probably the best-known variant of the model represented by equations (6 and 6'). It uses more or less restrictive assumptions concerning capital structure and the evolution of return on capital employed.

1. Principle

Under the excess earnings method, the value of a brand corresponds to the present value of the "abnormal" or excess profits it generates.

The basic tenet of the method is that a brand will enable a company each year to generate higher profits than a similar company without a brand (assuming that all the other assets contributing to economic profits are recognised by both firms). The difference between the profit earned by the company with a brand and that earned by a company without a brand represents the excess profits attributable to the brand.[5]

$$EP_t = NOPAT_{B,t} - NOPAT_{WB,t}, \tag{8}$$

where EP_t = excess profits attributable to the brand in period t;
$NOPAT_{B,t}$ = net operating profit after tax in period t of company with brand; and
$NOPAT_{WB,t}$ = net operating profit after tax in period t of company without brand.

The excess earnings method per se consists of identifying the excess profits attributable to the brand after deducting from total economic profits the contribution of all the other assets (contributory asset charges), as illustrated in details in the next section of this chapter.

As previously seen, when there is no brand, return on capital employed is assumed to be equal to the cost of capital. Value is neither created nor destroyed. The following relationship is implied:

$$ROCE = k, \tag{9}$$

where $ROCE$ = return on capital employed;
k = cost of capital employed.

Now, to the extent that

$$ROCE_{WB,t} = \frac{NOPAT_{WB,t}}{CE_{WB,\ t-1}}, \tag{10}$$

we obtain

$$NOPAT_{WB,t} = k \times CE_{WB,t\text{-}1}, \tag{11}$$

where $CE_{WB,t\text{-}1}$ = capital employed excluding brand at beginning of period t.

Excess profits earned by the brand are equal to the difference between actual post-tax operating profits and capital employed multiplied by cost of capital:

$$EP_t = NOPAT_{B,t} - k \times CE_{B,t-1}. \tag{12}$$

The brand's value can be estimated by discounting excess profits forecast over its expected useful life (which may be infinite):

$$V_{B,t} = \sum_{\tau=1}^{T} \frac{EP_{t+\tau}}{(1+k)^{\tau}}, \tag{13}$$

where $V_{B,t}$ = brand value at t.

The outperformance (the economic goodwill generated by the company) derives solely from its brand. However, because the recognition of internally generated intangibles in accounting is limited (see Chapter 3), companies usually own other significant intangible assets, the value of which may not be shown in the balance sheet, e.g., human capital, distribution networks, and technologies. These assets also contribute to economic outperformance.

The financial value of a brand does not, therefore, correspond to a company's total economic goodwill value, but only to residual goodwill once part of the outperformance has been attributed to the other contributing intangible assets. Equation (13) must then be modified to take account of this.

$$EP_t = NOPAT_{B,t} - (k \times CE_{WB,t}) - EP_I, \tag{14}$$

where EP_I = excess earnings attributed to other intangible assets not recognised in the balance sheet.

In practice, to the extent that the value of excess earnings deriving from other intangible assets is not necessarily known, but is estimated using different methods, equation (15) is applied.

$$V_{B,t} = \sum_{\tau=1}^{\infty} \frac{EP_{t+\tau}}{(1+k)^{t+\tau}} - V_{I,t}, \tag{15}$$

where $V_{I,t}$ = value of other intangible assets not recognised in the balance sheet in t.

2. Implementation—Valuation of a Consulting Firm's Brand

Consultancy Inc. is a management consultancy firm founded in the United States during the second half of the twentieth century. The firm is positioned as a top-end firm providing custom-made solutions to complex problems. The firm has a reputation for being innovative and today employs several thousand consultants worldwide.

2.1. Financial Performance of the Firm

The Consultancy Inc. brand needs to be valued as of December 2014. Table 4.1 shows the firm's financial performance for the previous three years.

As the variations in revenue show, the firm was severely affected by the departure of several key partners in 2013 who took important clients with them.

The firm's cost structure is mainly semi-fixed (salary costs and associated indirect costs). The number of consultants and offices cannot mechanically be adjusted as business conditions change; the consultancy sector incurs semi-fixed costs. The loss of clients, therefore, had an especially high impact on operating profit, because the level of business was insufficient to absorb fixed costs. The firm's directors were, as a result, forced to launch a restructuring plan to restore profitability.

Management expectations of the firm's financial performance for 2015 to 2019 are shown in Table 4.2.

As far as capital requirements of the business are concerned, a consulting business does not need large amounts of capital, as shown in Table 4.3. The only significant capital required is to finance working capital.

Table 4.1 Historical income statements of Consultancy Inc.

Millions of Euros	*2012*	*2013*	*2014*
Revenue	**170.0**	**110.0**	**115.0**
Consultants' salaries and direct costs	(119.9)	(83.9)	(88.6)
Operating margin	**50.1**	**26.1**	**26.4**
as % of revenues	*29.5%*	*23.8%*	*23.0%*
Support function and other indirect costs	(39.6)	(30.8)	(29.5)
Operating profit	**10.5**	**(4.6)**	**(3.1)**
as % of revenues	*6.2%*	*(4.2)%*	*(2.7)%*
Restructuring costs and other costs	(0.4)	(9.4)	(15.2)
EBIT	**10.1**	**(14.0)**	**(18.3)**
Finance costs (net)	(3.4)	(3.1)	(2.8)
Profit before tax	**6.6**	**(17.1)**	**(21.0)**
Taxation	(6.7)	(5.4)	1.0
Net profit/(loss)	**(0.1)**	**(22.5)**	**(20.0)**

Table 4.2 Forecast income statement of Consultancy Inc.

	Business Plan					
Millions of Euros	*2014*	*2015*	*2016*	*2017*	*2018*	*2019*
Revenue	**115.0**	**121.9**	**125.6**	**133.7**	**142.4**	**156.7**
Growth rate	*4.5%*	*6.0%*	*3.0%*	*6.5%*	*6.5%*	*10.0%*
Direct costs	88.6	90.2	90.4	94.9	101.1	111.2
Operating margin	**26.4**	**31.7**	**35.2**	**38.8**	**41.3**	**45.4**
as % of revenues	*23.0%*	*26.0%*	*28.0%*	*29.0%*	*29.0%*	*29.0%*
Indirect costs	29.5	30.5	30.1	29.4	29.9	32.9
Operating profits	**(3.1)**	**1.2**	**5.0**	**9.4**	**11.4**	**12.5**
as % of revenue	*(2.7)%*	*1.0%*	*4.0%*	*7.0%*	*8.0%*	*8.0%*

Table 4.3 Historical balance sheets of Consultancy Inc.

Millions of Euros	*Dec. 2012*	*Dec. 2013*	*Dec. 2014*
Fixed assets	2	2	2
Working capital	22	33	31
Capital employed	**24**	**35**	**33**
Equity	60	38	18
Net debt	(36)	(3)	15
Invested capital	**24**	**34**	**33**

Tables 4.2 and 4.3 show the low-capital intensity of the business. For every euro invested at the end of 2014, the firm expects to generate almost €3.7 of revenues in 2015 (= 121.9/33), a capital turnover of 3.7.

2.2. *Rate of Return of the Business*

The economic rate of return is the measure of the economic performance of a business. It is calculated by dividing the business's operating profit by the capital employed to generate that profit.[6] Table 4.4 shows the economic rate of return of Consultancy Inc. (ROCE).

Despite a relatively low operating margin, the firm is able to generate a high return on capital employed (ROCE): above 10% in 2016 and above 15% from 2017 onwards. The low-capital intensity of the consulting business enables such a high return to be earned.

2.3. *Excess Earnings Generated by the Business*

The brand contributes to a certain level of performance (NOPAT). In this respect, this performance should not take account of possible costs relating to the brand and its development. Double-counting must be avoided; otherwise,

Table 4.4 Forecast profitability and ROCE of Consultancy Inc.

	Business Plan						
Millions of euros	*2013*	*2014*	*2015*	*2016*	*2017*	*2018*	*2019*
Revenue [a]	110.0	115.0	121.9	125.6	133.7	142.4	156.7
growth rate		*4.5%*	*6.0%*	*3.0%*	*6.5%*	*6.5%*	*10.0%*
Capital employed (beginning of period) [b]	**24.0**	**34.5**	**33.0**	**35.0**	**36.0**	**38.4**	**40.9**
Growth rate		*(4.3)%*	*6.0%*	*3.0%*	*6.5%*	*6.5%*	*10.0%*
EBIT [c]	(8.6)	(3.1)	1.2	5.0	9.4	11.4	12.5
Corporation tax [c] × 30% = [d]	2.6	0.9	(0.4)	(1.5)	(2.8)	(3.4)	(3.8)
NOPAT [c] +[d] = [e]	**(6.0)**	**(2.2)**	**0.9**	**3.5**	**6.6**	**8.0**	**8.8**
ROCE [e] / [b]			**2.6%**	**10.1%**	**18.2%**	**20.8%**	**21.5%**
Turnover of employed capital [a] / [b]	*4.6*	*3.3*	*3.7*	*3.6*	*3.7*	*3.7*	*3.8*
EBIT margin [c] / [a]	*(7.8)%*	*(2.7)%*	*1.0%*	*4.0%*	*7.0%*	*8.0%*	*8.0%*
NOPAT margin [d] / [a]	*(5.5)%*	*(1.9)%*	*0.7%*	*2.8%*	*4.9%*	*5.6%*	*5.6%*

the value of the brand would be underestimated. Only costs relating to the maintenance and upkeep of the brand should be taken into account.

Once this adjustment has been made, a major step remains. It is clear that the economic performance thus calculated overestimates the brand's contribution, because other assets (tangible and intangible) have also contributed to this performance. A notional charge must be made for the use of these other contributory assets. How should this notional charge be determined? In fact, it will be equivalent to the return required by investors on those types of assets or, in other words, the cost of capital.

The excess earnings method entails comparing the actual economic performance (rate of return) delivered by the company with the return required by its investors (cost of capital). When a company is able continuously to earn a return higher than its cost of capital, we talk of excess earnings (economic rents). Brands are determining factors in the creation of economic rents.

Let us assume that in the last three years, Consultancy Inc. has spent no money on developing its brand. Its cost of capital is 7.5%.

The level of annual excess earnings of Consultancy Inc., calculated as the difference between actual NOPAT and the minimum NOPAT required by its investors, is shown in Table 4.5.

2.4. *Sustainability of Excess Earnings*

The firm generates excess profits in the business plan period. But the question remains as to the sustainability of these super profits. How long will the firm be able to maintain its economic rent?

Table 4.5 Estimation of annual excess earnings

	Business Plan						
Millions of Euros	*2013*	*2014*	*2015*	*2016*	*2017*	*2018*	*2019*
Capital employed (Beginning of period) [a]	24.0	34.5	33.0	35.0	36.0	38.4	40.9
Remuneration of capital employed [b]	7.5%	7.5%	7.5%	7.5%	7.5%	7.5%	7.5%
Required NOPAT [c] = [a] × [b]	1.8	2.6	2.5	2.6	2.7	2.9	3.1
Actual NOPAT [d]	(6.0)	(2.2)	0.9	3.5	6.6	8.0	8.8
Actual ROCE			*2.6%*	*10.1%*	*18.2%*	*20.8%*	*21.5%*
Excess earnings [d]–[c]	(7.8)	(4.7)	(1.6)	0.9	3.8	5.1	5.7
No of years discounted			0.5	1.5	2.5	3.5	4.5
Discount factor			1.0	0.9	0.8	0.8	0.7
Present value of excess earnings			(1.6)	0.8	3.2	4.0	4.1

A company without a particular competitive advantage, and operating in a sector with no real barriers to entry, will not be able to maintain a rate of return significantly higher than its cost of capital. Where there are no barriers to entry and the company has no special competitive edge, new players attracted by the possibility of interesting returns on their investment will enter the market. As a result, competition will become fiercer and return on capital employed will decrease towards the level of the cost of capital. If the rate of return became lower than the cost of capital, some market players would be led to reallocate capital invested to other more profitable activities. This would mechanically cause the rate of return to move back up to the level of the cost of capital. Where no entry barriers or competitive advantages exist, the normal rate of return of a business tends towards its cost of capital.

On the other hand, if barriers to entry exist or if certain players possess sound competitive advantages (brands or know-how, for example), it is more costly for new players to enter the market in question. The level of profitability at which it is economically worthwhile to enter the market is therefore higher. Existing market players, therefore, maintain a return on capital employed higher than their cost of capital and so protect their economic rent.

This implicitly raises the question of how durable a brand can be. A brand is an entry barrier to a market. As we saw in Chapter 1, a brand does not necessarily last forever. A brand may disappear. In the same way, the competitive advantage conferred by a brand may be more or less substantial or durable. These issues must be addressed through strategic and economic analyses of the brand's strength.

In our case study of the valuation of the Consultancy Inc. brand, we have assumed for the sake of simplicity that the brand, and therefore the firm's excess earnings, would last indefinitely. The firm and its brand were created several decades ago, and the reputation of the firm and its brand is well established. Our assumptions are therefore consistent with the strategy and outlook of the brand.

Calculation of Terminal Value

When a series of cash flows is infinite, we need to calculate a terminal value for the cash flows beyond the explicit projection period. Two approaches are possible:

1. The Gordon Shapiro method or Gordon growth model, where the terminal value equals the present value of maintainable (normalised) cash flows growing perpetually at rate g and discounted to infinity:

$$TV_T = \frac{CF_{Norm,T}}{k - g}, \tag{16}$$

where TV_T = terminal value beyond projection period (T);
$CF_{Norm,\,T}$ = normalised cash flows expected in the year after T, e.g., excess earnings from the brand;
k = discount rate;
g = growth rate of normalised cash flows (in perpetuity).

The terminal value (TV) is then discounted back to the valuation date:

$$TV_{t=O} = \frac{1}{(1+k)^T} \times \frac{CF_{Norm,T}}{k-g}. \tag{17}$$

It is also possible not to extrapolate to infinity and to calculate a terminal value which diminishes progressively to zero.

2. The second approach entails applying a multiple to a key performance indicator, such as operating profit. To estimate the multiple, the approach assumes that comparable brands exist with similar recognition and growth profiles to the brand being valued. For this reason, the first approach is more frequently used for brands.

2.5. *Valuation of the Consultancy Inc. Brand: First Step*

Once the brand's useful economic life has been estimated, the excess earnings it will generate throughout its life can be calculated. To reflect the business environment of Consultancy Inc., we include an "extrapolation period" between the years 2020 and 2030 over which the performance will converge towards normalised performance in the year 2030. We have assumed the business is an ongoing concern and the brand has an indefinite economic life. The total excess earnings generated by the business can be estimated at €83.8 million, as shown in Table 4.6. This represents the present value of the sum of future excess earnings.

Can this value be considered a realistic estimate of the value of the brand?

The answer is probably no because two elements are so far missing from the analysis. First, the brand's lifespan may be indefinite in principle, but in practice, its ability to generate excess returns for the firm is unlikely to be infinite. It would be more reasonable to include excess earnings over a finite period (say between 20 and 30 years). Second, the firm has other intangible assets, not recognised in its balance sheet, which contribute to these excess earnings: human capital (talent and know-how of its teams), organisational capital (efficiency of its organisation and support functions in carrying out its assignments), or unrecognised technologies.

In its calculation of total excess earnings, the valuation in Table 4.6 includes an extrapolation of the economic rents (the finite extrapolation

Table 4.6 Estimated excess earnings of the Consultancy Inc. business

	Business Plan					*Extrapolation*				*Maintainable*
Millions of Euros	*2015*	*2016*	*2017*	*2018*	*2019*	*2020*	...	*2029*	*2030*	*2031*
Capital employed (beginning of period) [a]	33.0	35.0	36.0	38.4	40.9	45.0	...	53.7	54.8	55.9
Remuneration of capital employed [b]	7.5%	7.5%	7.5%	7.5%	7.5%	7.5%	...	7.5%	7.5%	7.5%
Required NOPAT [c] = [a] × [b]	2.5	2.6	2.7	2.9	3.1	3.4	...	4.0	4.1	4.2
Actual NOPAT [d]	0.9	3.5	6.6	8.0	8.8	8.9	...	10.7	10.9	11.1
Actual ROCE	*2.6%*	*10.1%*	*18.2%*	*20.8%*	*21.5%*	*19.9%*	...	*19.9%*	*19.9%*	*19.9%*
Excess earnings [d]–[c]	(1.6)	0.9	3.8	5.1	5.7	5.6	...	6.7	6.8	6.9
No. of years discounted	0.5	1.5	2.5	3.5	4.5	5.5	...	14.5	15.5	15.5
Discount factor	1.0	0.9	0.8	0.8	0.7	0.7	...	0.4	0.3	0.3
Present value of excess earnings	(1.6)	0.8	3.2	4.0	4.1	3.7	...	2.3	2.2	2.3
Present value of excess earnings (2015–2019)	10.5									
Present value of excess earnings (2020–2030)	32.1									
Present value of excess earnings (terminal value: 2031 onwards)	41.1									
Present value of total excess earnings	83.8									

covers 2020 to 2030). One could argue that no excess profits would be earned beyond 2030 (Under this assumption, the sum of excess earnings would be reduced to €42.6 million.).

In total, cumulative excess profits amount to €83.8 million. It is probably reasonable to consider that only a fraction of this figure is attributable to the brand. The question is how to quantify this fraction: is the brand responsible for 40%, 50%, or 60% of excess earnings?

The second step will enable us to isolate excess profits which derive from the brand by deducting the contribution of the other unrecognised intangible assets.

2.6. Valuation of Consultancy Inc.'s Brand: Second Step

Let us assume that another intangible asset contributes to Consultancy Inc.'s excess earnings: the human capital represented by its consultants. It is a fact that for a consultancy firm, its workforce constitutes an essential asset that provides a competitive advantage but is not recognised in the balance sheet.

When using the excess earnings method, a company's profit must remunerate not only capital employed but also the availability of its workforce, which is a vital asset for the firm. This remuneration must be quantified and then subtracted from total excess profits to isolate the value of the brand.

The reproduction cost method is usually used to value human capital.[7] The method involves estimating the costs that would be necessary to put together an equivalent team of consultants. These costs are the following:

- Recruitment costs: these include the costs of recruitment firms and the costs of recruitment campaigns (for the more junior consultants). These costs are generally measured in number of months' salary of the recruited staff and depend on the level of experience of each consultant.
- Training and ramp-up costs: these correspond to the time needed to train newly hired consultants. They also take account of the time required for the teams to become fully productive. These costs are estimated using the total salary costs of each category of the firm's employees.

As presented in Table 4.7, these various assumptions result in the firm's workforce being valued at approximately €21.2 million.[8]

The firm's profit has to remunerate not only the capital employed shown in the balance sheet but also the unrecognised workforce. On this basis, the value of excess earnings generated by the firm is presented in Table 4.8.

We shall assume that the value of the workforce is constant in time (an alternative assumption could be that it varies in line with capital employed, for example).

Table 4.7 Value of Consultancy Inc.'s workforce

	Thousands of Euros	*Analysts*	*Managers*	*Senior Managers*	*Partners*	*Total Consultant*	*Support Functions*	*Total*
	Recruitment costs							
	Average salary (201er person including bonus)	50	100	150	275		50	
×	Recruitment cost (in number of months' salary)	1.0	2.0	3.0	4.0		2.0	
/12 =	**Recruitment cost**	**4.2**	**16.7**	**37.5**	**91.7**		**8.3**	
	Training and ramp-up costs							
	Average payroll cost (201er person including bonus and benefits)	70	120	180	340		65	
×	Training and ramp-up costs (in number of months)	6.0	3.0	3.0	2.0		2.0	
/12 =	**Training and ramp-up costs**	**35.0**	**30.0**	**45.0**	**56.7**		**10.8**	
	Number of consultants by category	250	80	90	50	**470**	100	**570**
	Recruitment cost	1,042	1,333	3,375	4,583	**10,333**	833	**11,167**
+	Training and ramp-up costs	8,750	2,400	4,050	2,833	**18,033**	1,083	**19,117**
=	**Gross value of workforce**	**9,792**	**3,733**	**7,425**	**7,417**	**28,367**	**1,917**	**30,283**
	Net value of workforce (after tax @30%)							**21,198**

Table 4.8 Estimated excess earnings from the Consultancy Inc. brand

Millions of Euros	*2015*	*2016*	*2017*	*2018*	*2019*	*2020*	...	*2029*	*2030*	*2031*
Capital employed (beginning of period)	33.0	35.0	36.0	38.4	40.9	45.0	...	53.7	54.8	55.9
Market value of workforce	21.2	21.2	21.2	21.2	21.2	21.2	...	21.2	21.2	21.2
Adjusted capital employed (beginning of period) [a']	**54.2**	**56.2**	**57.2**	**59.6**	**62.1**	**66.2**	...	**74.9**	**76.0**	**77.1**
Remuneration of capital employed [b]	7.5%	7.5%	7.5%	7.5%	7.5%	7.5%	...	7.5%	7.5%	7.5%
Required NOPAT [c] = [a'] × [b]	**4.1**	**4.2**	**4.3**	**4.5**	**4.7**	**5.0**	...	**5.6**	**5.7**	**5.8**
Actual NOPAT [d]	**0.9**	**3.5**	**6.6**	**8.0**	**8.8**	**8.9**	...	**10.7**	**10.9**	**11.1**
Actual ROCE	*1.6%*	*6.3%*	*11.4%*	*13.4%*	*14.1%*	*13.5%*	...	*14.3%*	*14.4%*	*14.4%*
Excess earnings [d]–[c]	**(3.2)**	**(0.7)**	**2.3**	**3.5**	**4.1**	**4.0**	...	**5.1**	**5.2**	**5.3**
No. of years discounted	0.5	1.5	2.5	3.5	4.5	5.5	...	14.5	15.5	15.5
Discount factor	1.0	0.9	0.8	0.8	0.7	0.7	...	0.4	0.3	0.3
Present value of excess earnings	**(3.1)**	**(0.6)**	**1.9**	**2.7**	**3.0**	**2.7**	...	**1.8**	**1.7**	**1.7**
Present value of excess earnings (2015–2019)	3.9									
Present value of excess earnings (2020–2030)	23.7									
Present value of excess earnings (terminal value : 2031 and +)	31.7									
Present value of total excess earnings	**59.3**									

If we use the same assumptions as previously used regarding brand lifespan and the development of the firm's business at the end of the explicit projections period, the brand is valued at €59.3 million.

Once again, for simplicity's sake, the residual excess profits, after remuneration of the capital employed (including the workforce), are attributed solely to the brand (although one could value other contributory intangible assets and include a charge for their use under a similar logic).

3. What Is the Return on Capital Needed to Finance a Brand?

One of the essential factors in the excess earnings valuation method is the cost of capital required to remunerate capital employed, which represents a *normal* level of profitability for the business. This is a major difficulty with this method. The reader will find in Appendix 1 methods traditionally used to estimate the cost of capital of an asset.

In practice, specific required rates of return may exist for different categories of assets. A separate required rate will exist for intangible assets, for tangible assets, and for working capital. This implicitly means assigning a level of risk to each asset or asset class of a company.[9] The weighted average of these required rates of return must equal the cost of capital.

Figure 4.1 explains how the Canadian Institute of Chartered Business Valuators (CICBV) implements this approach. The CICBV suggests how to estimate an appropriate cost of capital for each type of asset.

However satisfying it may be to break down required rates of return, this approach has a major drawback: it treats a company like a portfolio of financial assets. In a portfolio, every asset and class of asset has its own level

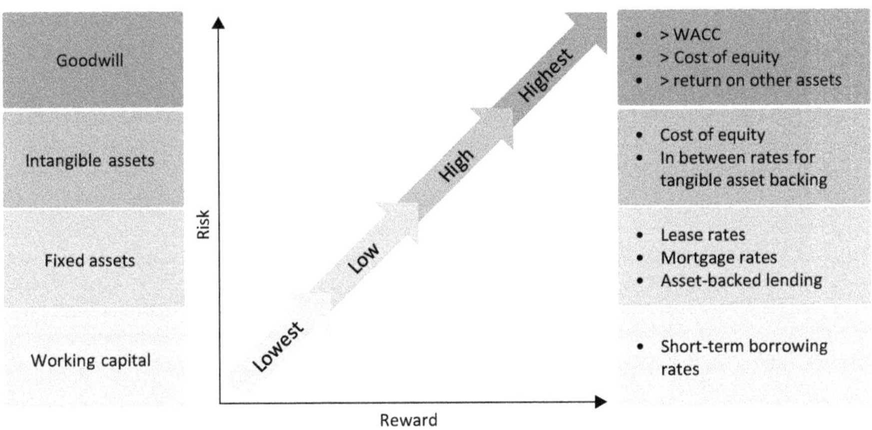

Figure 4.1 Cost of capital by asset category

Source: The Canadian Institute of Chartered Business Valuators (CICBV).

of risk and therefore its specific required yield. This abstract way of looking at a company stems from the Mean-Variance model resulting from the work of Markowitz (1952) and Sharpe (1964).

Such a vision is, however, inappropriate to a complete and organised set of productive resources. In an organised group of assets, the significance of one part of the group can vary according to its position in the structure; in other words, it varies according to how it interacts with other assets. The idea of remunerating each separate element of the organised set in isolation may therefore be considered theoretically unsound.

Conclusion

The excess earnings method is relatively challenging to implement, as it requires high quality data and a detailed analysis of several factors: the business plan, the return required by investors, excess profits, and unrecognised intangible assets. Defining the numerous necessary parameters involves mature economic and strategic analyses.

In practice, the excess earnings method is one of the intrinsic or income-based methods often used for brand valuation. Using several methods, if feasible, is usually preferable to using one. One other method is the revenue premium method, which is described in the following chapter. The main difference between these two methods is above all one of presentation. The excess earnings method involves quantifying economic profits attributable to the brand after deducting the proportion of earnings that are attributable to other assets. Under the revenue premium method, excess cash flows deriving from a brand are compared with those from a generic (unbranded) product. Each method is therefore based on a different approach using company cash flows to quantify the additional value created by a brand.

Notes

1. Here we assume that there is only net equity and no financial debt. In this case, the only capital providers are the shareholders.
2. The following relationships can also be derived under certain conditions if a company has financial debt. See Feltham and Ohlson (1995).
3. We shall return in Chapter 10 to the problems posed by the synergistic nature of brands.
4. EVA (*Economic Value-Added*) measures the value created by a company during an accounting period with the following formula: EVA = (ROI—WACC) × NOA, where NOA represents net operating assets, WACC is the weighted average cost of capital of the business and ROI (*Return on Investment or net operating assets*). MVA (*Market Value-Added*) is the difference between the market value of the company and the book value of net operating assets. EVA and MVA are trademarks of Stern Stewart & Co.
5. Whilst we do not identify the specific drivers of excess earnings here, we will illustrate the notion of revenue premium as a driver of excess earnings in Chapter 5.
6. Operating profit or EBIT measures the operating performance of a business. Operating profit net of tax is referred to as NOPAT (net operating profit after tax).

7. The reproduction cost method is covered in Chapter 8. The principles that are presented can be applied to value a company's workforce.
8. This amount is net of tax. There is a debate on this subject among valuers. Some consider that if human capital is an accounting asset, it should be recorded at its gross value. Others argue that the asset's market value is based on after-tax cash flows, because related costs are tax deductible.
9. This is referred to as the weighted average rate of return on assets (WARA).

References

Edwards E.O. and Bell P.W. (1961), *The Theory and Measurement of Business Income*, University of California Press, Berkeley and Los Angeles.

Feltham G. and Ohlson J. (1995), "Valuation and Clean Surplus Accounting for Operating and Financial Activities" *Contemporary Accounting Research*, Vol. 11 (2), pp. 689–731.

Markowitz H. (1952), "Portfolio Selection" *Journal of Finance*, Vol. 7 (1), pp. 77–91.

Ohlson J. (1995), "Earnings, Book Values, and Dividends in Equity Valuation" *Contemporary Accounting Research*, Vol. 11 (2), pp. 661–687.

Peasnell K.V. (1982), "Some Formal Connections Between Economic Values and Yields and Accounting Numbers" *Journal of Business Finance & Accounting*, Vol. 9 (3), pp. 361–381.

Sharpe W.F. (1964), "Capital Asset Prices: A Theory of Market Equilibrium Under Conditions of Risk" *Journal of Finance*, Vol. 19 (3), pp. 425–442.

5 Revenue Premium Method

The revenue premium method is part of a larger method called profit premium method. A brand may generate a profit premium for a company by increasing its revenues or reducing its costs. In the rest of this chapter, we will focus on the revenue premium method, which includes the price premium and the volume premium methods, and belongs to the family of intrinsic valuation approaches.

Unlike the excess earnings method, which analyses the total profits earned by a business, the revenue premium method focuses on the impact that a brand has on the two factors which determine revenue: price and volume. The idea is to assess how much a brand contributes to a company's revenue and cost structure and, thus, quantify the part of profits and cash flows that is directly attributable to the brand. The value of the brand is then calculated from the present value of the cash flows that it directly generates. The method is therefore based on a "marginal" approach to brand valuation.[1]

1. Principle

The first step of the revenue premium method is to quantify the incremental price (mark-up) attributable to the brand compared with an unbranded product: the price premium. A volume premium can be added to (or subtracted from) this price premium. If the volume premium is positive, the brand enables the company to win market share from competitors and sell higher volumes.

These price and volume differences result in additional revenue directly attributable to the brand. Costs specifically associated with maintaining and developing the brand and those variable costs arising from the additional revenue (taxes, variable salaries, or more simply production costs or increased working capital requirements in the case of a volume premium) are then subtracted from the additional revenue to obtain the net cash flows produced by the brand.

The branded business's incremental cash flows, compared with those of an unbranded business, are forecast over the estimated useful life of the brand. The estimated value of the brand is given by the sum of the present value of these incremental cash flows. Under this method, the brand's value is calculated by equation (1):

$$V_{B,t} = \sum_{\tau=1}^{\infty} \frac{\left(S_{B,t+\tau} - S_{WB,t+\tau} - C_{B,t+\tau} - C_{V,t+\tau}\right)}{\left(1+k\right)^{t+\tau}}, \tag{1}$$

where $V_{B,t}$ = value of the brand in period t;
$S_{B,t}$ = revenue (sales) of business with brand in period t;
$S_{WB,t}$ = revenue of unbranded business in period t;
$C_{B,t}$ = brand development costs in period t;
$C_{V,t}$ = variable costs of additional revenue in period t;
k = discount rate.

The key part of equation (1), which is specific to the revenue premium method, is the difference between $S_{B,t}$ and $S_{WB,t}$, i.e., the incremental revenue produced by the brand. This difference can be split into a price element or price premium and a volume element or volume premium.

2. Implementation—Valuation of a Consulting Firm's Brand (Continued)

The consultancy firm Consultancy Inc.'s brand was first valued in the previous chapter using the excess earnings method. We shall return here to this example to show how the revenue premium method could work in practice.

2.1. Determining the Price Premium

In order to determine the price premium (the mark-up made possible by the brand) enjoyed by Consultancy Inc., we must look at the market in which the firm operates and its positioning within that market. Its competitors—the least known or those without brands—can be used as a basis for comparison. An analysis of the market is also crucial to estimate the firm's future level of business.

2.1.1. Analysis of the Market

Consultancy Inc. operates as a strategy consultant. This business is part of a wider market: that of management and marketing consulting. This relatively large market covers strategy consulting as performed by Consultancy Inc., but also consulting in information technology, operational management, human resources, or outsourcing. Certain market players are specialised, whilst others operate in several market segments.

Consultancy Inc.'s competitors include large international strategic consulting firms, small consulting firms specialising in certain fields (e.g., building, healthcare, and media), departments of large IT consulting firms, and the consulting segments of large audit firms.

The structures of these firms depend on their size (usually expressed in number of consultants) and their average revenue per consultant. Specialised firms are smaller, and revenue per consultant for these firms and large strategy consulting firms is on average between two and four times higher than other market players. Consultancy Inc. is in an intermediate position. It is an international strategic consulting firm, but it is smaller than the world leaders.

Revenue per consultant is an indicator of the reputation and image of a firm in this market. The best-known firms attract the best consultants and create strong and lasting relationships with their clients, which enables them to maintain high prices. In the consultancy field, a strong image has two positive impacts. The first is internal: the firm attracts talent; the second is external: clients have a higher perception of the quality of service provided.

2.1.2. Quantifying the Price Premium

An analysis of the strategy consulting market shows that there is a wide disparity in prices charged by firms (measured in terms of average revenue per consultant) and that this disparity is due directly to the brand image of each firm.

To calculate the price premium attributable by Consultancy Inc.'s brand, we can use as a benchmark a sample of consulting firms with the least known names and, therefore, charging the lowest hourly rates in the market. Because of their low visibility, these firms are considered to be *unbranded*: their clients do not choose them for their reputation but for other reasons, such as the composition of their teams or the prices they charge. The names of these firms are not deemed brands because they bring no added value to their business model.

With revenues of €115 million and 570 consultants, Consultancy Inc. earned revenue per consultant of roughly €200,000 in 2014. Revenue per consultant for the four firms included in the sample of unbranded firms is shown in Table 5.1.

Table 5.1 Revenue per consultant

Thousands of Euros	*2014*
Alpha firm	174
Beta firm	165
Gamma firm	181
Delta firm	177
Average	**174**
Consultancy Inc. revenue per consultant	200
Consultancy Inc. price premium per consultant	**26**

Average revenue per consultant is €174,000 for the benchmark sample. Consultancy Inc.'s price premium is therefore estimated at €26,000 (€200,000 – €174,000) per consultant.

2.2. *Determining Cash Flows Generated by the Brand*

Costs to be deducted from the price premium in order to quantify the net cash flows produced by the brand are of two sorts:

- Brand upkeep costs; and
- Variable costs deriving from the price premium itself.

Brand upkeep costs consist mainly of marketing and communication expenses, which are estimated to be €25,000 per annum on average.

The incremental remuneration of consultants was on average 8% of revenue from 2012 to 2014. This rate of 8% is reasonably assumed to remain stable over the useful life of the brand.

Given a tax rate of 30%, net operating profit earned by the Consultancy Inc. brand in the first year of the business plan is valued at €9.527 million, as shown in Table 5.2.

This additional profit represents the net incremental cash flows earned by owning and using the Consultancy Inc. brand.[2]

2.3. *Duration of Brand Cash Flows and Discount Rate*

Cash flows generated by the brand must be estimated over its useful life. Due to strong competition in the consultancy market and the low marketing amounts spent by Consultancy Inc. on the brand (only €25,000 per year), we shall assume in our example that the price premium remains stable for 5 years and then decreases evenly to 0 after 15 years. These assumptions take account of the fact that new players enter the market regularly.

If we apply the firm's discount rate of 7.5%,[3] the Consultancy Inc. brand is valued at €66.1 million, as shown in Table 5.3.

Table 5.2 Operating profit generated by the Consultancy Inc. brand

Thousands of Euros	*2015*
Price premium per consultant	26
× Number of consultants	570
= Additional revenue generated by brand	**14,820**
– Variable salaries associated with price premium (8.0%)	1,186
– Brand maintenance costs	25
= Brand profits	**13,609**
– Tax on brand profits (@30.0%)	4,083
= Net operating profit of the Consultancy Inc. brand	**9,527**

Table 5.3 Discounted cash flows and value of the Consultancy Inc. brand

Thousands of Euros	*2015*	*2016*	*2017*	*2018*	*2019*	*2020*	*2021*	*2022*
Price premium per consultant	26	26	26	26	26	24	21	19
× Number of consultants	570	570	570	570	570	570	570	570
= Additional revenue generated by the brand	**14,820**	**14,820**	**14,820**	**14,820**	**14,820**	**13,473**	**12,125**	**10,778**
- Variable salaries associated with price premium (8.0%)	1,186	1,186	1,186	1,186	1,186	1,078	970	862
- Brand maintenance costs	25	25	26	26	27	27	27	28
- Tax on brand profits (@30.0%)	4,083	4,083	4,083	4,082	4,082	3,710	3,338	2,966
= Net operating profit of the Consultancy Inc. brand	**9,527**	**9,526**	**9,526**	**9,526**	**9,526**	**8,658**	**7,790**	**6,922**
Discount factor (@7.5%)	0.964	0.897	0.835	0.776	0.722	0.672	0.625	0.581
Present value of brand cash flows	**9,188**	**8,547**	**7,950**	**7,396**	**6,879**	**5,816**	**4,868**	**4,024**

Thousands of Euros	*2023*	*2024*	*2025*	*2026*	*2027*	*2028*	*2029*	*2030*
Price premium per consultant	17	14	12	9	7	5	2	-
× Number of consultants	570	570	570	570	570	570	570	570
= Additional revenue generated by the brand	**9,431**	**8,084**	**6,736**	**5,389**	**4,042**	**2,695**	**1,347**	-
– Variable salaries associated with price premium (8.0%)	754	647	539	431	323	216	108	-
– Brand maintenance costs	28	29	29	29	30	30	31	31
– Tax on brand profits (@30.0%)	2,594	2,223	1,851	1,479	1,107	735	363	(9)
= Net operating profit of the Consultancy Inc. brand	**6,054**	**5,186**	**4,318**	**3,450**	**2,582**	**1,714**	**846**	**(22)**
Discount factor (@7.5%)	0.541	0.503	0.468	0.435	0.405	0.377	0.350	0.326
Present value of brand cash flows	**3,274**	**2,609**	**2,021**	**1,502**	**1,046**	**646**	**296**	**(7)**
Brand value								66,055

3. Revenue Premium Method—Relevance and Limitations

3.1. Difficulties in Finding Comparable Unbranded Businesses

The revenue premium method belongs to the family of intrinsic (income) valuation approaches. It has, however, a feature in common with the market approach, as the price premium is determined by comparing the prices of branded products with those of competitors' unbranded products. For the method to be relevant, an unbranded business must be identified which is comparable to that of the brand being valued. Companies used as benchmarks should ideally operate in the same market sector, in the same geographical areas, and offer products of similar quality and a similar level of service. This generally makes it difficult to select unbranded competitors that are sufficiently comparable. Companies make every effort to distinguish themselves from the competition by making their products or services different from those of other market players so as to gain a competitive advantage and win customers.

It is therefore complicated to assess how much a brand contributes to price differences accepted by customers or to higher volumes sold, because factors other than the brand differentiate the product, such as performance, warranties, after-sales service, or distribution channels. The impact of the brand on price or volume, as well as on costs, is usually difficult to quantify. As is the case with the excess earnings method, the revenue premium method is only reliable if it is possible to define how much each intangible asset contributes and thus distinguish the price premium produced by a brand from that produced by other intangible (and tangible) assets.

In addition, a competing unbranded business has to be found. In practice, businesses without brands are rare except for certain generic consumer products. It is also often difficult to gain access to financial data for generic businesses. In the absence of such financial information, the premium may be calculated using a business in the same sector with a lesser-known brand. The resulting value will therefore be relatively prudent, meaning that the brand will be undervalued, because its value is estimated by deducting the value of the weakest brands in the market rather than the value of an unbranded business.

3.2. Difficulties in Estimating Volume Premium

It is difficult to identify and to quantify the volume premium. Estimating the theoretical volumes that a branded business would generate if it had no brand (the "but for" scenario) is a complicated exercise. The volume premium should ideally only include incremental demand arising from the brand. However, sale volumes do not depend solely on demand. Volumes sold depend on a company's productive capacity—its existing workforce, technical facilities, and the adaptability of its organisation to changes in demand (demand elasticity).

In addition, the impact of a brand on volumes is not necessarily positive, but may be negative, especially where there is a high price premium. Branded goods are often too expensive for certain customers who prefer to switch to cheaper products, even if they are less glamorous or of lower quality. This positive or negative relationship between price and volume premiums is often overlooked when valuing a brand using the revenue premium method.

3.3. *Forecasting Future Revenue Levels*

Once the revenue premium has been determined, forecast benchmark prices and volumes to which the premium will be applied must be estimated. This can be difficult for several reasons.

The evolution of the base price and of forecast revenue levels must be assessed with regard to expected prices and volumes in the relevant market as a whole. Does the company operate in a market where prices are regulated (e.g., gas, water treatment, or other public utilities)? Are volumes regulated (e.g., milk quotas or volume restrictions on controlled origin labels such as champagne)? Is there a risk that the product will become obsolete through technical innovation or changes in consumer behaviour? Are the products basic consumer goods which are always needed in theory (e.g., rice or sugar)? The future development of the market can vary considerably depending on the nature of the product and how sensitive it is to fashion, technological innovation, legislation, and market regulation.

Where a brand covers a large variety of products, the development of prices and volumes must be estimated for each sector. Price premium or volume premium must be quantified by product or product family. In the luxury goods sector, for example, a brand's price premium may not be the same in perfume, eyewear, or clothing. It is therefore essential to forecast future volumes and average prices generated using the brand, but also to determine the relative contribution of each product to overall revenues.

The question of the brand's lifespan and potential durability must also be addressed under the revenue premium method.[4] The premium must in fact be accounted for in light of the brand's strength, the competition, and the barriers to market entry.

Conclusion

The revenue premium method can rarely be implemented in entirely orthodox conditions. It is indeed difficult to identify unbranded companies that are sufficiently similar to the business of the brand being valued, and it is not easy to obtain relevant financial and management information about those companies. In practice, the valuer can use a sample of similar companies with weak brands.

The revenue premium method is particularly suitable when the products of the brand to be valued are standardised, because this means that identical or highly comparable products exist. This is true, for example, in the case of ordinary consumer goods, such as flour, beverages, or washing powder. However, price differences that are attributable to the brand must be highlighted without including the price differences due to product quality or presentation. Conversely, the method cannot be used in the case of specific products or services without identical competing products, as no adequate generic benchmarks would exist.

Notes

1. This can also be described as a "but for" analysis; in other words, it means comparing in a situation where no brand is owned.
2. For the sake of simplicity, we have ignored capital expenditure and the impact of increased revenue on working capital requirements.
3. See Chapter 2 on the subject of choosing the appropriate discount rate, as well as Appendix 1.
4. See the detailed analysis of issues relating to brand durability in Chapter 1.

6 The Relief-From-Royalty Method

The relief-from-royalty method entails valuing a brand at the present value of the future royalties that the business saves (or is "relieved from" paying) by virtue of owning a brand. Indeed, companies sometimes license the right to use brands for certain products or services. These brands are subject to detailed licensing agreements between the brand owner and the company wishing to use them.

The relief-from-royalty method applies, therefore, both an intrinsic logic by discounting future cash flows attributable to the brand and a comparables or market rationale, in that the appropriate royalty rate is estimated using market benchmarks.

1. Principle

The relief-from-royalty method adopts the perspective of a licensee who pays royalties to a brand owner or licensor. Brand royalties used are after tax and after deducting the overall costs associated with using the brand. They are calculated over the estimated useful life of the brand.

The value of the brand is then equal to the sum of the royalties or licence fees saved over the life of the brand, less costs incurred in using it.

$$V_B = \sum_{t=1}^{\infty} \frac{\left(R_t - C_{B,t}\right)}{\left(1+k\right)^t}, \tag{1}$$

where V_B = value of the brand;
R_t = royalty or licence fee in period t;
$C_{B,t}$ = costs (especially marketing) of using the brand in period t;
k = discount rate.

Five steps are necessary to determine the present value of the future royalties:[1]

1. Estimate the brand-specific revenue. This will be used as a basis for calculating royalties.

2. Determine the appropriate royalty rate. This is applied to forecast revenue to give gross annual royalties.
3. Estimate the annual costs of using the brand, which are subtracted from gross royalties to obtain net annual royalties. Tax is then deducted from the net royalties.
4. Estimate the useful life of the brand. The useful life determines the time period over which the royalty payments will be made.
5. Lastly, estimate the appropriate discount rate to apply to arrive at the present value of net royalties after costs and tax.

1.1. Estimating Revenue

The forecast revenue to which the royalty rate will be applied corresponds to the business covered by the brand. If the brand covers all of a company's business, the relevant revenue is equal to total company revenue, and management's business plan can then be used as a basis for the revenue estimate. If the brand covers only part of the company's business, relevant forecast revenue must be determined by analysing the brand's various markets.

The relevant forecast revenue is not only that of the brand's current scope, but it must include its future extension to other products and other geographical areas. The possibility of extension should be assessed in light of the brand's potential for development and sums invested in developing it. Development potential of a brand depends on how old it is and at what stage it is in its life cycle: its residual potential will be different if it is in the launch, maturity, or decline stage. It also depends on the nature of the business and the type of customers. Brands aimed at businesses, for example, tend to be more durable but less likely to expand than brands aimed at consumers.

Whatever future expansion assumptions are made about the brand, it is crucial that they be consistent with estimates of future expenditure to be incurred to expand the brand. Development has a cost, even for a brand with high growth potential, and it is important to ensure that this cost is included in the amount of investments taken into account in the valuation.

1.2. Estimating an Appropriate Hypothetical Royalty Rate

Different sources of information may be available to estimate the royalty rate depending on how the brand has been used in the past.

- Internal source: if the brand is operated under licence by a third party, the royalty rate in the licence agreement may be used as an initial estimate of market royalty rates. Brand licence agreements, however, often cover only a part of the business or a part of the geographies covered by the brand overall. In this case, the royalty rate in the agreement may not represent a suitable rate for the brand as a whole.

- External source: if the brand is only used by its owner, its value will be estimated using royalties which would theoretically be paid if the brand were licensed in. In this case, theoretical royalties will be determined by reference to royalties generated by a benchmark of comparable brands. Relevant royalty rate data may be downloaded from a number of proprietary databases accessible online for a fee. These databases extract royalty rates, royalty bases, type of intangible asset (e.g., brand, patent, technology), and other terms from licensing agreements, and they allow the data to be searched and filtered by the user who can then download the comparable licensing agreements. The comparable royalty rates then need to be adjusted to reflect differences between the subject brand and the brands and terms and conditions in the comparable licensing agreements.

1.3. Estimating the Costs of Using a Brand

The costs of using a brand are all those costs necessary for the licensee to use it. In general, these are mainly marketing costs linked to communication about the brand and any legal costs payable by the licensee. What is difficult is to identify those costs specifically related to the brand being valued. Additional development costs to be incurred to expand the business carried out under the brand can be taken into account during this step.

1.4. Estimating Brand Lifespan and Discount Rate

Royalties will be earned during the useful life of the brand. Estimating the duration of this useful life raises a number of issues, which were discussed in the section of Chapter 1 dealing with brand life cycles.

The discount rate used must be appropriate given the level of risk inherent in the brand. As for revenues, if the brand covers a company's entire business, the company's discount rate can be used as a reference point.[2]

2. Implementation—Case Study: Valuation of the Traveller Brand

2.1. Presentation of the Traveller Brand

The Traveller brand is a well-known brand created in 1952 in the luxury leather goods sector. The company of the same name sells under this brand a range of leather goods comprising mainly wallets, handbags, briefcases, and travel bags. All of the company's products are sold under the Traveller brand name. The brand is only used by the company and has never been licensed.

The Traveller brand has several strengths:

- Its products cover the whole range of leather goods.
- It has wide geographical coverage, with a presence on all continents, and is particularly strong in Europe, North America, and South-East Asia.
- Consumer perception is positive, which enables the company to apply high-end pricing. Traveller product prices are on average 15% higher than those of the competition. In addition, the company offers a 25-year warranty on its products, longer than that of its competitors.

The company wishes to value its brand as of 31 December 2014. The relief-from-royalty method is to be used.

2.2. *Determining Forecast Revenues*

The first step in implementing the relief-from-royalty method is to estimate the forecast revenues of the business covered by the brand, which will be used as a basis for calculating royalties. All company products are sold under the Traveller brand, so the relevant revenue to which royalties apply is the company's total forecast revenue.

Management's forecasts of company revenues in its latest five-year plan are shown in Table 6.1. Management is planning strong revenue growth from 2015 to 2019 through penetration of new markets, especially in South-East Asia and South America.

At the end of the plan period, revenue growth is extrapolated for three years and assumed to decrease evenly from 5% in 2019 to 1.5% in 2022. Perpetual annual growth of 1.5% is assumed from 2022 onwards (see Table 6.2).

Table 6.1 Forecast revenues 2015–2019

Millions of Euros	*2015*	*2016*	*2017*	*2018*	*2019*
Revenue	43.0	46.0	49.2	52.2	54.8
Annual growth rate		*7.0%*	*7.0%*	*6.0%*	*5.0%*

Table 6.2 Forecast revenues 2015–2022

Millions of euros	*2015*	*2016*	*2017*	*2018*	*2019*	*2020*	*2021*	*2022*
Revenue	43.0	46.0	49.2	52.2	54.8	56.9	58.4	59.3
Annual growth rate		*7.0%*	*7.0%*	*6.0%*	*5.0%*	*3.8%*	*2.7%*	*1.5%*

This forecast growth in revenue is consistent with macroeconomic projections of major forecasting institutions concerning markets relevant to Traveller (IMF, World Bank).

2.3. Determining the Royalty Rate

The brand has only been used by the company and has never been licensed. The expected royalty rate must therefore be estimated by reference to a benchmark of similar brands.

Data on a sample of four comparable brands in the leather goods sector has been collected. These brands are operated under licensing agreements, the content of which is publicly available. Contractual royalty rates for these four brands are 2.7%, 0.9%, 6.0%, and 8.4%, respectively.

These rates show a strong dispersion, which is typical for brand licensing agreements. To assess the appropriate rate for the Traveller brand within this range, a study carried out in 2013 by a marketing consultancy firm on brand awareness in the leather goods market has been used. The results of this study are shown in Table 6.3.

Awareness of the Traveller brand lies between those of brands C and D, which have the highest royalty rates, and those of brands A and B, which have the lowest rates. The brand is relatively mature and consumer perception is positive. These observations lead us to choose a royalty rate for Traveller brand in the middle of the range shown by the sample. The chosen royalty rate for the Traveller brand is therefore 4%. Gross future royalties shown in Table 6.4 are calculated by applying this royalty rate to the forecast revenues estimated in Table 6.2.

Table 6.3 Study of brand awareness in the leather goods sector

	Brand A	*Brand B*	*Brand C*	*Brand D*	*Traveller*
Unaided awareness	37%	25%	55%	62%	**46%**
Aided awareness	80%	75%	88%	96%	**80%**
Consumer perception	Elegant	Fragile	Robust	Prestigious, quality	**Elegant, quality**
Brand created	1997	1993	1948	1924	**1952**
Royalty rate	**2.7%**	**0.9%**	**6.0%**	**8.4%**	**?**

Table 6.4 Estimated gross royalties of the Traveller brand

Millions of Euros	*2015*	*2016*	*2017*	*2018*	*2019*	*2020*	*2021*	*2022*
Revenue	43.0	46.0	49.2	52.2	54.8	56.9	58.4	59.3
× Royalty rate	4%	4%	4%	4%	4%	4%	4%	4%
= Gross royalties	**1.7**	**1.8**	**2.0**	**2.1**	**2.2**	**2.3**	**2.3**	**2.4**

2.4. Estimating Net Royalties

Every year, the Traveller company incurs marketing costs for utilising its brand. Management estimates these costs at €0.8 million for 2015. It is assumed these costs will increase by 1.5% per annum. The applicable tax rate is 33%.

Net royalties, after deducting brand-use costs and corporate taxes, are shown in Table 6.5.

2.5. Discounting Royalties and Valuation of the Traveller Brand

The useful life of the Traveller brand is deemed to be indefinite, especially in view of its age and high visibility after 60 years of existence. Moreover, brands rarely merge in the leather goods market and tend to retain their distinctiveness.

The discount rate of the Traveller company is used to discount the forecast royalties of the Traveller brand, as the brand covers the company's whole business. This rate is estimated at 9.4%.

Applying this discount rate, the present value of net royalties is shown in Table 6.6.

The value of the Traveller brand under the relief-from-royalty method is therefore estimated at €11.2 million as shown in Table 6.7.

Table 6.5 Net royalties of the Traveller brand

Millions of Euros	*2015*	*2016*	*2017*	*2018*	*2019*	*2020*	*2021*	*2022*
Revenue	43.0	46.0	49.2	52.2	54.8	56.9	58.4	59.3
× Royalty rate	4%	4%	4%	4%	4%	4%	4%	4%
= **Gross royalties**	**1.7**	**1.8**	**2.0**	**2.1**	**2.2**	**2.3**	**2.3**	**2.4**
– Costs of use	0.8	0.8	0.8	0.8	0.8	0.9	0.9	0.9
= **Brand pre-tax royalties**	0.9	1.0	1.1	1.3	1.3	1.4	1.5	1.5
– Tax (@33%)	0.3	0.3	0.4	0.4	0.4	0.5	0.5	0.5
= **Net royalties**	0.6	0.7	0.8	0.8	0.9	0.9	1.0	1.0

Table 6.6 Present value of net royalties of the Traveller brand

Millions of Euros	*2015*	*2016*	*2017*	*2018*	*2019*	*2020*	*2021*	*2022*
Net royalties	0.6	0.7	0.8	0.8	0.9	0.9	1.0	1.0
× Discount factor	0.96	0.87	0.80	0.73	0.67	0.61	0.56	0.51
= **Present value of net royalties**	0.6	0.6	0.6	0.6	0.6	0.6	0.5	0.5

Table 6.7 Value of the Traveller brand

Millions of Euros	Value
Sum of present value of net royalties 2015–2022	4.6
+ Terminal value 2023[3]	6.5
= Value of the Traveller brand as at 31/12/2014	**11.2**

3. Relief-From-Royalty Method—Relevance and Limitations

3.1. Relevance of the Relief-From-Royalty Method

The relief-from-royalty method is one of the methods most often used in valuing brands. It is part of the income-based approach and, therefore, likely to result in an appropriate market value for a brand if the different inputs used are estimated correctly. The method is often preferred because it is relatively simple to use and because the information needed to estimate the different inputs and main assumptions is usually available.

The other advantage of the method is that it is a mixed approach. It is both part of the intrinsic/income approach (because it is based on business revenue and specific costs of use of the brand being valued) and of the market approach (because royalty rates are derived from actual rates observed for a sample of comparable brands). Determining the royalty rate using comparable brands enables available market information to be included, whilst applying the resulting royalty rate to the company's operational indicators takes account of the actual prospects of the business.

Combining market and intrinsic approaches guarantees a result that is both relatively objective and consistent with market benchmarks (as opposed to the cost-based method, for example) and which takes into account the brand's own characteristics. Creating a sample of comparable brands and positioning the brand being valued within that sample in order to estimate the appropriate royalty rate in effect makes use of criteria such as the brand's visibility and the way it is perceived by consumers.

As with other valuation methods, this method is only appropriate if all the necessary inputs can be reliably estimated. However, certain inputs cannot easily be quantified, and brand valuations using this method are extremely sensitive to changes in the main input, the royalty rate, which is precisely the most difficult input to estimate.

3.2. Implementing the Relief-From-Royalty Method—Issues and Challenges

Once the different inputs have been estimated, the relief-from-royalty method is simple to use, as it involves applying a royalty rate to forecast revenues, possibly subtracting certain costs, and discounting the resulting royalties. The complex part of the method is estimating its different inputs.

As we have seen, it can be quite difficult to forecast the future revenues of the branded business, especially if the brand covers only a part of a company's business or if the brand's product range is large and serves very dissimilar markets. In addition, the brand can be valued "as is" or by taking into account its future expansion. To know in which configuration the brand should be valued, its characteristics (in particular its age) and the context of the valuation must be taken into consideration. In an internal reorganisation context, a prudent stance can be taken by valuing the brand based on its current scope, without taking account of possible future expansion. However, in the context of an acquisition, the purchaser will generally aim to develop the business more aggressively, and the expected expansion of the brand can be taken into consideration.

It is also necessary under this method to estimate a royalty rate applicable to the brand based on rates found for a sample of comparable brands operated under publicly available licensing agreements. The valuer will face two difficulties here. The first will be to identify comparable licensed brands using the databases of licensing agreement that we referred to earlier. As an illustration, Table 6.8 shows a set of royalty rate benchmarks.

Once the sample is put together, the second difficulty is to choose a single appropriate rate for the brand being valued from an often wide range of rates, which may vary by a ratio of one to five. This dispersion is explained by the fact that brand licences often apply to non-core businesses rather than the core business of the brand. Royalty rates observed for theoretically comparable brands may in fact cover distinct businesses. For example, royalty rates charged by a fashion brand may only cover the sale of sunglasses. Licensing agreements must therefore be examined in detail to ascertain their exact scope and contractual terms in order to determine which rates are appropriate for the valuation. Estimating the right royalty rate is crucial, because the relief-from-royalty method is linear. If the rate varies by 100%, the resulting valuation of the brand will vary by just as much.

Finally, estimating brand-use costs is often difficult. It assumes that it is possible to identify marketing costs which are specifically related to using a given brand. This becomes more difficult the more brands a company owns.

In all, the major challenge of this method is to quantify the inputs to be used, such as the royalty rate in particular. This is often tricky and even more so because the value resulting from this method is extremely sensitive to changes in those parameters. This method should, therefore, only be used for brands of lesser importance or for business sectors where licensing agreements are commonplace.

Table 6.8 Ranges of royalty rates by sector and brand type—as a per cent of revenue

Brand Type	*Commercial Industrial*	*Mass Consumption*	*Services*	*Food and Drink*	*Clothing*	*Games, Toys, Entertainment*
Institutional		[6; 7.7; 10]				
Corporate	[0.25; 3.4; 5]	[1; 4.6; 10]	[1; 3.2; 6]	[1; 5.1; 15]	[5; 6.9; 10]	[4; 5; 6]
Fashion		[3; 6; 10]		[7; 7; 7]	[2; 5.5; 8]	
Celebrity		[6; 12; 15]		[10; 10; 10]	[10; 11; 12]	[3.5; 8.6; 10]
Person		[4; 8.6; 12]	[4; 4; 4]	[5; 5; 5]	[2; 8; 15]	[3; 8.4; 12]
Academic/ Sport		[8.5; 9.9; 15]		[2.5; 6.1; 10]	[4.5; 7.6; 15]	[6; 9; 12]

Note: [low, average, high] the first figure indicates the lowest value observed, the second the average, and the third the highest value observed.

Source: Smith (1996).

Royalty Rates, an Unreliable Benchmark

Based on an analysis of 300 licensing agreements, Smith (1996) illustrates the difficulty of reliably estimating a royalty rate. Within the same industry and for the same type of products, the range of rates observed can be remarkably wide (see Table 6.8).

In a more recent study, Smith and Richey (2013) show that brand royalty rates can be split into two categories:

- Business to business (B2B), showing rates between 2.7% and 3.4% of revenue;
- Consumer brands, showing higher rates between 7.6% and 9.3% of revenue.

Faced with such uncertainty, professionals often consider using rules of thumb before deciding. Thus, in a given industry, depending on the level of margin (before marketing costs), it can be considered that the maximum acceptable royalty rate (the investment required for the brand to produce the margin) cannot exceed a certain proportion of the business margin (an acceptable burden or investment level).

This line of argument was developed by Smith and Parr (2000) who drew up the 25% / 5% rule. According to the authors, who were writing about the pharmaceutical industry, royalties should not be greater than 25% of operational profit or 5% of revenues. There is a similar rule in Germany (developed by Helmut Knoppe), which states that the amount to be paid for a brand should be somewhere between one-fourth and one-third of the company's pre-tax profits (Salinas, 2009).

Whilst these simple rules do not constitute a real valuation method, comparing royalties to profits provides a relevant reasonableness check of the chosen royalty rate.

Conclusion

Aside from the difficulties in estimating certain inputs, the relief-from-royalty method has certain limitations. In particular, the method relies only on royalties paid and includes in the valuation of the brand only value saved by the brand user or licensee, while ignoring value earned by the brand owner or licensor. The method therefore takes account of only part of the economic benefits attributable to the brand.

Two parties generally enter into a contract because it is in their mutual interest to do so. The licensee gains from excess earnings (after deducting royalty payments) generated by the brand compared with an unbranded business. The licensee enters into the contract with the brand owner because he or she expects to obtain economic benefits from using the brand and is ready to share part of these benefits with the owner. The owner gains from the royalties he or she receives, which constitute a transfer of part of the economic benefits attributable to the brand. These are therefore shared between the licensee and the licensor. However, the relief-from-royalty method takes into account only the value earned by a brand user through royalty savings and in so doing, can lead to the brand being systematically undervalued.

Notes

1. In practice the best way to determine savings made by a brand owner is to compare two sets of cash flows: (1) the company's actual cash flows and (2) its cash flows if it did not own the brand but paid royalties to a third party to use it. Putting royalty costs to one side, the company would save legal and registration costs and even certain marketing costs.
2. For methods of estimating cost of capital, see Appendix 1. See also Chapter 11 for a discussion of possible differences between brand cost of capital and company cost of capital.
3. The terminal value is calculated as $(1.0 \times (1.015)/(9.4\% - 1.5\%)) / (1 + 9.4\%)^{7.5}$.

References

Salinas G. (2009), *The International Brand Valuation Manual: A Complete Overview and Analysis of Brand Valuation Techniques, Methodologies and Applications*, Wiley, Chichester, UK.

Smith G.V. (1996), *Trademark Valuation*, 1st edition, John Wiley & Sons, New York.

Smith G.V. and Parr R.L. (2000), *Valuation of Intellectual Property and Intangible Assets*, 3rd edition, John Wiley & Sons, New York.

Smith G.V. and Richey S.M. (2013), *Trademark Valuation*, 2nd edition, John Wiley & Sons, New York.

7 The Market-Based Approach

> Forecasts may tell you a great deal about the forecaster; they tell you nothing about the future.
>
> Warren Buffett[1]

As forecasting future economic benefits is a complex and highly subjective task, the market-based approach relies on using available comparable trading multiples or transaction multiples to infer the value of a company. It is worth noting that the relief-from-royalty method discussed in the previous chapter also uses market information, i.e., royalty rates from comparable licensing agreements to value brands, which makes it a mixed approach. As mentioned earlier, there is no active market for buying and selling standalone brands. However, it has been suggested that in some cases we can, nonetheless, observe certain transactions (deals) involving companies whose value is mostly driven by their brand(s). The same reasoning could also be developed when observing the market value of a subset of listed companies whose value is also mostly driven by their brand(s).

The objective of this chapter is to show the rationale behind the market-based approach and its limitations. Given the difficulty in isolating the value of a brand from the value of other assets in the prices paid for acquired companies or in the prices of listed companies, we consider that this approach cannot be used to value brands as such. It may only be used in rare cases (i.e., when the brand is the most valuable asset of a company) to cross-check the brand value obtained using other valuation methods.

1. Principle

The principle underlying the market-based approach is fairly simple and can be briefly summarised as follows:

$$V_B \text{ or } V_C = \frac{V_{Benchmark} \text{ or } V_{Transactions}}{VD_{Benchmark} \text{ or } VD_{Transactions}} \times VD_B \text{ or } VD_C, \tag{1}$$

where V_B or V_C = Value of subject brand (V_B) or value of subject company (V_C);
$V_{Benchmark}$ = Value of benchmark companies;
$V_{Transactions}$ = Value of benchmark transactions;
$VD_{Benchmark}$ = Fundamental value driver of benchmark companies;
$VD_{Transactions}$ = Fundamental value driver of benchmark transactions;
VD_B or VD_C = Fundamental value driver of subject brand or company.

The first step involves selecting the benchmark-listed companies or transactions that will be used. They should be as comparable as possible to the subject brand/company to be valued. That generally means finding brands/companies in the same industry or sector and finding brands/companies at a similar point in their development and life or growth cycle.

The second step involves choosing the fundamental value driver(s). Value drivers are generally taken from 1) the income (profit and loss) statement or 2) the cash flow statement. From the income statement, valuers take either the top line, sales, or some measure of profitability: operating profit or EBIT, EBITDA, or NOPAT.[2] Theory developed in Chapter 4 would argue that NOPAT is the most appropriate value driver. Using sales is the most problematic, as a certain level of sales does not always lead to the same profitability. However, sales may be the only driver available for early stage companies that have yet to generate profits. In these cases, non-financial drivers may be used, such as Internet traffic, units sold, or backlog.

From the cash flow statement, one could choose cash flows from operations or free cash flows (cash flows from operations minus Capex). Theory presented in Chapter 2 would suggest that free cash flows is the more appropriate value driver of the two.

The third step involves obtaining the subject company's fundamental value driver selected in the second step. For both the benchmark companies and the subject company, care should be exercised in selecting the value driver. In theory, value is based on discounted future expected profits or cash flows. In forecasting these future expected profits or cash flows, generally starting with current profits or cash flows, non-recurring items should be eliminated (e.g., one-off gains or losses such as restructuring charges) to get as close as possible to recurring or normalised future profits or cash flows.

Finally, we need to be careful that the market values (prices) of the listed benchmark companies as of the valuation date, or the comparable transaction prices close to that date, are not unduly affected by irregular market conditions, such as those experienced during major crises (likely undervalued) or bubbles (likely overvalued).

2. Implementation

2.1. Trading Multiples

Many data providers (e.g., Bloomberg and Thomson Reuters) track the trading multiples of publicly listed companies. The current share price is often divided by either the last twelve months (LTM) or forecast earnings per share for the next year (FY1) to arrive to price-earnings or P/E ratios or by the per share book value of equity to arrive to price-to-book or P/B ratios. Alternatively, these data providers will also calculate trading ratios based on enterprise value (EV), i.e., the market value of the whole business (by extension the market value of the net debt and market value of shareholders' equity).[3]

Table 7.1 presents some trading multiples of a set of listed companies with well-known brands in the luxury apparel sector. On 7 October 2015, these companies' EVs were on average equivalent to 2.57 times FY1 Sales, 11.30 times FY1 EBITDA, and 14.19 times FY1 EBIT.

For example, if one were to use these multiples to value an unlisted company in the same sector, Company Brand X, with an estimated FY1 EBIT of €10 million, then its value would be around €142 million (ten times the average EV/EBIT of 14.19). In selecting the appropriate multiple to apply to the subject company, some valuers prefer to use median rather than average multiples so as to exclude the impact of outliers (e.g., companies experiencing a temporary negative earnings shock and therefore trading at relatively

Table 7.1 Trading multiples of companies in the luxury apparel sector (7 October 2015)

Name	*Ticker*	*EV/Sales FY1*	*EV/EBITDA FY1*	*EV/EBIT FY1*
Burberry Group	BRBY-LN	2.20	9.92	12.97
Christian Dior	CDI-FR	1.53	6.82	8.18
Coach	COH-N	1.74	8.15	10.26
Ferragamo	SFER-MI	2.99	13.30	16.02
Hermès	RMS-FR	7.08	20.17	22.36
Hugo Boss	BOSS-XE	2.68	12.29	15.87
Jimmy Choo	CHOO-LN	2.07	11.95	17.66
Kering	KER-FR	2.20	12.10	14.71
LVMH	MC-FR	2.46	10.62	13.32
Michael Kors Holdings	KORS-N	1.59	5.48	6.22
Prada IT	1913-HK	2.50	10.00	14.40
Ralph Lauren Corporation	RL-N	1.27	8.17	10.98
Richemont	CFR-VX	2.89	10.67	12.73
Ted Baker	TED-LN	3.25	19.44	23.79
Tiffany & Co.	TIF-N	2.48	10.11	12.54
Tod's	TOD-MI	2.27	11.57	15.11
Mean		**2.57**	**11.30**	**14.19**
Median		**2.37**	**10.64**	**13.86**
High		**7.08**	**20.17**	**23.79**
Low		**1.27**	**5.48**	**6.22**

EV = Enterprise Value; FY1 = One Year Ahead Forecast Value; EBITDA = Earnings Before Interest, Tax, Depreciation and Amortisation; EBIT = Earnings Before Interest and Tax.

Source: Thomson One.

high multiples). In this case, the median EV/EBIT is 13.86, which is close to the average of 14.19. Alternatively, some valuers remove high and low multiples from the list. For example, in this case, we could remove 1) Hermès, which is trading at very high multiples (excellent brand value but also some speculation about a potential M&A deal) and 2) Ralph Lauren Corp., which is trading at low multiples (recent announcement of sales slow-down plus Ralph Lauren stepping down and naming a new CEO who may shift the business model to higher volume but lower margins). The resulting mean and median EV/EBIT multiples would be almost identical at 13.85.

2.2. *Transaction Multiples*

Many financial data providers, e.g., Thomson Reuters and Bureau van Dijk, have specific databases of mergers and acquisitions from which transaction multiples can be collected. In Table 7.2, we set out multiples from five recent transactions involving target companies with well-known brands in the sports apparel sector. On average, acquirers paid 1.22 times sales, 12.46 times EBITDA, and 13.22 times EBIT.

As these transaction multiples are typically based on the prices paid for whole businesses, isolating the value of the brand would require adjustments similar to those performed in the excess earnings method presented in Chapter 4. For example, in the case of the Reebok acquisition by Adidas, trademarks and other intangible assets represented over 70% of the purchase price. These represented over 65% of the value of acquired assets in the Umbro acquisition by Nike (see Figure 7.1 and Figure 7.2 for the presentation of the corresponding purchase price allocation disclosures).

Table 7.2 Transaction multiple on recent sports apparel companies

Date Effective	*Target Name*	*Acquirer Name*	*Deal Value Inc. Net Debt (EV) ($ Million)*	*EV / Sales*	*EV / EBITDA*	*EV / EBIT*
01/31/2006	Reebok International	Adidas-Salomon	4,288.05	1.07	12.29	14.06
10/20/2005	Adidas-Salomon	Amer Sports	623.96	0.74	na	na
03/03/2008	Umbro	Nike Vapor	568.75	1.89	11.50	12.38
10/17/2008	Moncler	Fuori dal Sacco	547.14	1.63	13.60	na
04/30/2013	K-Swiss	Eland World	127.67	0.76	na	na
Average				1.22	12.46	13.22

EV = Enterprise Value; EBITDA = Earnings Before Interest, Tax, Depreciation and Amortisation; EBIT = Earnings Before Interest and Tax. Enterprise value is the market value of the whole business, na = not available.

Source: Thomson One.

Reebok's Net Assets at the Acquisition Date Millions of euro	Pre-acquisition carrying amount	Fair value adjustments	Recognised value on acquisition
Cash and cash equivalents	539	-	539
Accounts receivable	453	-	453
Inventories	447	55	502
Other current assets	103	(3)	100
Property, plant and equipment, net	293	(33)	260
Trademarks and other intangible assets, net	68	1,674	1,742
Long-term financial assets	-	4	4
Deferred tax assets	198	44	242
Other non-current assets	16	-	16
Borrowings	(506)	-	(506)
Accounts payable	(109)	-	(109)
Income taxes	(59)	-	(59)
Accrued liabilities and provisions	(329)	(30)	(359)
Other current liabilities	(418)	-	(418)
Pensions and similar obligations	(7)	-	(7)
Deferred tax liabilities	(11)	(578)	(589)
Other non-current liabilities	(2)	-	(2)
Minority interests	(3)	-	(3)
Net Assets	**673**	**1,133**	**1,806**
Goodwill arising on acquisition			1,165
Purchase price settled in cash			**2,971**
Cash and cash equivalents acquired			539
Cash outflow on acquisition			**2,432**

Figure 7.1 Purchase price allocation of the Reebok acquisition.

Source: Adidas Group Annual Report 2006.

"Based on our purchase price allocation, identifiable intangible assets and goodwill relating to the purchase approximated $419.5 million and $319.2 million, respectively. Goodwill recognized is deductible for tax purpose. Identifiable intangible assets include $378.4 million for trademarks that have an indefinite useful life, and $41.1 million for other intangible assets consisting of Umbro's sourcing network, established customer relationships, and the United Soccer League franchise. These intangible assets will be amortized on a straight line basis over estimated lives of 12 to 20 years. The following table summarizes the allocation of the purchase price, including transaction costs of the acquisition, to the assets acquired and liabilities assumed based on their estimated fair values (in millions)."

Current assets	$87.2
Non-current assets	90.2
Identified intangible assets	419.5
Goodwill	319.2
Current liabilities	(60.3)
Non-current liabilities	(279.4)
Net assets acquired	**576.4**

Figure 7.2 Purchase price allocation of the Umbro acquisition.

Source: Nike form 10-K 2008.

3. Market-Based Valuation Methods—Relevance and Limitations

The market approach appears relatively easy to implement, but is in reality subject to a number of challenges:

1) Selecting the benchmark companies can be quite difficult, because companies can be different in size, type of product and market segmentation, and at different growth stages. Most trading or transaction multiples are calculated based on information disclosed by publicly listed companies, which are typically more mature and larger than most.
2) EV-based multiples will also be biased if companies have very different levels of debt to equity.
3) The fundamental value drivers, whether they be profits or cash flows, need to be adjusted for one-off items, because value is driven by future maintainable profits or cash flows.
4) Multiples of sales are probably the least relevant, as sales do not always mean positive profits or cash flows.

5) Trading multiples can be sensitive to short-term market swings or longer-term market imbalances, such as asset bubbles or financial crises.
6) Similarly, transaction multiples can be sensitive to whether the mergers and acquisitions market is in a buoyant phase or not.
7) Trading or transaction multiples give a value for whole businesses, not for specific assets of those businesses such as their brand. In addition, few companies are single-brand companies.

Conclusion

Applying trading or transaction multiples of comparable companies to value subject companies can be relatively easy and quick to do, although it requires the exercise of great care, as discussed in the limitations section earlier. The main technical drawback of the approach is the absence of perfectly comparable companies: the value obtained is only as good as the relative comparability of the subject company with the chosen comparable companies and the extent to which the selected value drivers are representative of maintainable earnings/cash flows.

More importantly, the approach is rarely used to value brands, because it would require the brand to be the most significant—if not the only—asset of the company. Otherwise, as is usually the case, the market approach results in the total market value of a subject company and not directly that of its brand. Consequently, this approach, even if it is sometimes theoretically discussed, is almost never used in practice to value brands.

Nonetheless, with the application of IFRS 3, we have recently seen an increase in the number of, and the amount of detail disclosed in, purchase price allocation notes in the financial statements of acquiring companies (such as those reproduced in Figures 7.1 and 7.2). As a result, one way the market approach could be applied to value brands directly is to review the purchase price allocation notes in the financial statements of companies that acquired comparable companies to the one whose brand is being valued, as these notes may show the value of the brands of the acquired companies. Multiples could then be calculated to express these brand values in relative terms (e.g., relative to revenue or profit) and apply them to the revenue or profit of the brand being valued (after appropriate adjustments to reflect the differences between the subject brand and the comparable brands). Binder and Hanssens (2015) examine 6,000 purchase price allocations between 2003 and 2013. They report that the average percentage of the purchase price allocated to brands has decreased over the period from about 18% to 10%, whereas the average percentage of the purchase price allocated to customer relationships has increased from 9% to 18%. The authors argue that customers still value strong brands but, as information is more easily accessible, decisions have become less driven by mere brand image than by more objective facts and customer experience. It is also possible that M&A activity has been shifting away from brand-centric businesses to more customer-centric businesses.

Notes

1. http://eu.wiley.com/WileyCDA/Section/id-817935.html.
2. Net profit or income is more logically used to arrive at equity value than EV, the value of the company as a whole (see Chapter 4).
3. Enterprise value is generally calculated in databases as the market capitalisation of a company plus the book value of net debt. Data providers use the *book value* of net debt because it is generally assumed that the *book value* of net debt is close to its *market value*.

Reference

Binder C. and Hanssens D. (2015), "Why Strong Customer Relationships Trump Powerful Brands" *Harvard Business Review*, April, available at: https://hbr.org/2015/04/why-strong-customer-relationships-trump-powerful-brands (accessed 26 December 2015)

8 The Cost-Based Approach

> The value of a commodity, or the quantity of any other commodity for which it will exchange, depends on the relative quantity of labour which is necessary for its production [. . .].
>
> Ricardo (1819)

The cost-based approach to brand valuation relies upon estimating the amount it would be necessary to spend on creating and developing a similar brand. This notion of value evokes the "labour theory of value", an old concept dating back to classical economists such as Adam Smith and David Ricardo. This approach can prove useful in certain cases where limited forecasts of financial information are available.

1. Principle

A brand is a decisive vector of value creation for a company. Company managers are willing to invest large amounts to create and develop brands: time spent on the initial conception and integration of the brand into company strategy, internal or external expenditures on its distinctive features (logo or design, colour, sound, smell), marketing costs (advertising, sponsoring), costs to promote and maintain the brand, for legal protection, and to monitor brand awareness.

The cost-based approach to brand valuation entails analysing this "investment"[1] to assess how much it would cost to reproduce a similar brand at the date of valuation. The value of a brand under this approach is therefore directly linked to the amount it costs to create the brand.

In practice, there are two types of possible methods under the cost-based approach: the first relies on the actual historical cost of a brand; the second is based on the costs that would have to be incurred to develop a similar brand (reproduction costs).

1.1. Historical Cost Method

The historical cost method measures the value of a brand by reference to the costs actually spent on developing the brand from its origins (if developed internally) or from its recognition (if acquired) until the date of valuation.

Valuation at historical cost is a time-honoured approach, which is traditionally used in accounting. It is true that before the arrival in Europe of the concept of "fair value" in financial reporting for certain assets in 2005, tangible and intangible assets were stated in accounts at historical cost (see Chapters 3 and 9), because the verifiability of the figures used in financial statements was of paramount importance to accounting standard-setters.

Under the historical cost method, the value of a brand corresponds to the total costs incurred in its development from its origin until the valuation date. These costs are expressed in present value terms using a capitalisation rate to aggregate past costs. The approach is formalised in equation (1).

$$V_T = \sum_{\tau=1}^{T} C_\tau (1+k)^{T-\tau}, \tag{1}$$

where V_T = brand value at date T;
C_τ = costs (after tax) attributable to the brand in period τ;
T = date of brand valuation;
k = capitalisation rate.

Costs C_τ comprise two elements: first the costs of creating or acquiring the brand and second the costs of developing the brand. Costs of maintaining the brand are, however, excluded because they do not increase the brand's value. This method consequently requires an efficient management accounting system to identify costs that are relevant to the brand.

The costs to create and launch a brand can include:

- internal marketing costs and salaries of those managers who helped to draw up the brand specification and determine its place in company strategy;
- advisory fees to define the brand's distinctive features: name, colour, logo (or any other distinguishing characteristics);
- legal fees to register the brand;
- advisory fees and internal marketing costs to put together the brand launch campaign; and
- payment for advertising space and other external marketing costs.

In later stages, marketing investment may be required to develop the brand, which may include in particular:

- developing new advertising campaigns;
- buying advertising space; and
- redrawing the logo and the visual symbols of the brand if they are not in line with the sought-after image.

The capitalisation rate *k* enables costs incurred in the past to be expressed in present value terms. This rate reflects not risk but cost inflation through time. In general, the capitalisation rate is estimated using price indices for the relevant category of costs.

Under the historical cost method, the value of the brand is equal to the aggregate costs incurred in its development. The brand is deemed to have attained its present status by virtue of those costs. However, not all investment is effective, and the historical cost method takes no account of the possible ineffectiveness of certain expenditure.

1.2. Reproduction Cost Method

The reproduction cost method entails estimating all the costs that would be incurred to replicate a brand—that is, to develop a brand as similar as possible to the one being valued. The characteristics of the hypothetical brand must be identical to those of the brand to be valued, in particular market share, brand awareness, brand image, brand loyalty, and its degree of legal protection.

The first step in applying this method is to analyse in detail the characteristics of the brand. The second step is more complicated and involves assessing the costs which would be required to reproduce these distinctive features.

One of the key points of the method is how to take account of the brand's life cycle at the date of valuation, as the point is not to value the brand as if it were created *ex nihilo* today, but to value it as it really is. As we saw in Chapter 1, brand value does not in fact remain constant throughout a brand's life cycle. It goes through periods of growth and decline depending on how effective the brand strategy is. The expenditure used in the reproduction method must be estimated as that which is necessary to create a brand similar to the one being valued, taking account of its level of obsolescence, which is not always easy.

2. Implementation—A Case Study

2.1. Historical Cost Method

In 2007, the company MeubleDesign created a brand of exotic wood furniture, the "Acajou" brand. Let us suppose that this brand needs to be valued as at 31 December 2014. The following costs were incurred in the first year to create and launch the brand:

- *Design costs*:
  - identifying the products whose images are to be conveyed by the new brand; in this case, the products are the range of tropical wood furniture distributed by the company;
  - analysing strategically the target market to determine how to position the brand. The brand is aimed at customers looking for solid

exotic wood furniture that is both elegant and hard-wearing. They are prepared to pay a higher price for a higher quality product;
- defining the brand message: elegant and hard-wearing furniture, made from exotic wood; and
- choosing the brand name, "Acajou", and designing a logo representing a tree.

Costs incurred comprised salary costs of employees in the marketing and strategy departments (two people for 150 days at an average daily rate of £400 per person, i.e., £120k) and communication agency fees (£43k). Total design costs for the brand in the first year, therefore, amounted to £163k.

- *Marketing costs*: developing an advertising campaign to make the brand visible.

These costs comprised salary costs of employees in the marketing department (50 days at an average daily rate of £400, i.e., £20k), advertising agency fees (£51k), and acquisition of television and Internet advertising space (£70k). Total marketing costs for the brand in the first year, therefore, amounted to £141k.

- *Legal costs*: registering the brand in the intellectual property register for £5k and £2k per annum thereafter.

An initial advertising campaign launched the brand in 2007. MeubleDesign carried out two further advertising campaigns in order to increase brand awareness. In 2008, the company spent £97k, including £12k salary cost, £35k in fees, and £50k for advertising space. In 2009, the company spent £105k, including £12k salary cost, £40k in fees, and £53k for advertising space. We shall assume for simplicity's sake that the same amount was spent every year up to 2014.

The total costs that the company incurred to develop the "Acajou" brand are summarised in Table 8.1.

To apply the historical cost method, total expenditure must be expressed in present value terms as of 31 December 2014. To do so, the inflation rate of the country in which the company operates is used as the capitalisation

Table 8.1 Creation and development costs of the "Acajou" brand

Thousands of £	*2007*	*2008*	*2009*	*2010*	*2011*	*2012*	*2013*	*2014*
Brand design	163	–	–	–	–	–	–	–
Marketing	141	97	105	105	105	105	105	105
Legal fees	5	2	2	2	2	2	2	2
Historical costs of the Acajou brand	309	99	107	107	107	107	107	107

Table 8.2 Valuation of the "Acajou" brand at capitalised historical costs

Thousands of £	*2007*	*2008*	*2009*	*2010*	*2011*	*2012*	*2013*	*2014*
Historical costs of the Acajou brand	141	97	105	105	105	105	105	105
Tax (@35%)	(49)	(34)	(37)	(37)	(37)	(37)	(37)	(37)
Net costs	92	63	68	68	68	68	68	68
Annual inflation rate	4%	4%	4%	4%	4%	4%	4%	4%
Capitalisation factor	1.34	1.29	1.24	1.19	1.15	1.10	1.06	1.02
Capitalised costs of the Acajou brand	123	81	85	81	78	75	72	70
Estimated value of the Acajou brand								666

rate. This rate should therefore reflect the time value of money without a risk premium. This is because the historical costs of the "Acajou" brand are known with certainty and are therefore not risky. Let us assume that inflation was 4% per annum throughout the period.

The value of the "Acajou" brand under the historical cost method is £666k, as shown in Table 8.2.

2.2. Reproduction Cost Method

How much would it cost today to reproduce a brand equivalent to "Acajou"; in other words, what would be the cost to produce a brand with the same positioning, visibility, and image?

The "Acajou" brand was created in 2007 and is quite recent. It is therefore probable that the same steps would have to be followed to create a similar brand today, i.e., in the first year design, registration, and a launch campaign, with further advertising in the following years to increase the brand's visibility until maximum visibility is attained. It is also probable that the brand would become known more rapidly.

The question we must ask is: would the costs of these steps be identical to the costs incurred by MeubleDesign in developing its brand? It is conceivable that the brand could become as well known as it is today more quickly through several more costly and probably more ambitious advertising campaigns. It is possible that in the past company management, out of caution or lack of resources, hesitated to invest in a large-scale advertising campaign. In addition, past investment may not always have been well spent, and the costs borne by the company to develop the "Acajou" brand may have been excessive.

To take account of the first factor, it is possible to estimate the cost of a more ambitious campaign to accelerate the positioning and awareness of the brand. The second factor requires an assessment of how effective actually spent costs were.

Table 8.3 Reproduction costs of the "Acajou" brand

Thousands of £	*2015*	*2016*	*2017*
Brand design	173	–	–
Marketing	145	100	108
Legal costs	6	–	–
Reproduction costs of the Acajou brand	324	100	108
Tax (@35%)	(114)	(35)	(38)
Estimated value of the Acajou brand			346

Let us assume that for the "Acajou" brand, these costs could have been incurred over a shorter period without any impact of inflation. Let us assume also that these costs will be particularly well spent. Costs which would have to be incurred to develop a similar brand today are set out in Table 8.3.

As we have said, we shall ignore inflation, because we are dealing with a short period. If we apply the reproduction cost method, the "Acajou" brand value is estimated at £346k (after tax).

It is not surprising that the value of the "Acajou" brand using the reproduction cost method (£346k) is much lower than that obtained using the historical cost method (£666k).

There is a bias in the reproduction cost method as to the length of time necessary to build up an equivalent brand to the one being valued. Is having a brand from December 2014 onwards (historical cost method) equivalent to reproducing a similar brand which will only be as well known as the "Acajou" brand in 2017 (reproduction cost method)? Certainly not, because in the second case, the company will forego earnings for three years. And what about an old brand that only achieved the status of reference brand after ten years' development? This point is discussed in the following section, which deals with the various limitations of cost-based methods.

3. Cost-Based Valuation Methods—Relevance and Limitations

3.1. Historical Cost Method

The main advantage of the historical cost method is that, in principle, it is objective and reliable. Because it is based on actual past costs, it is, in principle, anything but arbitrary. A historical cost valuation should yield similar results, regardless of the valuer and the assumptions made. However, the application of this method in practice can be much more complicated. The costs on which the method is based have indeed been incurred in the past, but they are difficult to identify.

The first difficulty is to identify all the costs attributable to a brand. Such costs are, in general, not shown separately in a company's management accounting system. In addition, where the brand is old, data must be collected over a long period of time, because this approach, when the *historical cost* method is used, requires costs incurred because of the creation or acquisition of the brand to be taken into account. It is often complex to isolate all the costs that are specifically related to a recently created brand. When a company holds a large portfolio of brands, it is difficult to allocate company costs to each brand. Once costs relating to a brand and its product line have been isolated, it is not simple to distinguish between the costs of the brand and the costs of the product. How does one separate, for example, marketing expenses to develop the brand from expenses to sell the product?

The second problem is that the method requires the costs of maintaining a brand to be separated from the costs of developing it, because only development costs can be taken into account in the valuation. The aim of the historical cost method is to assess the present value of the brand using only those costs that have contributed to its value. Costs directly attributable to the brand but which have not enhanced its value should therefore be excluded. Development costs and maintenance costs for a brand differ in the same way that capital expenditure on expanding an industrial plant differs from amounts spent on maintaining or renewing that plant. Capital expenditure increases the value of the plant, whilst maintenance costs cover the asset's depreciation charge. It is also difficult sometimes to distinguish between these types of expenditure in the case of brands. For example, in the case study used in Section 2 of this chapter, all advertising spend was deemed to represent the cost of developing the brand and was included in the brand valuation. In practice, a part of this cost probably helped to maintain the visibility of the brand, whilst only part of it increased its value.

Rather than estimating the value of a brand, the historical cost method essentially gives a brand's minimum value. It is true that if a brand's value is lower than its cost, it would lose money for the company and the brand should have been repositioned if management strategy had been effective.

The method proves more relevant when applied to brands that are recent or still being launched. In this case, costs incurred best reflect the stage of development of the brand, which has not yet grown or declined significantly and has not yet created (or destroyed) value. Furthermore, in valuing a new and immature brand, it is difficult to apply forward-looking methods, as benchmarks for future revenues attributable to the brand and their evolution over time are not available. The historical cost method is in this case easier and more reliable to use than methods based on future brand revenue, which were presented in Chapters 4 to 7.

In general, this method gives an order of magnitude of brand value. Comparing costs spent each year on marketing and advertising with total company costs and with the value of the company as a whole can provide a rough order of magnitude of brand value.

3.2. Reproduction Cost Method

The reproduction cost method proves even more complicated to put into practice than the historical cost method. What references are to be used to estimate those costs which would have to be incurred today to develop a brand in the same stage of development, having the same image and power, and commanding the same customer loyalty? Costs spent on developing a brand do not guarantee its success or its potential to attract and win customer loyalty. In addition, a brand is not created overnight, so how should the time wasted by the company be treated?

The reproduction cost method can easily be applied to tangible assets that are standard and interchangeable. It is less applicable in the case of brands, which are unique and highly specific intangible assets. The method takes little account of a brand's life cycle. Market prices or internal company costs are abundantly available for tangible assets. These external references can be revised downwards to reflect the obsolescence of the assets being valued. This does not work for a brand whose lifespan is unknown and whose obsolescence is not linear. Contrary to most assets, a brand does not have its highest value when it is "new". Similarly, a brand is not subject to wear and tear which gradually erodes its value; in fact, it is quite the contrary. Brands often show strong growth in the first years of their existence and then may decline more or less rapidly as a result of sometimes inappropriate strategic decisions.

The topic of the time it takes to develop a brand is often overlooked when applying the reproduction cost method. The development process for a brand is usually lengthy, and a reference brand cannot be generated in several months. To reproduce a brand similar to the one in question may take a decade, depending on its stage of development. For a company, purchasing a mature brand, which it can use immediately, is not equivalent to developing internally a similar brand that will reach maturity a decade later. The earnings lost by the company as a result of the extra time needed to develop the new brand cannot be quantified using a cost-based method, which takes no account of the earnings generated by a brand.

The idea of estimating the value of a brand by referencing the theoretical costs of reproducing a similar brand is justified from an economic viewpoint by the underlying premise that an investor is unwilling to pay more for an asset than it would cost to develop it himself internally. The maximum price that an investor who is considering buying a brand is prepared to pay is the cost to develop a similar asset internally. This approach is all the more relevant if the investor really possesses the market capacity to reproduce a similar brand in a reasonable time frame.

However, the practical difficulties and the lack of objectivity inherent in implementing this method remain, including those involved in the identification of the reproduction costs and the duration of the development phase, as well as those involved in taking account of the brand's life cycle.

Conclusion

Cost-based valuation methods in general lead to assets being undervalued. Brands valued using this method are no exception. Estimating the value of a brand based on its cost implies that the benefits from using the brand are identical to its development costs. In other words, the approach assumes that brands do not contribute to the creation of company value.

Cost-based valuation methods assume that a given type of expenditures will always yield the same return on investment. For example, for a given cost, all advertising campaigns have equal success and result in the same increase in earnings from the sale of products or services. In practice, certain extremely costly advertising campaigns fail dismally, whilst others with limited budgets succeed in spurring interest for the products among consumers. The power of a brand does not systematically depend on the amounts spent on creating and launching it.

In conclusion, unless they are used in the case of a brand which is recent, is being launched, or is just beginning to generate profits, cost-based methods should generally be set aside in favour of more theoretically sound financial methods, which were described in Chapters 4 to 7.

Note

1. Investment can comprise capital expenditure that is capitalised in the balance sheet and then depreciated in the profit and loss account, or expenses that are written-off immediately.

Reference

Ricardo D. (1819), *On the Principles of Political Economy and Taxation*, 1st edition, John Murray, Albemarle-Street, London.

9 Brands and Valuation Standards

> Intangible assets are recognized as highly-valued properties. Arguably the most valuable but least understood intangible assets are brands.
>
> ISO Standard 10668 (2010), Introduction

> Scandals, crises, and growing accountability demands have triggered an unstoppable march toward higher quality fair value measurements, provided by better qualified valuation practitioners.
>
> Forsythe (2015)

The disparity in valuation methods used and the growing importance of intangible assets, and brands in particular, have led certain organisations to publish standards specifically covering financial valuation. These standards have three purposes:

- lay down best practice for preparers of financial statements and independent valuers in order to enhance the quality of valuations in the absence of a common methodology;
- help users of valuations understand the underlying financial techniques and assumptions;
- ensure that valuations of intangible assets are consistent and of a high enough quality to restore public confidence, which was undermined by the financial crisis of 2008–2009.

As we emphasised in Chapter 2, brand valuations are required in different contexts: legal disputes, taxation, preparation of financial statements, securitisation, and commercial or strategic transactions. The need for credible references to define good valuation practice has been accentuated in certain circumstances, especially in the context of disputes. In a dispute, quantifying the loss suffered relies essentially on valuation techniques. In such a context, the quality and independence of the valuation report are critical. Courts therefore asked early on for standards to be established. The first rules were thus laid down by courts and tax authorities (in particular the Internal Revenue Service (IRS) in the United States). These first valuation "standards" accepted by the IRS, however, do not provide a complete economic and financial analysis of valuation methods, but rather a general guide for its own internal use.[1] It is more a checklist for employees of the IRS than detailed standards that prescribe the use of specific valuation methods.

Advanced valuation methods evolved informally and only recently gave rise to standards of good practice. It was only after 2008 that the general demand for precise technical standards to serve as a practical reference for brand valuation was met.

Among those who have created a body of standards are the accounting standard-setters: the IASB and the FASB, both of which have published standards on "fair value" measurement as part of the process of convergence between the two sets of standards. Other international bodies have contributed by publishing specific documents on valuation: the International Valuation Standards Council (IVSC) and the International Organization for Standardization (ISO). Certain national bodies have also produced guides to best practice in valuing intangible assets: external financial auditors in Germany (IDW), the Appraisal Foundation (TAF) and the American Society of Appraisers (ASA) in the United States, the Royal Institution for Chartered Surveyors (RICS) in the United Kingdom, and in France AFNOR (French Association for Standardisation), which is a member of ISO. These organisations, associations, or institutions do not all possess the same legitimacy, the same competence, or even the same determination to put forward detailed valuation methods for intangible assets. The quality and usefulness of the documents produced are therefore variable. The standards issued by the IVSC, the ISO, and the accounting standard-setters are relatively detailed. Those organisations that have published more succinct documents (ASA, TAF, and AFNOR) often refer to the standards and to the major institutions.

In this chapter, we will first describe the context in which these valuation standards for intangible assets have emerged and the issues they raise. We list and analyse standards on brand valuation published by these organisations. We look at international standards and then national standards. We criticise certain positions taken and discuss the relationships between these organisations.

1. Emergence of Brand Valuation Standards—Context and Issues

After the crisis of 2008–2009, market regulators and, in particular, the Securities and Exchange Commission (SEC), the powerful American regulator, examined valuations carried out by professionals in the sector. Valuation at fair value, advocated by American and international standards, was severely criticised and sometimes considered responsible for the crisis (Laux and Leuz, 2010). Professional valuers also came under criticism.

Since 2008, there has been a certain distrust of professional valuers in a context where fair-value valuations shown in financial statements became disconnected from market values. The use of fair value in financial statements has been seen by some as a source of accounting manipulation (Ramanna and Watts, 2009). It is true that valuation models used to measure fair value often rely on assumptions that are impossible for financial auditors to verify. For certain valuations, doubt focused on certain fair-value estimates referred to in IFRS or US GAAP as level 2 or level 3 (see next section). These estimates are based on assumptions made by management rather than on observable market information. Certain critics do not hesitate to describe the valuation of assets and liabilities based on level 3 inputs as "marked-to-myth" rather than "marked-to-market" (Kolev, 2008).

After 2008, the latent overvaluation of many balance sheet items was so blatant that the capacity of impairment tests to ensure prudent fair-value estimates was called into doubt (see Filip *et al.*, 2015; Li and Sloan, 2015; and Figure 3.2 in Chapter 3 for FTSE 100 companies). The SEC did not hesitate to demand that listed companies reconcile the values of their reporting units (or "cash-generating units" under IFRS) with their market capitalisation.

Figure 9.1 shows the variation between 2005 and 2010 in the proportion of listed companies in Europe (STOXX 600) and in the United States (S&P 500) having a higher book value than market value.

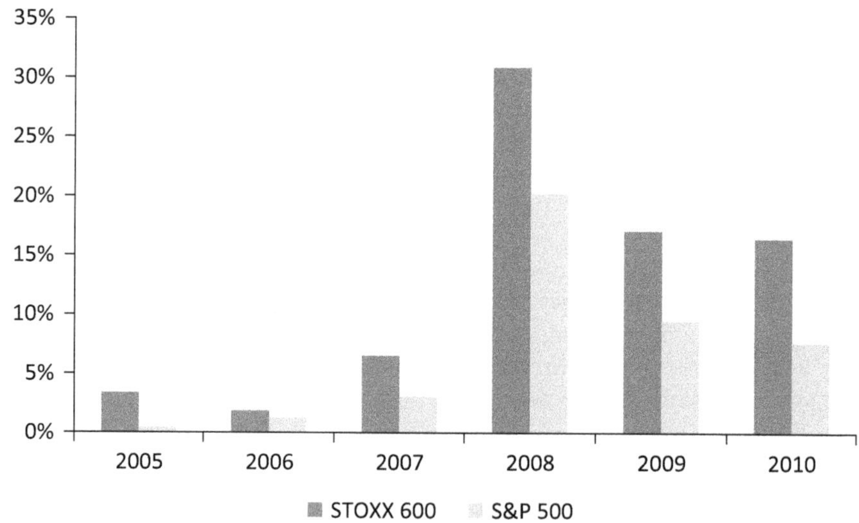

Figure 9.1 Variation in 2005–2010 in the number of companies with a higher book value than market capitalisation (as a per cent of the number of companies making up the two indices).

Source: American Society of Appraisers (2012), *ASA Advanced Business Conference 2012*, "Raising the Bar for the Valuation Profession".

During the financial crisis of 2008, more than 30% of listed European companies and more than 20% of US companies had a book value higher than their market capitalisation, despite the impairment testing mechanisms presented in Chapter 3, the aim of which is precisely to ensure that financial statements are drawn up prudently (conservatively)!

After 2008, the underlying economic depreciation had not impacted net assets but was factored into market values. This overstatement of net assets still exists, especially in Europe, because in 2009 and 2010, more than 15% of STOXX 600 companies still showed net assets higher than market value compared with only about 10% of S&P 500 companies. The more persistent phenomenon in Europe can be explained by the fact that market regulators are less vigilant on this subject, although the European Securities and Markets Authority (ESMA), the counterpart of the SEC in Europe, voiced some concerns in 2013 (ESMA, 2013). In both areas, however, there is resistance to bringing book values more in line with market values.

Market regulators, especially the SEC, started to address the question of the independence and consistency of valuation reports. Given the number of professional organisations offering certifications for valuers,[2] and the disparity in standards, the SEC indicated that it would be in the public interest to standardise certain aspects of the profession: (1) common requirements for training and experience for professional certification, (2) a common code of ethics and good practice, and (3) one set of valuation standards reflecting best practice (see Beswick, 2011).

In addition, the American and European market regulators (the AMF in France or the BaFin in Germany) called upon external financial auditors to be increasingly vigilant when auditing documentation supporting fair-value measurements and, in particular, impairment tests.

The issues at stake have therefore provoked much thought on the part of all those involved in valuations and especially the accounting standard-setting bodies: the IASB and FASB.

2. International and US Accounting Valuation Standards: Valuation at "Fair Value"

2.1. *General Principles of Fair-Value Measurement Under Accounting Standards*

IFRS 13, "Fair Value Measurement", was published by the IASB in May 2011 as part of the process of convergence between the IASB and the FASB, which issued FAS 157 (ASC Topic 820) "Fair Value Measurements" in September 2006. The two boards succeeded in converging in these two standards with a common definition of fair value and a common method of measuring it.[3]

Over and above the aim of achieving convergence between international and American financial reporting standards, the standard on fair value has three main objectives:

- Provide a single definition of fair value. Prior to the publication of IFRS 13, guidance on fair value was found in many standards, for example, IAS 39 ("Financial Instruments: Recognition and Measurement") or IAS 36 ("Impairment of Assets").
- Provide guidance on valuation practices. IFRS 13 explains how to measure fair value for financial reporting.
- Require disclosure enabling users of financial statements to understand the valuation method used, the assumptions made, and the subjectivity of the valuation. The aim is to help users assess how reasonable the valuation is.

The standard attaches great importance to two basic principles arising from a questionable choice of methodology (particularly in the case of brand valuation):

- fair value is measured at an "exit price"; in other words, it is measured on the assumption that an asset would not be used by an entity but sold to a third party;
- the valuation is carried out on the assumption that the use of the asset is its highest and best use; in other words, no account is taken of the specificity of the entity owning the asset or liability.

The definition of fair value reflects these principles: it is "the price that would be received to sell an asset or paid to transfer a liability in an orderly transaction between market participants at the measurement date" (IFRS 13). The notions of exit price and market participant are both present in this definition.

To summarise, an asset's value is measured in practice as if it were put to its best use (to maximise future economic benefits) and by a hypothetical market participant who is well informed and freely willing to enter into the agreement (under no compulsion to do so).

In terms of valuation, IFRS 13 distinguishes three possible approaches to measuring fair value from the viewpoint of a market participant: (1) the market approach using market transaction prices, (2) the replacement (reproduction) cost approach, and (3) the income approach involving discounting future cash flows. IFRS 13 does not favour one approach but states that the appropriate approach shall be one for which quality data is available.

Whilst the standard does not rank the valuation methods, it does establish a hierarchy of data available as inputs to a valuation. IFRS 13 lists three categories of inputs, from the most reliable (which should be preferred) to the least reliable (to be used only if better data cannot be used):

- Level 1 inputs: quoted prices (unadjusted) observed at the measurement date in active markets for identical assets or liabilities.
- Level 2 inputs: market data that can be observed directly or indirectly, other than quoted prices included in level 1. IFRS 13 gives the example of quoted prices for identical or similar assets in non-active markets or prices for similar assets in active markets.
- Level 3 inputs: these are unobservable inputs, which should only be used if level 1 or level 2 inputs are not available. The valuing entity may use specific data it has itself developed.

Brands are nearly always valued using level 3 inputs.

2.2. *Criticism of the Fair-Value Approach to Brand Valuation in Accounting Standards*

The position taken in accounting standards on brand valuation is to use the value of a brand to a market participant (exit price) who is maximising the brand's potential (highest and best use). Two criticisms can be levelled against using the market participant's viewpoint (1.) and the exit price logic (2.):

1. Brands are highly specific assets, often inseparable from other assets (distribution network or human capital, for example). In practice, it is impossible to ignore the specificities of the brand owner. For example, if a company acquires a competing brand during a business combination, the brand must be valued at its fair value in the purchase price allocation process (IFRS 3). The acquiring company seeks to eliminate a competitor and has no intention of operating the brand. A market participant, however, would be ready to pay to obtain control of the brand and operate it (highest and best use). Oddly, the company will therefore have to value and capitalise the brand using the market participant rationale and then write it off from the balance sheet at the next impairment test.
2. Referring to an exit price for a brand presupposes that the readers of financial statements are looking to see brands valued as if they were stand-alone assets of a company, which is a strong, and probably erroneous, assumption. Investors, who are considered the primary users of financial statements by the IASB and the FASB, are probably more interested in assessing the economic prospects of a brand operated by a company as an ongoing concern than as an asset to be potentially disposed of. For brands, which are highly specific assets, the value of

which depends greatly on their use by management, measurement of fair value in this way is potentially uninformative.

In addition, the question of brand valuation methods is dealt with by IFRS 13 only in the light of fair-value measurement. In other words, the standard answers the question "If I must measure fair value, how shall I do it?" but ignores the question of whether fair value needs to be measured ("Is fair value the right valuation basis?"). In other words, IFRS 13 brings no correction to the inconsistency between the way purchased brands and internally developed brands are dealt with in financial statements. Brands developed internally are therefore still valued at (legal) registration cost, whereas a fair-value measurement would be more appropriate for readers of the financial statements.

As stated earlier, accounting standards are not the only regulatory standards dealing with the valuation of intangible assets. International bodies such as the International Valuation Standards Council (IVSC) and the International Association of Consultants, Valuators, and Analysts (IACVA) have also published guidance on brand valuation.

3. Standards and Recommendations of the IVSC and the IACVA

3.1. International Valuation Standard No. 210—Intangible Assets

The IVSC is an international body, founded in 1981 and based in London, whose role is to establish international valuation standards to encourage professional best practice. The body has high ambitions because its goal is to deal with the valuation of all types of assets, regardless of valuation context. The council has been chaired since 2012 by Sir David Tweedie, former chairman of the International Accounting Standards Board from 2001 to 2011 and one of the most active promoters of fair value in the preparation of financial statements.

When it presented International Valuation Standard 201 (IVS 210), "Intangible Assets", the IVSC stated that one of its aims was to demystify the valuation process for intangible assets, such as brands, goodwill, and intellectual property.[4] The recommendations of the IVSC do not only apply to financial reporting issues or IAS/IFRS. They can be used in other contexts and especially in transfer pricing analyses. The IVSC's credibility is growing and it acknowledges that it works in collaboration with the Appraisal Foundation (TAF) in the United States (see the following section).

Contrary to international accounting standards, the IVSC is more open to taking into account the valuation context and selects several bases of valuation:

- "Market value" is defined as, "The estimated amount for which an asset or liability should exchange on the valuation date between a

willing buyer and a willing seller in an arm's length transaction, after proper marketing and where the parties had each acted knowledgeably, prudently and without compulsion." This valuation basis is the closest to fair value under financial reporting standards (market participant perspective, exit price) (IVSC, 2103).
- "Investment value" is defined as "the value of an asset to the owner or a prospective owner for individual investment or operational objectives." The valuation basis is specific to the party that controls (owner) or would control (prospective owner) the brand. Therefore, for the owner of a brand, this valuation basis is similar to the "value in use" of the reporting entity, as used in some IFRS, such as IAS 36 (IVSC, 2103).
- "Fair value" is the estimated price for the transfer of an asset or liability between identified knowledgeable and willing parties that reflects the respective interests of those parties. This basis differs from market value in that it takes account of the specificities of the two parties. It also, therefore, differs from fair value under financial reporting standards.

The valuation of an asset can, therefore, differ according to the context and the valuation basis used. Thus, if a brand is valued for commercial strategic reasons, the investment value basis would, for example, be more relevant than market value, which would require imagining a theoretical market for a highly specific asset. Estimating the value of a brand in a transaction context would occur by reference to market value or to fair value (as defined by the IVSC) if the identity of the purchaser was known.

IVS 210 "Intangible Assets" is the result of a process that begun in 2006 and which saw the first version of the standard being published in 2007. The standard was subsequently amended, and the latest version of IVS 210, which dates from 2011, was effective from 1 January 2012. IVS 210 makes a distinction between identifiable and unidentifiable intangible assets, the latter generally being called "goodwill". According to the standard, an intangible asset is identifiable if (1) it is separable (it can be sold, licensed, or exchanged) or (2) it arises from contractual or other legal rights. The four principal classes of identifiable intangible assets are as follows:

1. marketing-related intangible assets—brands belong to this class;
2. customer or supplier-related intangible assets;
3. technology-related intangible assets;
4. artistic-related intangible assets.

Three approaches to brand valuation are discussed in IVS 210: (1) the market approach, in which value is determined by reference to market transactions, (2) the income approach (relief-from-royalty, premium profits, excess earnings), and (3) the cost approach. Brand valuation is explicitly addressed to illustrate the adjustments necessary to reflect the differentiating characteristics of a brand when using the market approach.

In a discussion paper published in 2007 that deals with intangible asset valuation for financial reporting under IFRS, the IVSC sets out numerous practical examples of the use of these methods for brand valuations (IVSC, 2007). The IVSC emphasises that it is important to use several approaches to value intangible assets and proposes a hierarchy of applicable valuation methods. This hierarchy is different from that put forward by IFRS 13, which is based on source inputs, because in practice the valuation of brands always relies on level 3 inputs. The IFRS 13 hierarchy is therefore of limited interest for brand valuation.

We have reproduced a table contained in the IVSC (2007) discussion paper (see Table 9.1), which shows the approaches available for brand valuation depending on data available and the proposed hierarchy of methods for fair-value measurement under IFRS.

Table 9.1 Available data and valuation methods applicable to brands

Data Type	*Availability*	*Reliability of Data*	*Impact on Valuation Methods Available*
Comparable transaction prices and valuation multiples	Two transactions in similar asset available—each more than one year before the valuation date	Low—assets are not closely comparable	Market transactions method available as supporting, not primary, method
Prospective financial information	Forecasts could be made based on reporting entity's expectations adjusted to exclude entity-specific factors	Medium/high—reporting entity is a market participant and there are few entity-specific factors to adjust for	Income capitalisation methods may be available depending on other data required
Royalty rate	Details of ten comparable licensing arrangements are available	High	Relief-from-royalty method could be used as primary method
Premium profits	A comparable unbranded business is identified in the market, but it would not be possible to obtain a forecast for this business	Not available	Premium profits method is not available

Data Type	*Availability*	*Reliability of Data*	*Impact on Valuation Methods Available*
Capitalisation multiples	Price/earnings multiples of other branded businesses are available	Medium—some adjustments required between market P/Es and subject-brand capitalisation multiples	Multiples could be used for market transactions method or income capitalisation method
Discount rates	Could be calculated using the build-up method by reference to WACC for quoted companies using similar brands and the WACC of the reporting entity	High	Can use an income capitalisation approach
Contributory asset charges	The capital value of the assets contributing to cash flow is needed. However, one of those other assets is customer relationships—these are not known	Not available as one of the inputs, cannot be estimated	Multi-period excess earnings method is not available, as value of customer relationships is not known
Replacement cost	No replacement evidence available	Not available	Cost approach not available

Source: IVSC Discussion Paper (2007), Section VII.

According to this example given by the IVSC, the relief–from-royalty method (see Chapter 6) may be used as the primary method to estimate the fair value of a brand. Transaction multiples could then serve as a cross-check to support the primary approach. The IVSC proposes the following hierarchy of methods for valuing intangible assets:

1. sales comparison method for intangible assets traded in an active market; then if (1) is unavailable:

2. either a cost, sales comparison in an inactive market or income capitalisation method as the primary approach depending on data availability;
3. then, where possible, the value obtained by the primary approach should be cross-checked for reasonableness against another valuation method that uses either the same or a different valuation approach.

Method 1 is typically unavailable for brands. The IVSC therefore requires that a primary valuation be carried out using available data of reasonable reliability and that the value obtained be tested by a secondary method.

3.2. *The International Association of Consultants, Valuators, and Analysts*

The International Association of Consultants, Valuators, and Analysts (IACVA) is an international association created in 2010 with two objectives: (1) provide guidance on the uniform application of valuation theory, approaches, methods and models and (2) encourage the development and dissemination of the best techniques for the detection and prevention of fraud. The organisation seeks to achieve these objectives through training professionals. It issues two accreditations: one in business valuation (CVA—*Certified Valuation Analyst*) and the other in fraud deterrence (CFD—*Certified in Fraud Deterrence*).

The association also publishes standards that constitute guidelines and are less detailed than those of the IVSC. The IACVA's professional standards deal mainly with questions of professional ethics and address briefly the available valuation methods and the contents of valuation reports. The IACVA's professional standards document issued in 2011 contains only 21 pages. In reality, the IACVA encourages the adoption of standards published by the IVSC for the valuation of intangible assets and intellectual property, as well as those of the FASB and the IASB for financial reporting.

The IACVA's mission is not, therefore, to develop detailed standards, but rather to bring together valuation professionals within an international association.

4. Standard of the International Organization for Standardization—ISO 10668 "Brand Valuation"

The International Organization for Standardization (also known by the initials ISO) is a member organisation based in Switzerland, made up of 162 national standards bodies. It is the world's largest developer of international standards, with nearly 19,500 standards covering subjects as diverse as agriculture, building, mechanical engineering, transport, communication technologies, and, recently, brand valuation.

According to Catty (2011), the ISO has several missions: (1) make development, manufacture, and sale of products and services more efficient, safer, and ecological; (2) facilitate fairer exchanges between countries; (3) provide public authorities with technical rules on health, security, and respect for the environment; (4) propagate innovation; (5) protect consumers; and (6) make life easier for users of standards by offering solutions to common problems. Catty (2011) argues that the move toward standardisation of brand valuation was motivated by wide disparities between valuation estimates of brand values.

The ISO develops worldwide standards that are intended to "give world-class specifications for products, services and systems, to ensure quality, safety and efficiency." The standards "are instrumental in facilitating international trade" and aim at ensuring "that products and services are safe, reliable and of good quality."[5] ISO certification can be seen as a credible signal to consumers, thus ISO standards help businesses gain market share by reducing information asymmetries between potential customers and producers of goods and services.

Because of the wide range of subjects covered by its standards, the ISO could be perceived as less credible on valuation than the IVSC. ISO 10668, however, makes a significant contribution to standardising brand valuation. The standard deals only with monetary brand valuation and is the first ISO standard on financial valuation. It results from a process launched in 2006 by an international consultation at the initiative of the DIN (German Standardisation Institute), together with the French Association for Standardisation (AFNOR). An international work group met from May 2007 until 2008. Finally, it was not until 2010 that ISO 10668, "Brand Valuation—Requirements for Monetary Brand Valuation", was published.

ISO 10668 contains 11 pages and covers eight aspects of the requirements that need to be met for a valuation report to be ISO-certified. They are summarised by Catty (2011) as follows:

- Transparency: valuation processes must be transparent; the report must include information on data inputs, assumptions, and sensitivity analyses where necessary.
- Validity: data input and assumptions made must be valid and relevant to the valuation date.
- Reliability: valuation models used should be reliable and give reconcilable results.
- Sufficiency: valuations should be based on sufficient data and analysis to form reliable conclusions.
- Objectivity: the valuer should be free from any form of biased judgement.
- Parameters: appropriate behavioural, legal, and financial parameters should be used when performing the valuation.
- Purpose: the valuation report should specify its intended use, the audience addressed, the identity of the brand (including a full description of the brand), the date at which the brand has been valued, the date of the report, and the position of the valuer.

- Conformity with value concept: the brand value should represent the economic benefits conferred by the brand to the owner over its expected useful economic life. Generally, these benefits are calculated by reference to cash flows, earnings, economic profits, or cost savings.

The standard distinguishes three classes of valuation methods similar to those described by other standard-setters: (1) income approach (price premium, volume premium, income split, excess earnings, incremental cash flows, and relief-from-royalty), (2) cost approach (replacement (reproduction) cost or historical cost), and (3) market approach. ISO 10668 covers several technical points concerning the first class of methods; in particular, it covers the questions of the appropriate discount rate and useful life of the asset, the question of tax benefits (*Tax Amortisation Benefits*, see Appendix 3), or that of the long-term growth rate.

In addition, the standard requires that certain key characteristics of the brand be analysed and disclosed in the valuation report. For example, the brand's positioning, arrangements for its legal protection, consumer awareness of the brand, and the way in which it brings economic benefits to its owner, should be analysed and disclosed in the report.

In conclusion, ISO 10668 addresses quite comprehensively the issues involved in brand valuation and can be viewed as a relevant reference document for valuers.

5. Standards Published by National Bodies: United States, United Kingdom, France, and Germany

Over and above these international institutions, there are a number of national institutions who also play a role in standardising brand valuation. In general, national bodies tend to converge on brand valuation with the main international bodies, the IVSC and the ISO. There are, therefore, very few really distinctive local standards.

In the United States, the Appraisal Foundation (TAF) is a foundation whose objective is to promote expertise among valuation professionals and bolster public confidence. The foundation was created by the merger of eight professional associations (including the American Society of Appraisers) in 1987, just after the American savings and loans crisis when public confidence in real estate valuations was shaken. The organisation is recognised as a standard-setter by the American Congress. Historically, TAF has issued standards concerning real estate valuation in particular. In 2006, TAF and the IVSC declared they had a common objective of establishing a unique set of standards that were easy to understand and to apply. Both organisations have created work groups to identify and remove points of divergence between their respective standards.

The French Association for Standardisation (AFNOR), founded in 1926, contributes to standardising a large number of activities in France. This association is entrusted with a public service mission to organise and coordinate standardisation in France. It took part in the preparation of ISO 10668 for brand valuation in France.

In Germany, the Deutsches Institut für Normung (DIN), the equivalent of AFNOR, launched the development of ISO 10668 on brands. In addition, German Public Auditors have established standards on business valuations (IDW Standard: Principles for the Performance of Business Valuations). This document does not, however, deal specifically with intangible assets.

In the United Kingdom, the British Standards Institution (BSI) is also a member of the ISO. The Royal Institution for Chartered Surveyors (RICS) also publishes standards for valuations, historically of land, property, and construction. RICS has recently moved to the valuation of businesses and intangible assets (RICS, 2014). RICS is a member of IVSC and complies with international valuation standards with regard to intangible assets (IVS 210). It provides additional commentary on the practical implementation of IVS 210, "Intangible Assets".

Conclusion

In this chapter, we started by describing the context in which valuation standards for intangible assets have emerged and the issues they have raised. We listed and analysed standards on brand valuation published by a number of organisations, including international and US accounting valuation standards, standards and recommendations of the IVSC and the IACVA, the standard of the International Organization for Standardization—ISO 10668 "Brand valuation", and standards published by national bodies in the United States, United Kingdom, France, and Germany. We also criticised certain positions taken and discussed the relationships between these organisations. In the next chapter, we analyse *ad hoc* valuation models.

Notes

1. See: https://www.irs.gov/irm/part4/irm_04-048-005.html (accessed 22 February 2016).
2. In North America, the following organisations offer certifications and training for valuers: the International Association of Consultants, Valuators, and Analysts (IACVA), the American Society of Appraisers (ASA), the American Institute of Certified Public Accountants (AICPA), and the Canadian Institute of Chartered Business Valuators (CICBV).
3. Despite a number of notable successes such as business combinations (IFRS 3R/FAS 141) or fair value and some projects nearing completion (lease contracts and revenue recognition), there is currently no new project on the boards' agendas.
4. See IVSC press release of March 1, 2010: http://www.ivsc.org/news/article/ivsc-publish-revised-guidance-for-the-valuation-of-intangible-assets (accessed 26 December 2015).
5. See www.iso.org (accessed 26 December 2015).

References

Beswick P.A. (2011), "Prepared Remarks for the 2011 AICPA National Conference on Current SEC and PCAOB Developments" Deputy Chief Accountant, US Securities and Exchange Commission, Washington DC, December 5, available at: http://www.sec.gov/news/speech/2011/spch120511pab.htm (accessed 26 December 2015)

Catty J.P. (2011), "ISO 10668 and Brand Valuations: A Summary for Appraisers" *Business Valuation Update*, BVR, Vol. 17 (4), April, pp. 1–7.

ESMA (2013), *European Enforcers Review of Impairment for Goodwill and Other Intangible Assets in the IFRS Financial Statements,* European Securities and Markets Authority, Paris.

FASB (2001), *Statement of Financial Accounting Concepts No. 141: Business Combinations*, Financial Accounting Standards Board, Norwalk, CT.

FASB (2006), *Statement of Financial Accounting Standard No. 157, Fair Value Measurements*, Financial Accounting Standards Board, Norwalk, CT.

FASB (2007), *Statement of Financial Accounting Concepts No. 141R: Business Combinations—Revised*, Financial Accounting Standards Board, Norwalk, CT.

Filip A. Jeanjean T. and Paugam L. (2015), "Using Real Activities to Avoid Goodwill Impairment Losses: Evidence and Effect on Future Performance" *Journal of Business & Accounting*, Vol. 42 (3–4), pp. 515–554.

Forsythe G. (2015), "Valuation in the Fair Value Era. Higher Quality Can Help Companies Reduce Risk and Enhance Shareholder Value" Deloitte Financial Advisory Services LLP, available at: http://www2.deloitte.com/us/en/pages/advisory/articles/valuation-fair-value-article.html# (accessed 26 December 2015)

IASB (2003), *International Reporting Financial Standards (IFRS) No. 9: Financial Instruments: Recognition and Measurement,* IASC Foundation Publications Department, London.

IASB (2004), *International Reporting Financial Standards (IFRS) No. 3: Business Combinations,* IASC Foundation Publications Department, London.

IASB (2009), *International Accounting Standards No. 36: Impairment of Assets,* IASC Foundation Publications Department, London.

IASB (2011), *International Financial Reporting Standards (IFRS) No. 13: Fair Value Measurement,* IVSC Discussion Paper, IASC Foundation Publication Department, London.

International Organization for Standardization (ISO) (2010), *International Organization Standard No. 10668—Brand Valuation—Requirements for Monetary Brand Valuation*, The International Organization for Standardization, Geneva, Switzerland.

IVSC (2007), *Discussion Paper: Determination of Fair Value of Intangible Assets for IFRS Reporting Purposes*, International Valuation Standard Council, London.

IVSC (2011), *International Valuation Standard (IVS) No. 210: Intangible Assets,* International Valuation Standard Council, London.

IVSC (2013), *International Valuation Standards (IVS) 2013: Framework and Requirements,* International Valuation Standard Council, London.

Kolev K. (2008), "Do Investors Perceive Marking-to-Model as Marking-to-Myth? Early Evidence from FAS 157 Disclosure" *Working paper Stern School of Business*, New York University.

Laux C. and Leuz C. (2010), "Did Fair-Value Accounting Contribute to the Financial Crisis?" *CFA Digest*, Vol. 40 (2), pp. 33–34.

Li K.K. and Sloan R.G. (2015), "Has Goodwill Accounting Gone Bad?" *Working paper.*

Ramanna K. and Watts R. (2009), "Evidence on the Effects of Unverifiable Fair-Value Accounting" *Harvard Business School Working Paper* No. 08–014, available at: http://ssrn.com/abstract 1012139

RICS (2014), *Valuation—Professional Standards* January (Red Book), available at: http://www.rics.org (accessed 26 December 2015)

10 *Ad Hoc* Valuation Models

As a result of the rapidly growing need for brand valuations in various contexts, a structured offer of brand valuation services came into being. This market emerged during the 1990s and developed strongly in the following decade as accounting standards on purchase price allocation were issued (SFAS 141 in the United States in 2001 and IFRS 3 in Europe in 2005). From this point on, business combinations gave rise to the recognition and, therefore, the valuation of brands which had previously been considered integrals parts of goodwill.

Before the 1990s, there was little call for brand valuation. Nevertheless, there are some examples of brands being valued in the United Kingdom where the accounting rules for recognition of intangible assets were vague at the time. Grand Metropolitan Plc, active in the food and drinks sector, was the first company ever to recognise on its balance sheet the value of an acquired brand. In 1987, the Smirnoff vodka brand was thus recognised following the acquisition of Heublein.[1] In 1988, the management of the food group Rank Hovis McDougall Plc (today RHM) quoted on the London Stock Exchange, was faced with a hostile takeover bid. Rank Hovis management decided that year to value and capitalise its portfolio of acquired and internally developed brands to highlight their value to its shareholders. In pursuit of this strategy, perceived at the time as defensive, the portfolio was valued by Interbrand. The operation also resulted in the Interbrand firm becoming more widely known. The Australian company behind the bid, Goodman Fielder, which held 30% of RHM shares, finally decided to withdraw its offer.[2]

Since the 1990s, many consultancy firms have developed proprietary brand valuation models. These different models are based on the valuation methods presented in Chapters 4 to 8. What characterises these models, which are generally named after the firm or consultant who developed them, is their attempt to standardise the analytical approach and the estimation of parameters with a precise aim. The aim in general is to develop an objective approach so as to create brand league tables. In absolute terms, these models are neither good nor bad, and their suitability depends on the context in which they are used. It depends also on the objective of the valuation: is it to identify and capitalise the brand on the company's balance sheet? Is it to measure its fair value prior to a sale?

Table 10.1 Advantages and disadvantages of *ad hoc* brand valuation models

Advantages	*Disadvantages*
• Consistency/uniformity of valuation method • Consistent over time • Possibility to rank brands • Main factors taken into account (depending on models) • Protect the valuing firm's market (advantage for the valuer)	• Standardisation and simplification • Certain factors may be overlooked • Models lack specificity • False impression of rigour • Black box/subjectivity (depending on models) • Ignore the need to cross-check the valuation against other approaches

Ad hoc valuation models are, therefore, useful in certain contexts but can lead to errors caused by an over-systematic analysis. They do, however, have certain advantages: consistency of method helps brands to be ranked because, although *ad hoc* models can be considered biased, all brands are similarly affected, and the relative value of each brand compared with other brands does not change. In addition, *ad hoc* models can also prove useful when a manager wishes to measure whether/how his actions influenced a brand over time. The pertinence of a valuation at a given moment matters less than the relative progression of the brand's value.

Nevertheless, the use of *ad hoc* models can lead to errors being reproduced and inappropriate analysis being applied. Brands are highly specific assets. There is no guarantee that an *ad hoc* approach that is relevant for a consumer brand and meets management needs will also be relevant for the valuation of an industrial brand for purchase price allocation purposes within the strict framework of accounting standards. For an exercise aimed at quantifying the value of a brand, it is preferable to use a primary approach and then to cross-check it against a second or even a third approach. In theory, challenging the relevance of a standard valuation model in order to detect inconsistencies and avoid omitting important parameters can only be a good thing.

In this chapter, we present and discuss the major *ad hoc* valuation models for brands.[3] One of the oldest and best known was developed by the firm Interbrand and is derived from the excess earnings method. The firm of Stern Stewart (known for having developed the EVA excess earnings indicator) has also devised a brand valuation model based on this approach. Other models, such as those of BrandFinance or BBDO, rely on other approaches such as royalties or multiples.

1. *Ad Hoc* Valuation Models Based on Excess Earnings

1.1. *The Interbrand Model: Principles*

The valuation model developed by Interbrand is an adaptation of the excess earnings method. Interbrand considers brands to be business assets used in the medium/long term. The model therefore only takes into account the way in which management is likely to develop the use of its brand. This definition of the value of a brand differs from that put forward by accounting standards in that no reference is made to the amount that could be received if the brand was exchanged between knowledgeable and willing parties in an arm's length transaction, where the brand's future prospects might be different from those perceived by management. In certain circumstances and, in particular, where fair value or market value are being measured, the Interbrand method is not necessarily the most suitable.

Interbrand uses a method with three steps:

1. The first step is to estimate the *economic profits* that a company will generate. It should be noted that economic profits (referred to as excess earnings in Chapter 4) represent wealth created after remunerating all production factors (including capital) and is calculated as

   Economic profits = Net operating profit after tax –Capital charge.

   The amount subtracted from net operating profit after tax (NOPAT) is a notional capital charge to account for the capital used to generate the brand's revenues, calculated using the industry's WACC. Interbrand typically analyses past economic profits, which it extrapolates five years into the future and to which it adds a terminal value (implicitly assuming the useful economic life of brands to be indefinite).[4]
2. The second step is to assess the role played by the brand in generating economic profits. The idea is to measure how much of the consumer's decision to purchase the branded product rather than an unbranded product is attributable to the brand—that is, excluding other aspects of the offer, such as product features or price. This important step derives, depending on the brand, from one of three methods: primary research, a review of historical roles of brands for companies in that industry, or expert panel assessment. This step is clearly subjective.

   Interbrand calculates the profits attributable to the brand (*branded earnings*) by multiplying the excess earnings by a percentage ascribable to the brand:

   Branded earnings = Economic profit × Role of brand.

3. The last step is to measure *brand strength*, i.e., the ability of the brand to deliver expected future earnings. Interbrand bases its analysis on ten factors that affect brand strength, which it measures on a scale from 0 to 100. This score, when applied to a proprietary algorithm, impacts negatively the discount rate used to calculate the net present value of total future profits of the brand. The stronger the brand, the lower the discount rate.

   Brand value = Branded earnings × Discount rate based on brand strength.

   This last step is also subjective.

Table 10.2 describes the four "internal" and the six "external" factors which Interbrand states it uses during the third step in its 2011 *Best Global Brand* report.[5]

The four internal factors (clarity, commitment, responsiveness, and protection) measure the consistency of management's strategy for developing the brand within the company. The six external factors (relevance, authenticity, differentiation, consistency, presence, and understanding) reflect how the brand is perceived by current and potential consumers. For each criterion, brand strength is measured relative to other brands in the same industry sector. Once a score for brand strength on a scale of 0 to 100 is obtained, a discount rate is calculated. Interbrand does not disclose the detail of the calculation, but simply explains that an algorithm that is proprietary to Interbrand is used.

Table 10.3 shows the Interbrand ranking of the ten highest-value brands in 2014 and their rankings and annual valuations from 2005 to 2014.

Table 10.2 Factors impacting the Interbrand discount rate

Internal Factors	*External Factors*
1. Clarity of brand in internal communication (values, target market, and positioning are known throughout the organisation).	1. Relevance of brand to consumer expectations, needs, and desires.
2. Commitment of management to develop and defend the brand.	2. Brand authenticity, i.e., the ability to meet (high) consumer requirements.
3. Responsiveness of brand to change and its ability to evolve and renew itself.	3. Differentiation of brand against other brands, distinctive character.
4. Brand protection (legal, geographical, protection of industrial secrets).	4. Consistency of brand in different formats and contexts.
	5. Presence: ability of the brand to exist positively in traditional and new media.
	6. Understanding: the brand is not only known, but fully understood by the consumer. Consumers can also understand the brand company.

Source: Interbrand Best Global Brand (2011).

Table 10.3 Interbrand ranking of the ten highest-value brands (2005–2014)

Year	*2014*	*2013*	*2012*	*2011*	*2010*	*2009*	*2008*	*2007*	*2006*	*2005*
Apple	118.9	98.3	76.6	33.5	19.5	15.4	13.7	11.0	9.1	8.0
Rank	*1*	*1*	*2*	*8*	*17*	*20*	*24*	*33*	*39*	*41*
Google	107.4	93.3	69.7	55.3	43.6	32.0	25.6	17.8	12.4	8.5
Rank	*2*	*2*	*4*	*4*	*4*	*7*	*10*	*20*	*24*	*38*
Coca-Cola	81.6	79.2	77.8	71.9	70.5	68.7	66.7	65.3	67.0	67.5
Rank	*3*	*3*	*1*	*1*	*1*	*1*	*1*	*1*	*1*	*1*

(*Continued*)

Table 10.3 Continued

Year	*2014*	*2013*	*2012*	*2011*	*2010*	*2009*	*2008*	*2007*	*2006*	*2005*
IBM	72.2	78.8	75.5	69.9	64.7	60.2	59.0	57.1	56.2	53.4
Rank	*4*	*4*	*3*	*2*	*2*	*2*	*2*	*3*	*3*	*3*
Microsoft	61.2	59.5	57.9	59.1	60.9	56.6	59.0	58.7	56.9	59.9
Rank	*5*	*5*	*5*	*3*	*3*	*3*	*3*	*2*	*2*	*2*
GE	45.5	46.9	43.7	42.8	42.8	47.8	53.1	51.6	48.9	47.0
Rank	*6*	*6*	*6*	*5*	*5*	*4*	*4*	*4*	*4*	*4*
Samsung	45.5	39.6	32.9	23.4	19.5	17.5	17.7	16.9	16.2	15.0
Rank	*7*	*8*	*9*	*17*	*19*	*19*	*21*	*21*	*20*	*20*
Toyota	42.4	35.3	30.3	27.8	26.2	31.3	34.1	32.1	27.9	24.8
Rank	*8*	*10*	*10*	*11*	*11*	*8*	*6*	*6*	*7*	*9*
McDonald's	42.3	41.9	40.1	35.6	33.6	32.3	31.0	29.2	27.5	26.0
Rank	*9*	*7*	*7*	*6*	*6*	*6*	*8*	*8*	*9*	*8*
Mercedes-Benz	34.3	31.9	30.3	27.4	25.2	23.9	25.6	23.6	21.8	20.0
Rank	*10*	*11*	*11*	*12*	*12*	*12*	*11*	*10*	*10*	*11*

Source: Interbrand, in $ billions.

In 2014, five information technology companies (Apple, Google, IBM, Microsoft, and Samsung) appeared in the top 10. In 2005, however, only three of these companies were ranked in the top ten (IBM, Microsoft, and Intel), whereas Nokia, another IT company ranked number six in 2005, disappeared from the 2014 top ten (it was ranked number 98 in 2014). These changes illustrate the growing importance and volatility of the information technology sector in today's world economy. The value of some IT brands evaporates in a relatively short period of time, whereas other brand values skyrocket.

Four groups stand out during the period 2005–2014:

1. Brands showing very high growth: Apple, whose value was multiplied by 14.9 in nine years; Google, whose value was multiplied by 12.7; and Samsung, whose value was multiplied by 3 over the same period.
2. Brands with significant growth: Toyota, McDonald's, Mercedes-Benz, and IBM.
3. Brands showing relative stability: Microsoft and Coca-Cola, whose secret recipe and international renown makes the famous drink invincible (the brand accounted for 44% of Coca-Cola Co.'s market capitalisation at the 2014 year-end).
4. Brands in relative decline: the GE brand of American conglomerate General Electric.

Figures 10.1 to 10.4 show the movement in the value of one brand in each of these four groups since 2001. The evolution of the brand owners' market capitalisation over the same period is also shown.

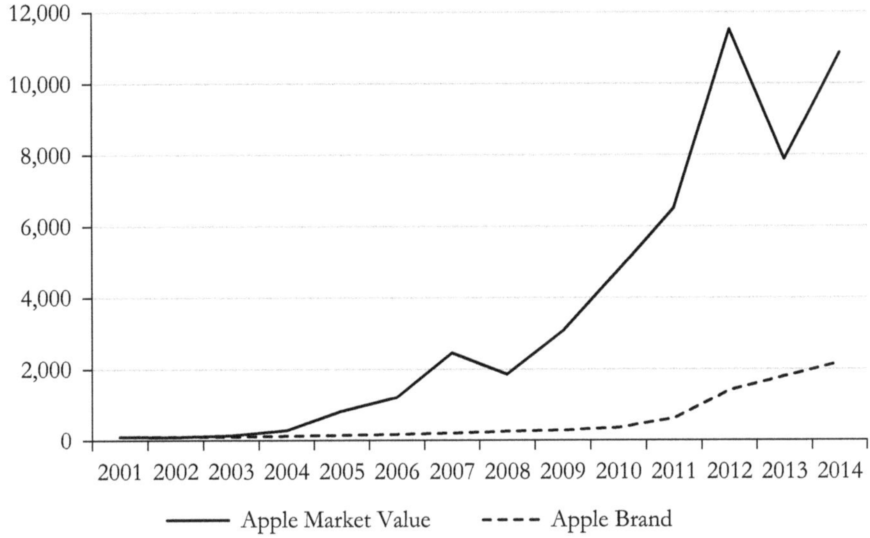

Figure 10.1 Movements in Apple brand value and market capitalisation (Base 100 in 2001).

Sources: Interbrand, Compustat.

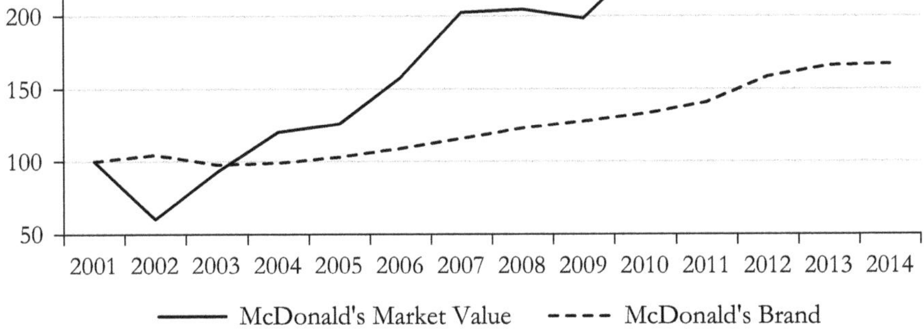

Figure 10.2 Movements in McDonald's brand value and market capitalisation (Base 100 in 2001).

Sources: Interbrand, Compustat.

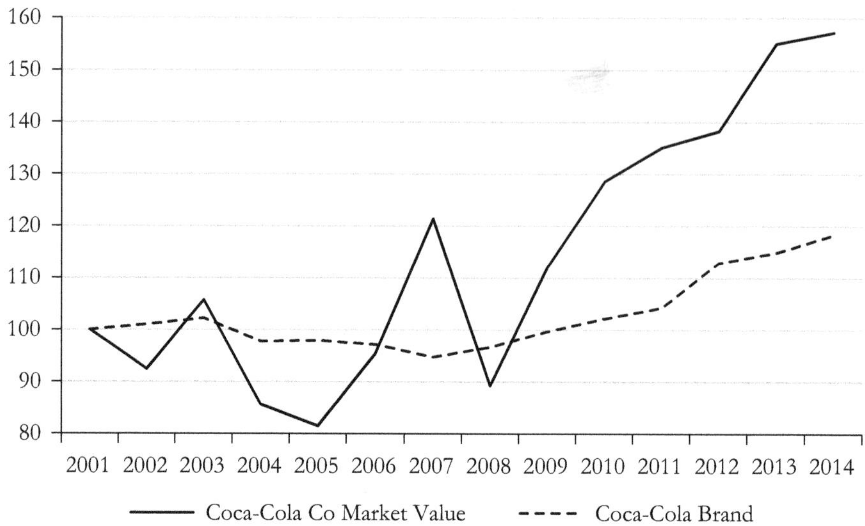

Figure 10.3 Movements in Coca-Cola brand value and market capitalisation (Base 100 in 2001).

Sources: Interbrand, Compustat.

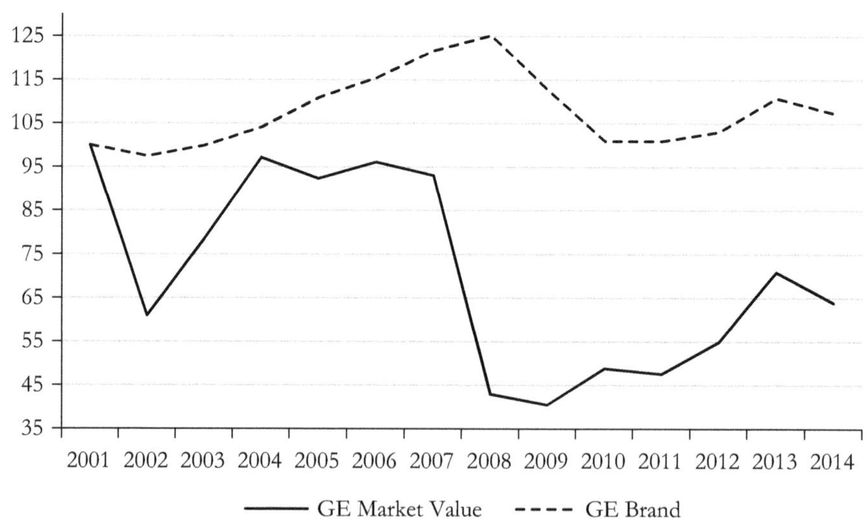

Figure 10.4 Movements in GE's brand value and market capitalisation (Base 100 in 2001).

Sources: Interbrand, Compustat.

According to Interbrand, the value of the Apple brand grew strongly over the period and increased from $5.5 billion in 2001 to $118.9 billion in 2014 (the value of the brand was multiplied by 21.7). This growth seems relatively low, however, compared to the growth of the company's market capitalisation, which increased from $5.4 billion in 2001 (similar to the value of the brand) to more than $590 billion at the 2014 year-end. The market capitalisation was multiplied by 108 in 13 years. According to Interbrand, the Apple brand is, therefore, not the main source of Apple's wealth creation. It is true that the company was a world leader during the period with its disruptive technological innovations (personal stereo: iPod; legal downloading: iTunes; smartphones: iPhone; tablets: iPad; and more recently watches: iWatch), all of which generated excess profits.[6]

Interbrand estimates that McDonald's fast food brand value increased by almost 67% in 13 years, whilst its market value increased by 166% (with a fall in the last three years).

The Coca-Cola brand grew by 18% over the 13-year period, whilst the company's market capitalisation increased by 57%, but fluctuated significantly. The Interbrand valuation method results in the value of the Coca-Cola brand being fairly stable as a result of the medium/long-term *business asset* approach used. The brand value represented 59% of Coca-Cola Co.'s capital employed in 2001 and only 44% in 2011.

The brand value of the American group GE, diversified in technologies, media, and financial services and employing more than 300,000 people worldwide, has increased by 7% since 2001. Managing a brand across several sectors is more complex than a brand present in a single sector, such as drinks or electronics, as not only does General Electric sell consumer products (especially household appliances), it also produces television programmes (NBC Universal). According to Interbrand, the group's strategy has not been successful in increasing the value of the GE brand. In terms of group value, GE was severely affected by the 2001 Internet bubble burst and the 2008 financial crisis, and the group's market capitalisation fell by 36% in 13 years.

1.2. The Interbrand Valuation Model: Discussion

Our discussion suggests that brand valuation under the Interbrand model remains a highly subjective exercise. Reliance is placed on specific assumptions and forecasts made by the consultancy firm when estimating the parameters needed to calculate brand earnings, i.e., the proportion of excess earnings attributable to the brand in the second step and then measuring brand strength in the third step. It is possible that these estimations may be very different from those that would be made by a market player in the context of a transaction. The extent of such differences is generally highlighted by resorting to a second valuation method.

The valuation model devised by Interbrand does, however, mean that non-financial parameters are systematically taken into account in a valuation. Analysis of factors that affect brand strength in various geographical areas, medias, or product formats enables comparisons to be made and enhances management's understanding and eventually control of value creation. The Interbrand model has been approved by the international standards agency ISO and was awarded the ISO 10668 certification in December 2010 (ISO, 2010). ISO considers that the Interbrand valuation model takes account not only of financial and market parameters but also of the legal and behavioural characteristics of a brand and thus meets the requirements of this standard (see Chapter 9).

When implementing the classical excess earnings method, the main factors determining brand strength as calculated by Interbrand, and which it uses to arrive at a discount rate, are taken into account in the estimation of the profile and duration of future cash flows. A rigorous and discerning application of the excess earnings method does not ignore these criteria, but incorporates them with more flexibility into the cash flows. The valuer can think critically about which factors are most likely to affect the brand's durability and its level of risk given its distinctive characteristics. The Interbrand model, therefore, makes valuation more mechanical by including all the non-financial criteria in the discount rate rather than by considering their impact on future cash flows.

1.3. The BrandEconomics Model (Stern Stewart & Co.): Principles and Discussion

The Interbrand valuation model is not the only model based on excess earnings. The consultancy firm Stern Stewart & Co. has developed a model called "BrandEconomics", which uses a simple econometric approach to measure the portion of excess profits that is attributable to a brand (step 2 of the Interbrand method). Like Interbrand, the Stern Stewart & Co. model comprises three steps:

1. Determination of the excess profits earned by the brand-owning company using the *economic value added* (EVA) model developed and registered by Stern Stewart, the idea of which is to measure economic profit (creation of value after remuneration of resources, including capital employed).
2. Determination of the role played by the brand in its market sector using linear regression between EVA and "brand health" (measured by the *Brand Asset Valuator* (BAV) of the Young & Rubicam advertising agency) for companies operating in the same sector as the brand being valued. The parameters a and b of the following regression are estimated:

   $$EVA = a + b \times BAV + \varepsilon.$$

BAV is measured by Young & Rubicam using a scale incorporating four parameters:

- differentiation;
- relevance;
- esteem; and
- knowledge.

These parameters are measured by consumer surveys. The regression coefficient *b* between the EVA and BAV represents, therefore, the average relationship for the sector (assumed to be linear) between the health of a brand and its contribution to the EVA of the brand-owning company.

3. Finally, the excess earnings of the brand being valued are calculated as a product of the average coefficient *b* for the sector and the brand's specific BAV score. The value of the brand is then simply equivalent to the present value of future excess profits deriving from the brand.

Stern Stewart attempts to rationalise its method of estimating the portion of excess earnings that is attributable to the brand by carrying out a statistical estimation of the link between brand performance (BAV) and excess earnings. This approach is meant to be objective, but it is underpinned by several questionable assumptions: (1) the portion of excess profits attributable to a brand is the same for all companies in a given sector (use of the average coefficient *b*); (2) the relationship between excess profits and brand performance is linear and constant in time; and (3) the linear model is simple; in other words, excess earnings depend solely on brand performance.

Assumptions (1), (2), and (3) are probably erroneous, because excess earnings also depend on other factors. In addition, the relationship between excess earnings and brand performance is certainly specific to each company and is not necessarily linear or constant over time.

2. *Ad Hoc* Valuation Models Based on Royalties

Valuation firms that use royalty-based models generally do so for several reasons: (1) the approach is accepted by legal and fiscal authorities because it relies on actual transactions between third parties (assumptions are less subjective), (2) information concerning licence agreements is readily available (so a valuation can be more easily checked), and (3) the approach is consistent with the notion of fair value as defined by accounting standards and the IVSC.

Certain firms, including BrandFinance, Intangible Business, Consor, or Brandient have developed their own valuation models based on the relief-from-royalty method. The particularity of these models is that they apply an indicator that reflects the "strength" or the "performance" of a brand compared with its competitors to either the royalty rate or the discount rate, or both. To illustrate this, we present and discuss the model developed by BrandFinance.

The distinguishing feature of the BrandFinance model is that it determines a "brand strength" indicator that influences both the estimated royalty rate and the discount rate. This indicator is derived by means of a comparative study of a brand and competing brands that focuses on certain aspects (in particular, market share, reputation, international presence, and profitability). Brand strength is used to estimate the royalty rate from within a range of rates observed in licensing agreements of competing brands.

Table 10.4 shows the different ratings used by BrandFinance to describe brand strength. As we can see, the logic is similar to that used by credit rating agencies.[7]

The highest royalty rates will therefore be those of brands rated AAA, whilst rates for those rated DDD-D will be close to zero. This step is of paramount importance, because under the relief-from-royalty method, brand value is extremely sensitive to the royalty rate used. A variation of a few basis points can result in large differences in brand value (see Chapter 6).

Brand strength also affects the beta coefficient used to obtain the discount rate (see Appendix 1) by means of an undisclosed calculation. This feature of the model reflects the assumption that brand strength is an indicator of a brand's durability and of the risk associated with the expected future royalty flows.[8]

Table 10.5 shows BrandFinance's ranking of the 25 most valuable global brands in 2014, together with the difference in value for those brands also covered in the Interbrand ranking for the same year.

Table 10.4 Definition of BrandFinance ratings

Rating	*Meaning*
AAA	Extremely strong
AA	Very strong
A	Strong
BBB-B	Average
CCC-C	Weak
DDD-D	Failing

Table 10.5 BrandFinance (2014) ranking and comparison with Interbrand ($ billion)

Ranking 2014	*Brand*	*Industry Group*	*Brand Value*	*Sept. 2014 Brand Rating*	*Interbrand–BrandFinance*
1	Apple	Technology	104.7	AAA	14.2
2	Samsung	Conglomerate	78.8	AAA	–33.3
3	Google	Technology	68.6	AAA+	38.8
4	Microsoft	Technology	62.8	AAA	–1.6

Ranking 2014	*Brand*	*Industry Group*	*Brand Value*	*Sept. 2014 Brand Rating*	*Interbrand– BrandFinance*
5	Verizon	Telecoms	53.5	AAA–	–
6	GE	Technology	52.5	AA+	–7.1
7	AT&T	Telecoms	45.4	AA	–
8	Amazon.com	Technology	45.1	AAA–	–15.7
9	Walmart	Retail	44.8	AA+	–
10	IBM	IT Services	41.5	AA+	30.7
11	Toyota	Automobiles	34.9	AAA–	7.5
12	Coca-Cola	Beverages	33.7	AAA+	47.8
13	China Mobile	Telecoms	31.8	AA+	–
14	T (Telekom)	Telecoms	30.6	AA	–
15	Wells Fargo	Banks	30.2	AAA–	–
16	Vodafone	Telecoms	29.6	AAA–	–
17	BMW	Automobiles	29.0	AAA	5.3
18	Shell	Oil & Gas	28.6	AA+	–22.3
19	Volkswagen	Automobiles	27.1	AAA–	–13.3
20	HSBC	Banks	26.9	AAA	–13.7
21	Bank of America	Banks	26.7	AA+	–
22	Mitsubishi	Conglomerate	26.1	AA	–
23	McDonald's	Restaurants	26.0	AAA–	16.2
24	Citi	Banks	24.5	AA+	–15.8
25	The Home Depot	Retail	24.3	AA–	–

Sources: BrandFinance Global 500—Best Global Brands and Interbrand 100 Best Global Brands—2014.

Table 10.5 shows that the BrandFinance ranking is totally different from that of Interbrand, both in terms of brand ranking and estimated values. These differences are the result of divergences in forecasting and methodology, and they highlight the fact that these models are fragile due to the considerable uncertainty surrounding brand values.

Both firms also approach valuation from different perspectives. The definition given by BrandFinance is close to fair value, whereas Interbrand considers a brand as a *business asset* affected by management expectations. It is difficult to explain the reasons behind these disparities, as both models derive largely from a "black-box" approach.

Given the information available, comparing the two rankings is purely illustrative. We observe seven brands to which Interbrand assigns a higher value than BrandFinance and eight brands to which Interbrand assigns a lower value than BrandFinance. For instance, Interbrand's estimated value of the Coca-Cola brand is almost $48 billion higher than that of BrandFinance. This can be the consequence of differences in methodology: excess earnings model versus relief-from-royalty model, as the latter typically undervalues brands (see Chapter 6).

The brands covered by the two firms are also different. BrandFinance is a firm that generally has more business and clients in Europe than Interbrand. The Tesco brand, for example, is not covered by Interbrand, no doubt because it is better known in Europe and in the United Kingdom in particular. This is also the case for Airbus and ALDI.

3. Other *Ad Hoc* Valuation Models

Other firms have developed their own valuation models. Most of them do not explain their methodology precisely and settle for giving certain indications as to the approach used and the main parameters taken into account. Information that is available on these models shows that:

- Almost all these models are based on the main valuation methods discussed in Chapters 4 to 6: revenue premium, excess earnings, or relief-from-royalty.
- These models in general use a composite indicator to reflect a brand's non-financial characteristics (e.g., market share, brand image, growth potential, international profile). This indicator is calculated from a scorecard covering a set of qualitative criteria for a brand. It is usually incorporated in the valuation model as a multiple or as a determinant of the discount rate applied to brand cash flows.

The *Brand Equity Evaluation System* (BEES) model of the firm BBDO, which is based on the use of a multiple, is a good illustration of this type of *ad hoc* model. The model identifies eight factors of brand value, of which four are financial and four non-financial.

The scores given to a brand for each of the criterion are weighted to obtain a multiple which is then applied to the brand's pre-tax profit to estimate its value.

The aim of these models is to ensure that non-financial characteristics of a brand are systematically taken into account in a standardised manner, which technically meets the requirements of ISO 10668. However,

Table 10.6 Criteria included in the Brand Equity Evaluation System to determine the pre-tax profit multiple

Financial Criteria	*Non-financial Criteria*
1. Brand revenues	5. Perspectives of brand development
2. Net operating margin	6. International orientation
3. Pre-tax earnings	7. Brand strength in sector
4. Advertising expenditure	8. Brand image

Source: BBDO (2001) Brand Equity Excellence.

standardisation makes it more difficult to recognise the specific features of each brand and assumes that the relative importance of each factor is the same for all brands, whatever their age, market, sector, etc.

In conclusion, these *ad hoc* models suffer from the arbitrary and undisclosed way in which the score sheet that supposedly reflects brand strength is designed, because awarding a brand a score for each of the relevant criterion remains a highly subjective exercise.

Conclusion

In this chapter, we have presented and discussed the major *ad hoc* valuation models for brands. First, we reviewed one of the oldest and best-known models that was developed by the firm Interbrand and which is derived from the excess earnings method. Second, we discussed the brand valuation model of the firm Stern Stewart based on the EVA excess earnings indicator it made popular in the 1990s and 2000s. Third, we briefly presented other models, such as those of BrandFinance or BBDO, which rely on other approaches, such as royalties or multiples.

Whereas these models may appear at first glance to ensure a degree of uniformity in valuation across companies because they are based on internally developed methodologies and are applied consistently, they must be viewed with caution. Standardisation may lead to over-simplification, and in the absence of details on underlying assumptions and algorithms, they remain to some extent black boxes. We have argued throughout the book on the need for triangulation, i.e., using multiple techniques to determine value.

The next chapter discusses the causes of brand value volatility and puts forward ideas to improve existing financial valuation models.

Notes

1. Grand Metropolitan, Annual Report 1988.
2. We thank Professor Stephen Zeff of Rice University for these two examples.
3. Salinas (2009) and Salinas and Ambler (2009) provide a more complete overview of these models.
4. See Chapter 4 for calculation of terminal values.
5. The number of factors analysed by Interbrand varies from year to year. In 2000, there were only seven factors.
6. These products also have their own brands.
7. The objective of credit rating agencies is to assess the risk of default by governments or companies (and also bonds issued by governments and companies). Investors are informed of this risk by means of "ratings" ranging from AAA for virtually non-existent risk of default to D for an insolvent company. There are three main credit rating agencies: Standard & Poor's, Moody's, and Fitch Ratings.
8. BrandFinance explains that size, geographical coverage, and brand reputation affect a brand's discount rate and therefore implicitly systematic risk.

References

BBDO (2001), *Brand Equity Excellence* BBDO Group, Germany, November.

BrandFinance (2011), *BrandFinance Global 500—The Annual Report on the World's Most Valuable Brands*, March, Brand Finance Plc, London.

BrandFinance (2014), *BrandFinance Global 500—The Annual Report on the World's Most Valuable Brands*, February, Brand Finance Plc, London.

FASB (2001) *Statement of Financial Accounting Concepts No. 141: Business Combinations*, Financial Accounting Standards Board, Norwalk, CT.

FASB (2007) *Statement of Financial Accounting Concepts No. 141R: Business Combinations—Revised*, Financial Accounting Standards Board, Norwalk, CT.

IASB (2004), *International Reporting Financial Standards (IFRS) No. 3: Business Combinations,* IASC Foundation Publications Department, London.

IASB (2008), *International Reporting Financial Standards (IFRS) No. 3: Business Combinations—Revised,* IASC Foundation Publications Department, London.

Interbrand (2011), *Best Global Brand 2011,* Interbrand, London.

Interbrand (2014), *Best Global Brand 2014—The Definitive Guide to the 100 Best Global Brands*, Interbrand, London.

International Organization for Standardization (ISO) (2010), *International Organization Standard No. 10668—Brand Valuation—Requirements for Monetary Brand Valuation*, The International Organization for Standardization, Geneva, Switzerland.

Salinas G. (2009), *The International Brand Valuation Manual: A Complete Overview and Analysis of Brand Valuation Techniques, Methodologies and Applications*, Wiley, Chichester.

Salinas G. and Ambler T. (2009), "A Taxonomy of Brand Valuation Practice: Methodologies and Purposes" *Journal of Brand Management* Vol. 17, pp. 39–61.

11 Volatility of Brand Values

By now the reader will have obtained many answers to the questions raised by brand valuation. However, one question has been implicit so far throughout this book: how can we understand the volatility of brand values? To be more precise, is this volatility the result of valuation methods that lack rigour or are insufficiently sophisticated, or is it due to an inherent uncertainty associated with brands and intangible assets in general?

We should remember that brands as described in Chapter 1 are assets possessing attributes that set them apart from most other economic assets. They are idiosyncratic (specific) assets without an organised market to indicate their price. Brands are embedded in the network economy and have strong potential to interact with other tangible and intangible assets. When combined with the other assets of a company, they produce value that is greater than the sum of the parts and, therefore, provide substantial economic leverage for their owners. As we have seen, the risk profile of brands is also complex to assess because their life cycle is neither linear nor stable. The economic trajectory of a brand is marked by several phases: they are launched, they accelerate, they may suffer accidents, and sometimes they reach orbit.

In parallel, the financial techniques used to value brands, the rationale of which was described in Chapter 2, rely basically on estimations of future cash flows and the risk associated with them. These techniques derive directly from the paradigm used to value financial assets (shares, bonds, options, swaps, and other derivatives) in the asset portfolio theory developed by Markowitz, Sharpe, and Lintner (Markowitz, 1991).

Brands are unique not only because they are not financial assets but also because they combine many specificities which introduce a high level of uncertainty into their valuation. The financial valuation techniques used are admittedly able to deal with these difficulties. However, there are so many uncertainties involved when valuing brands, and these uncertainties have such a potential impact on brand value, that the various models inevitably lead to a range of values for a given brand.

These ranges of values are extremely sensitive to changes in the key underlying assumptions. Brands are therefore assets with volatile values.

This is not due to the financial techniques employed, but rather to the intrinsic characteristics of brands.

Brands share this economic attribute with most other intangible assets. Uncertainty as to value exists also for human capital, organisational capital, and relational capital.

This chapter is split into three sections. The first discusses the causes of brand value volatility, and the second and third put forward ideas to improve existing financial valuation models.

1. Why Are Brand Values Volatile?

Brands are particularly volatile economic assets. As we have seen, they are born, grow, and sometimes die. A brand that is all the rage one day can disappear a few months later. This economic instability inevitably leads to valuations that are volatile. If a brand value is volatile, this is due to the brand itself and not to the valuation models.

To understand this volatility, we must return to the principles of valuation: the market value of an asset is a well-defined notion. It is the price at which an asset could be exchanged between willing and well-informed parties on an arm's length basis. To value a brand, we rely on this definition, and the models discussed in this book value a brand as if it were a standard financial asset being exchanged like any other asset.

It should also be noted that the theoretical principles from which most valuation models derive are underpinned by a number of restrictive assumptions about financial assets:

- Financial assets are perfectly divisible. They are fungible; an investor can purchase any financial asset he wishes to. A single company share is readily available, because there exist thousands (or millions) of identical shares.
- Information about assets in the marketplace is complete, free, and accessible to all. The equilibrium market price consequently reflects this information (informational efficiency is relatively high).
- Financial assets are liquid. To use the definition by Keynes (1936), they can be "disposed of in the short term, with more or less certainty". Once his decision is taken, a financial investor can very easily buy or sell a financial asset without major uncertainty as to its price.

In practice, as we saw in Chapter 1, brands are not financial assets and thus have other characteristics: indivisibility, absence of conflict in their utilisation (non-rivalry), network effects, absence of an organised market, different risk profile, and synergies with other tangible and intangible assets.

These factors have an important effect on the level of cash flows attributable to brands and their inherent risk, and they explain why brand values are often more volatile than the values of traditional financial assets (such as shares or bonds). The following paragraphs present some of the features of brands that generate volatile values.

1.1. An Asset About Which Little Information Is Available

Regardless of what financial theories say, the most obvious characteristic of brands is that, for the reasons explained in Chapter 1, they are not exchanged on organised markets. In addition, companies do not possess internal financial information systems for intangible assets. Consequently, neither the market (external) nor the company's information systems (internal) provide adequate information regarding the past performance of a brand or expectations of its future performance. As a result, we lack information on brands, both on those being valued and on those used as comparables, which are very useful to estimate an appropriate royalty rate, for example.

At the same time, in the absence of financial information, we have at our disposal a large body of disparate data regarding brands, e.g., marketing studies, studies of brand image, sectorial analyses, market research, and competition surveys. The job of the valuer is, therefore, to "translate" this data into financial language. This is precisely the aim of the *ad hoc* models described in Chapter 10. These models, each of which focuses on specific criteria, (e.g., cost of capital, brand rating) provide standardised ways of translating non-financial information.

It is therefore not surprising that we arrive at a relatively wide range of possible values for a brand. In keeping with the golden rule of all models—garbage in, garbage out—if information is lacking, the results given by valuation models, however sophisticated they may be, will inevitably contain relatively large estimation errors.

1.2. Absence of Conflict in the Use of Brands

Economics is the science of rare resource allocation; in other words, it focuses on goods which, if consumed by one individual, cannot be consumed by another (Malinvaud, 2005). Brands, on the contrary, can be used by several individuals at the same time (they are non-rival) and are ubiquitous. They are used every day by companies in many ways. How then should assets whose use is not limited, such as brands, be allocated?

Unsurprisingly this characteristic is problematic for financial models, which have difficulty integrating an asset that can be put to many uses which do not interfere with or contradict one another.

As we have seen, most valuation models rely on a brand's development prospects. However, once a brand can be used in different ways, its future is particularly complex to model. Even worse, its development potential can change significantly depending on the context and the acquirer.

Once again this basic characteristic (ubiquity) of brands lends significant uncertainty to brand values, which vary according to the prospects foreseen by the brand owner or acquirer. Results given by valuation models thus faithfully reflect forecast brand prospects in a given context. The disparity in results is simply the consequence of the differences between different brand prospects in different contexts.

1.3. An Asset Subject to Network Effects

Brand value is affected by network effects, also referred to as "positive demand externalities" in economics. We have seen that this is defined as an increase in the value of an asset caused by knowledge and use of this asset by consumers. For example, the value of brands (and the technologies linked with those brands) developed by Twitter and Facebook have rocketed due to the positive externalities generated by increased use of the services available through these applications. The network effect comes from the way this phenomenon is magnified: success breeds success, and the more users there are, the more new users will be drawn to the network.

Brands benefit from these network effects because their value increases exponentially as their notoriety increases. These network effects are unpredictable and lead to "winner-takes-all" type gains; in other words, the gains are enormous in case of success and virtually or totally non-existent for companies that have developed competing technology brands or distribution network brands. There are few world-renowned brands and many that struggle to survive.

This phenomenon has an important effect on the volatility of brand values and explains the extreme variations in value which can occur at the "tipping points" described in Chapter 1. The value of a brand will remain modest until the brand is so well known (it reaches the "tipping point") that it becomes a must-have brand. The whole valuation model and development prospects change dramatically at this point. Whereas before the brands expected life was quite logically considered to be limited, it now becomes an icon, almost everlasting. Whereas before the brand's growth may have been limited to a number of key markets, it now has the potential to take on markets worldwide.

Once again, the valuer becomes a translator whose job it is to transcribe economic reality into a financial model. The volatility of values obtained from these models purely reflects the uncertainties as to the potentially explosive impact of these network effects. We are faced here with extreme events that economics and finance have difficulty conceptualising.[1]

In response to these limitations and difficulties, academics and practitioners have proposed new ways of measuring brand value. These proposals are explained and discussed in the following two sections.

2. Brands Seen as Financial Options

Brands are not the only assets with volatile values. Financial options in particular have a number of similar characteristics. Brand value volatility can be understood with the help of option valuation theory (see framed text).

Financial Options, a Special Type of Asset

An option is a contract that confers the right, but not the obligation, to buy or sell an asset on or before a specified date, at a fixed price (the exercise price), against the payment of a premium. A contract that gives the right to buy an asset is called an option to buy or *call*, and one that gives the right to sell an asset is called an option to sell or *put*.

If the right (to buy or to sell) can only be exercised on a given date, the option is referred to as European-style. If the option can be exercised at any time until the expiry date, it is referred to as American-style.[2] More exotic options with more complex characteristics also exist.

The asset on which the option is based is referred to as the "underlying asset".

It is important to distinguish the premium paid initially to purchase the option from the price paid at the expiry date to buy or sell the underlying asset (the exercise price).

The basic feature of all options is the asymmetry between the potential profit (unlimited) they offer for the owner of the option and the risk of loss (usually limited to the premium paid to purchase the option).

The possible outcome for the owner of an option is, therefore, completely asymmetrical: at worst he or she will lose his or her initial investment (the premium paid to purchase the option), at best he or she will earn a lot of money. An option owner will therefore have a large appetite for risk: the more risky the underlying asset, the higher the potential gain. It does not matter to him or her that this gain is improbable or that the market price of the underlying asset may collapse (for the owner of a call). He or she is protected from a fall in the value of the underlying asset; only the magnitude of his or her potential profit matters.

Option theory enables this asymmetrical gain potential, the essential characteristic of options, to be valued. In many cases, the option may be worth nothing; in some cases, it may be worth a great deal. If we thus look at the volatility of the option value (and for once not at that of the underlying asset), we see that it is very high, much greater than the volatility of the underlying asset itself.

Options are an example of assets that are particularly difficult to value using the standard approach of discounting risk-adjusted cash flows. First, risk is not constant over time and depends on the relationship between the underlying asset value and the exercise price. Second, options present considerable financial leverage and thus have a high-risk adjusted cost of capital, which varies over time.

Many events and situations feature gain asymmetry in the corporate world. For example, a company may hit the jackpot if it is the first to enter a new market. However, it can also invest a limited amount, take time to review the results, and invest more heavily later on if it considers it worthwhile. This is the typical behaviour of an option owner.

Myers (1977) proposes the use of option theory to value certain real assets, in particular those with high growth potential such as brands or research and development. He develops an analogy between investment projects and financial options. "Real options theory" applies financial market option valuation techniques to corporate finance issues. Using option valuation methods, real options theory aims to assess and quantify decision-making flexibility in an uncertain environment.

The launch of a brand has financial aspects similar to real options. Initial investment in the creation of a brand provides the opportunity, subsequently, to develop and launch new products under the brand name. Further investment in the brand will enable it to strengthen its position. This flexibility has value to management: the possibility to take advantage of future opportunities.

As Table 11.1 shows, brands can be valued similarly to options. It is necessary at first to determine the different parameters of an option (as shown in Table 11.1) and then to value the option using traditional option valuation models. A distinction is normally made between the continuous probabilistic models of Black, Scholes, and Merton and the discrete-time binomial models of Cox-Ross-Rubinstein.

It has even been suggested that real options theory models should be used to value brands (Damodaran, 1996). Information on certain financial parameters is needed in order to apply option valuation models including the risk-free rate, implicit volatility of the underlying asset, option exercise price, financial value of the underlying asset, and option expiry date. A real option valuation is therefore quite difficult to carry out, because these parameters are fairly uncertain.

Nevertheless, real options theory does explain the volatility of brand value when uncertainty is high. This is because the value of an option (financial or real) increases as the uncertainty (volatility) of the underlying asset (or project) increases. The riskier the development prospects for new branded products, the greater the value of the real option (brand). In this respect, the analogy with real options is more useful as a heuristic tool to understand brand value volatility than as a brand valuation technique.[3]

Table 11.1 Similarity between options and brands

Option	*Brand*
Option to purchase a share (call)	**Option to enter a new market**
Share price (underlying asset)	Net present value of future cash flows (if the project succeeds)
Exercise price	Investment cost
Expiry date	Time before opportunity disappears
Share price volatility	Uncertainty of future cash flows
Risk-free interest rate	Risk-free interest rate

3. Brands Seen as an Intertwined Asset[4]

3.1. The Role of a Brand in a Group of Assets

An economic model based on the creation, deployment, and upkeep of a strong brand creates strong synergies between the various assets of a company. The value of a distribution network is therefore considerably enhanced if it can rely on a strong brand, which in turn increases the brand's value (this is a positive "externality"). Similarly, if a company's workforce adheres to the image and values promoted by the brand, the value of its human capital will necessarily rise. For when one works for a company with a strong brand, one can recognise oneself in the image of expertise, likeability, or other positive connotations of the brand. Prestigious academic institutions such as Harvard or Yale have strong images that make the skills and intrinsic expertise of their students more attractive in the job market. Conversely, students from unknown institutions will have to promote more actively their own skills in the job market. A brand is also an effective tool to advertise an economic project to employees and ensure they share ownership of that project. A brand can encourage commitment and motivation, and it enhance the value of a company's workforce, and this in turn increases the brand's value in a positive feedback loop. This is also the case for brands connected with prestigious institutions: their alumni benefit from the name of their institution, feel committed to the brand name and the image of excellence it conveys, and strive to contribute to this excellence through the quality of their work. This further reinforces the strength of the brand.

Synergies operate between brand and human capital when they are positive (when the brand conveys positive values which enhance workforce value), but also when they are negative (when the brand conveys negative elements which reduce workforce value). The image presented by the BP brand owned by the group of the same name after the environmental disaster in the Gulf of Mexico in 2010 certainly decreased the value of its workforce, which had been painstakingly built up over a long period by the group. In France, Orange (called France Telecom prior to 2013) experienced a wave of employee suicides from 2010 to 2012 after the launch of its NeXT strategic plan, which had negative effects on its workforce and brand.

These effects also explain why brand values are volatile. Far from being an asset isolated from other company resources, brands are closely linked to all the other assets and are therefore directly affected by what may impact any one of them. However, unlike many other assets, the effects of such events on brand value are magnified for the reasons explained earlier.

The synergies that exist between various assets make it difficult to isolate brand value from the intricate layers of resources deployed by a company. It is often impossible to disconnect a brand from other assets to estimate its value. The appropriate type of approach for this type of asset seems to be more a combinatory approach (assets are valued as a whole) than a traditional additive approach (each asset is valued separately). The validity of these approaches is shown in Table 11.2.

Transaction cost theory (Coase, 1937) explains why a company is sometimes more efficient than the market in achieving an economic objective. According to the resource-based view (Hamel and Prahalad, 1990), a company represents a collection of resources or "core competencies", and this collection enables sustainable wealth creation. These two theories suggest that intangible assets, and brands in particular, have a combinatory nature. According to the resource-based view, a brand is a particular resource that generates synergies with other assets and, according to transaction cost theory, a brand can only be combined with other resources within a company.

The rule of representation (Ijiri, 1975) explains the process of measurement, i.e., the numerical representation of the dimensions of an object, such as the value of a company. This rule highlights that it is essential in the measurement process to conserve the structure of the "principal" or, in other words, the object represented numerically. Consistent measurement should maintain the combinatory aspect of brands when their values are represented numerically. The standard valuation model underlying the "sum-of-the-parts" approach assumes that the value of a group of assets is equal to the sum of each individual asset value in the group. It is represented graphically in Figure 11.1.

In Figure 11.1, measuring the value of the company by the function m (.), i.e., the numerical representation of its financial value, leads to the company being represented as the sum of the values of financial assets assessed in isolation from one another. The values of productive assets of the company are added together without taking into account interactions between them. This approach ignores by construction the combinatory value of brands, in other words their value, taking into account the positive and negative synergies with other assets of the company. This is the logic that is applied when brands are valued as simple financial assets.

Table 11.2 Validity of additive and combinatory models

Market	*Organisation*
No synergy expected between resources	Interaction expected between resources
Additive valuation model	Combinatory valuation model
"Sum-of-the-parts" valuation	Combined resources approach
Revalued net assets	Very strong synergy between assets (positive or negative)
Little synergy between assets	

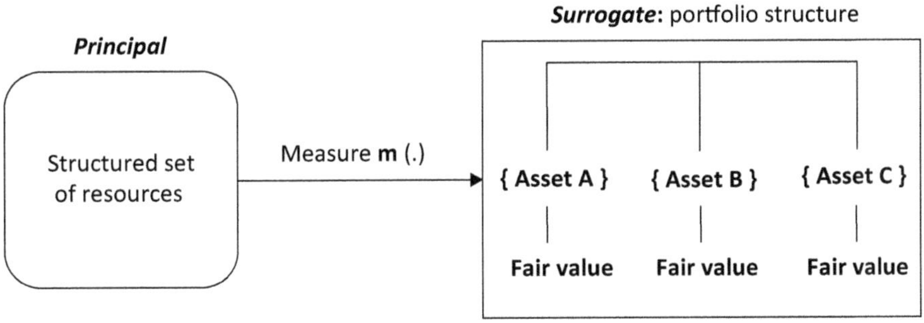

Figure 11.1 Standard valuation model and representation rule.

Many academics have objected to this simplistic view of companies. Thus, according to Miller (1973), "[n]o valuation of a business can be obtained by any summation of individual values of its separate but unfree parts" (p. 283). This is impossible because the approach does not recognise the company as a system: "[a] system is an operating structure comprising interrelated elements of events, objects, and attributes regulated to attain activity goals" (Miller, p. 281). The sum of the values of a system's elements is by definition the result of an aggregation process that implicitly makes no attempt to recognise the complexity of the relations between the various elements of the system. Miller adds:

> [s]ystems may be most complex. Some are almost incomprehensible as aggregates of elements because interactions of the parts result in synergy which manifests itself in the unique behavior of whole systems unpredicted by any behaviors of their component functions taken separately.[5] (p. 281)

3.2. *Thoughts on a Consistent Brand Valuation That Reflects the Combinatory Nature of Intangible Assets*

To assume that a company's assets are completely interchangeable and that they have no interaction with one another (in short that they are all financial assets) is rather unrealistic. Combining effectively a company's resources (e.g., brands, distribution channels, production capacity, competencies, and workforce) is at the heart of management skills and strategy in general. It is precisely because a company is more than a sum of assets, of adjacent resources, that its value is greater than the sum of its parts valued separately.

Within an organised set of resources, the value of one of the elements of the set can vary according to its place within the structure or, in other words, within the network of interactions between resources. A company should then be seen as a structured set of resources in which the interactions between the various resources can be a source of wealth creation (Casta and Bry, 1998; Casta and Ramond, 2005). It is therefore necessary to be able to model in general a situation in such a way that the value of the whole is greater than the sum of the values of the constituent parts.

With this in mind, it is necessary to develop a methodology that models the possible interactions between all of a company's resources and recognises the relative importance of each by attributing weights to each subset of resources. Let us consider a company which has a set of resources X consisting of three assets A, B, and C. The principal (the object to be valued) and the interactions between the resources can be represented as a lattice[6] defined as the set P(S) of the parts of the set S (see Figure 11.2).

This lattice shows the most general form of structure. It depicts all the possible relationships between the three assets (considered individually, two by two, and all together). At each node, the intensity of the interaction between assets is given by the function μ (positive, neutral, or negative). In order to satisfy the constraints of modelling synergy between the resources and quantifying their relationship, the function must possess specific properties that model one of (1) neutrality (as in the additive model), (2) value-creating synergies, or (3) value-destroying inhibition. Recognising the depth of the organisation opens the possibility of analysing the impact of structure on value.[7]

Non-additive models are still in their development stage today, but they can explore a valuation logic that is consistent with the specific nature of intangible assets. Brands are difficult to separate from a company's other assets: know-how, technologies, and products. In any event, they are not financial assets, which are perfectly divisible or exchangeable. Traditional valuation models, unfortunately, do not yet recognise this property.

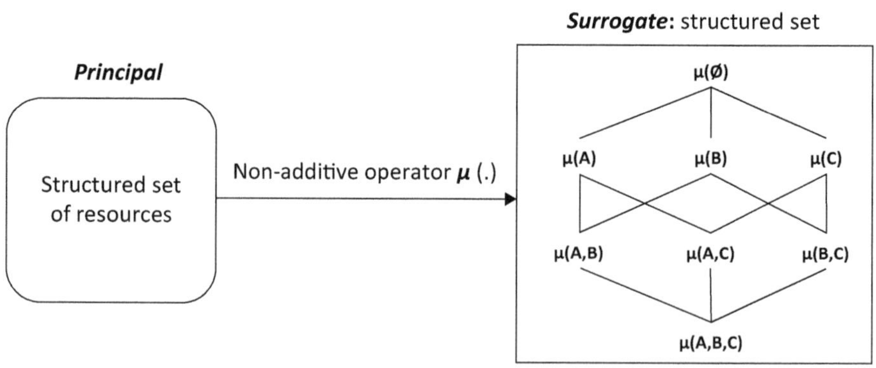

Figure 11.2 Valuation reflecting the combinatory nature of intangible assets.

Conclusion

In this chapter, we first discussed the causes of brand value volatility, namely the little information existing about brands, the absence of conflict in the use of brands, and the network effects to which brands are subject. We then put forward ideas to improve existing financial valuation models: financial options models and intertwined asset models. The next chapter offers our concluding remarks of the book.

Critique of the Weighted Average Return on Assets (WARA) Analysis

As we have seen in the preceding chapters, valuation methods treat brands as ordinary financial assets that can easily be separated from the rest of the company.

As an illustration, when applying the excess earnings method (see Chapter 4), the valuer sometimes assesses each category of a company's assets (e.g., goodwill, brands, tangible assets, working capital) in isolation. He then seeks to identify the risk and liquidity profile of each of these asset categories. In this way, he can determine the return required for each category.

In this context, the valuer generally works from the premise that the higher an asset's risk and the lower its liquidity, the higher the required rate of return will be. The required return on the main types of asset is thus often ranked as follows:

- Working capital and tangible assets are thought to be less risky than the company as a whole, to the extent that they can be sold in the relatively short term, with tangible assets being less liquid and thus considered riskier than working capital.
- Goodwill, a non-transferable asset which has no value outside the collection of assets held by a company, is thought to be riskier than the company as a whole.
- Intangible assets are usually ranked between goodwill and tangible assets.

In certain accounting exercises this type of analysis is formalised in the weighted average return on assets (WARA) model, which assigns a specific rate of return to each asset class and then tests the consistency between the company's cost of capital (WACC) and the weighted average of the specific rates of return (see Chapter 4).

We can see that this exercise is of limited interest in the case of intangible assets. The notion of specific rates of return has little meaning, because the value of intangible assets derives from their combination with the other assets of the company (see Figure 11.2). Such an analysis implicitly refutes the combinatory value of intangible assets.

Notes

1. For thoughts on how to overcome these difficulties (e.g., economics of extremes, black swans, fractals), see Zajdenweber (2009) and Taleb (2010).
2. These terms obviously bear no relation to the location in which these transactions are carried out or the nationalities of the parties carrying them out.
3. For an analysis of the limitations of real options analysis and its usefulness as a heuristic tool rather than a valuation tool, see Philippe (2004).
4. This section draws on Paugam *et al.* (2015).
5. Miller is quoting Buckminster Fuller (1970).
6. In mathematics, a lattice is a partially ordered set in which every two elements have at a least upper bound and a greatest lower bound.
7. For further thoughts on the application of a non-additive valuation model, see Paugam *et al.* (2015).

References

Casta J-F. and Bry X. (1998), "Synergy, Financial Assessment and Fuzzy Integrals", *in Proceedings of IVth Congress of International Association for Fuzzy Sets Management and Economy* (SIGEF), Santiago de Cuba, No. 2, February, pp. 17–42.

Casta J-F. and Ramond O. (2005), "Intangibles Mismeasurement, Synergy and Accounting Numbers: A Note" *Cahier de recherche du CEREG*, Université Paris-Dauphine, Vol. 27 (7).

Coase R.H. (1937), "The Nature of the Firm" *Economica*, Vol. 4 (16), pp. 386–405.

Damodaran A. (1996), *Investment Valuation: Tools and Techniques for Determining the Value of Any Asset*, John Wiley & Son, New York.

Fuller R. Buckminster (1970), *Utopia or Oblivion: The Prospects for Humanity*, Allen Lane, The Penguin Press, London.

Hamel G. and Prahalad C.K. (1990), "The Core Competence of the Corporation" *Harvard Business Review*, May–June, Vol 68 (3) pp. 79–91.

Ijiri Y. (1975), *Theory of Accounting Measurement*, American Accounting Association, Studies in Accounting Research No. 10.

Keynes J.M. (1936), *The General Theory of Employment, Interest and Money*, Macmillan (reprinted 2007), London.

Malinvaud E. (2005), *Leçons de théorie microéconomique*, 4th edition, Dunod, Paris.

Markowitz H. (1991), "Foundations of Portfolio Theory" *The Journal of Finance*, Vol. 46 (2), pp. 469–477.

Miller M.C. (1973), "Goodwill-An Aggregation Issue" *The Accounting Review*, Vol. 73 (2), pp. 280–291.

Myers S.C. (1977), "Determinants of Corporate Borrowing" *Journal of Financial Economics*, Vol. 5 (2), pp. 147–175.

Paugam L. Casta J-F. and Stolowy H. (2015), "Measuring Value Creation from Synergies Between Assets" *Working paper.*

Philippe H. (2004), "Les options réelles—Modèle financier ou modèle de gestion?" PhD Thesis, Université Paris-Dauphine, Paris.

Taleb N.N. (2010), *The Black Swan—The Impact of the Highly Improbable*, 2nd edition, Random House Trade Paperbacks, New York.

Zajdenweber D. (2009), *Économie des extrêmes—krachs, catastrophes et inégalités*, 2nd edition, Flammarion, Paris.

Conclusion

Since the beginning of the 1990s, Western economies have become massively intangible (Nakamura, 2004). This trend is illustrated by the companies that have gone public recently, as their business models rely heavily on intangible assets (Srivastava and Tse, 2015). Today, human capital, technological capital, customer relationships, and organisational capital are key vectors of growth and success.

Managing these assets implies the ability to analyse and measure their value. It is therefore important to grasp the nature of intangible assets, to understand their different facets, and to know what actions to take to increase their chances of success in today's competitive environment. These constraints for managers are made more complicated by the evolution of accounting standards. IFRS and US GAAP have recently moved towards greater recognition of intangible assets.

In the intangible landscape, brands are the best known and most often valued assets. They are seen as being of immediate and fundamental value to a company. Many players have even devised specific valuation methods and publish annual rankings of the most valuable brands. For example, the Coca-Cola brand is valued by Interbrand at almost $82 billion. Standard-setters (IVSC and ISO, for example) have in turn issued recommendations on their preferred valuation methods among the wide choice of possible methodologies.

Numerous questions have arisen from these developments: how should brand value be understood? What should we think of the values arrived at by certain valuers? Are they objective enough? Are existing valuation standards appropriate? How and when should they be applied? More importantly, is today's manager sufficiently well equipped to grasp the economic nature of brands and capitalise on the current economic environment in which they play a leading role?

This book has attempted to provide answers to these questions, to present and explain the relevant tools of brand valuation, and to help the reader understand the intangible economy and the place of brands therein. The main aim of this book was to present, analyse, and demonstrate the advantages and limitations of the financial models currently used to value brands.

Beyond methodological aspects, the objective of this book was to go further in the analysis of brand value. Understanding the intangible economy helps us see the uses and limitations of financial valuation models for managers. The reader will have realised that the volatility of brand values reflects the complex nature and inherent risk of the economic "objects" being valued. It is in no way due to the financial models being irrational, unreliable, or inadequate.

The reader will also note that this book forms wider-reaching conclusions. Brands belong to a specific type of economic resource, that of intangible assets. Most of the financial models described in this book, including their shortcomings, can apply to other types of intangible assets: workforce, technology, organisational capital, or relational capital. These assets possess similar characteristics to brands: complexity, network effects, synergies, and non-linear useful economic lives. By respecting the financial logic developed throughout the book, the reader may value these other intangible assets in a similar manner to valuing brands.

Finally, the reader may have been struck by the fact that an enormous amount of data on brands exists (e.g., market surveys, competitive analysis, awareness surveys), but related financial information is scarce. Oddly enough, it is not the mechanism of the calculations, which are relatively unsophisticated and similar to financial valuation models in general, that makes brand valuation difficult. The difficulty lies in translating the economic reality and development prospects of brands into financial terms. For the valuation of traditional financial assets, organised financial markets usually provide essential information on those assets concerning value, risk, and development outlook. Brands belong to a special type of assets for which no financial markets exist. We are thus deprived of a crucial source of financial information. This lack of information explains the proliferation of *ad hoc* valuation models for brands. The "expertise", "experience", and homespun "know-how" of the proponents of *ad hoc* models are substitutes for hard financial information normally provided by financial markets, but which here is lacking.

The reader will also have gathered that brand valuation has taken us to the boundaries of modern financial valuation techniques, which are based on the premise that the asset being valued can be considered a financial asset having all the characteristics normally associated with it (e.g., liquidity, exclusive ownership). Based on this premise, each asset of a company can be treated as a financial asset in isolation from the company's other resources, as in the weighted average return on assets (WARA) presented (see Chapter 11). This assumption implies that each asset has its own financial value, its own level of risk, and its own cost of capital. Many of the difficulties of brand valuation derive from this approach. A brand is essentially valuable because it is an asset that is intertwined with the company's other assets. It is therefore awkward to attempt to measure the value of this asset on its own. In the same way, it is difficult to determine the cost of capital of this asset in isolation.

The reader is now able to judge how appropriate the brand valuation methods that he or she may encounter in practice are. By dissecting these methods, as well as the *ad hoc* models proposed by certain firms, the aim of this book has been to enable the reader to find his or her way around these different methods, to examine them critically, and to adapt them to his or her own situation whilst being fully aware of their limitations.

References

Nakamura L. (2004), "A Trillion Dollars a Year in Intangible Investment and the New Economy", *Federal Reserve Bank of Philadelphia's Paper*, *in* Hand J.R.M. et Lev B., *Intangible Assets: Values, Measures, and Risks*, Oxford University Press, Oxford, pp. 19–47.

Srivastava A. and Tse S.Y. (2015), "Why Are Successive Cohorts of Listed Firms Persistently Riskier" *Working paper*.

Appendix 1

Cost of Capital

1. Definition of Cost of Capital

The cost of capital reflects the rate of return required by lenders and investors on money they have invested. The rate of return depends on two factors: the "time value of money", i.e., the remuneration for providing money over a period of time, and a "risk premium", which increases as the investment risk increases.

Traditionally the cost of capital is derived from the Capital Asset Pricing Model (CAPM).

$$K = r_f + \beta \times MRP, \tag{1}$$

where r_f = risk-free rate of return;
β = systematic risk of the investment;
MRP = market risk premium.

Not surprisingly, the CAPM equation includes the two components of cost of capital, the time value of money or risk-free rate of return (r_f), and the asset's risk premium ($\beta \times MRP$). As we shall see later, the first component is relatively straightforward.

The second component, which measures the risk of the investment, is more difficult to understand and to quantify, because the market risk premium used in CAPM does not correspond to the total risk of the asset. Total risk is the equivalent of the standard deviation of returns expected from a financial asset, also referred to as volatility (σ). CAPM is based on the financial theory of portfolio diversification. The theory assumes that any investor is easily able to reduce the risk of his portfolio by diversification. By including carefully selected financial assets, an investor can reduce the risk of his portfolio to an asymptotic level that represents the risk of the market as a whole. Therefore, when investing in a financial asset, an investor considers not the total risk of the asset, but the way in which it reflects the risk of the market as a whole (or systematic risk). This reasoning can be seen in the CAPM formula: beta (β) indicates either higher or lower volatility than the market, and the second factor (MRP) corresponds to the market risk for financial assets as a whole.

2. Estimating the Different Parameters of CAPM

The risk-free rate, r_f, is the expected yield on an asset which is not exposed to risk of default. The closest equivalent is the yield on bonds issued in a "strong" currency by a government considered to be solid (e.g., the United States, the United Kingdom, or Germany). The maturity date of the bond chosen must be similar to that used to estimate the market risk premium.

The beta (β) of an investment is a measure of the risk arising from exposure to general financial market variations (systematic risk), as opposed to specific factors ("idiosyncratic" or "specific" risk). Financial markets are represented theoretically as a portfolio comprising all types of assets (e.g., shares, bonds, property, commodities, precious metals, and derivative products). As we have said, beta measures the investment risk that cannot be reduced by diversification, i.e., systematic risk. Idiosyncratic risk can be diversified away (eliminated) in a portfolio containing a sufficient number of investments.

In practice, beta is obtained by linear regression of variations in the share price and variations in a benchmark (e.g., S&P 500, FTSE, Eurostoxx 600), which represents a theoretical market portfolio. The beta of an asset is equal to the ratio between the covariance of the return of an asset and the return of the market portfolio, as well as the variance of the market portfolio:

$$\beta_A = \frac{Cov(r_A, r_M)}{Var(r_M)}, \qquad (2)$$

where r_A = financial return on the share;
r_M = return on the benchmark representing the market;
$Cov(x, y)$ = covariance of variables x and y;
$Var(y)$ = variance of variable y.

A beta equal to one means that the share price varies in line with the market. A beta below one can mean two things: either that the asset price varies less than the market, i.e., the asset is relatively less volatile (e.g., government bonds), or that price variations are uncorrelated to the market (e.g., the price of gold). A beta above one means, on the contrary, that share price variations are greater than those of the market; in other words, the systematic risk of the share is high (e.g., large technology companies and businesses that are highly dependent on economic conditions).

When the investment being valued is not quoted, its beta is estimated by reference to betas of a sample of comparable quoted companies. To the extent that the beta of a quoted company is affected by financial leverage, the betas of comparable companies must be deleveraged.

There are a number of different formulae that model how financial leverage transfers risk between shareholders and creditors. As an example, Hamada's equation (1972) allows the unlevered beta of a company to be calculated from the observed beta of a share (levered) and vice versa:

$$\beta_L = \beta_U \, [1 + (1 - T) \times D/E], \tag{3}$$

$$\beta_U = \frac{\beta_L}{\left[1 + (1 - T) \times D / E\right]}, \tag{3bis}$$

where β_U = unlevered beta;
β_L = levered beta;
E = market value of equity financing;
D = market value of debt financing;
T = tax rate.

The market risk premium represents the additional return that an investor will require compared with the risk-free rate for investing in a risky asset rather than a risk-free asset. Different approaches are used to estimate the market risk premium: historical, forward-looking, or adjusted historical. The historical approach uses actual observed premiums over a long period of time to estimate a future expected premium (assumed to be constant). This approach is, however, open to criticism due to the high volatility of historical premiums. Under the forward-looking approach, an implicit market risk premium is deduced from forecast data on a sample of companies. The reliability of this method depends upon the quality of analysts' projections and on the extrapolation method used beyond the forecast period. The adjusted historical approach, developed in particular by Dimson *et al.* (2002), involves stripping out from historical premiums the impact of exceptional economic events (in particular speculative bubbles). The resulting market risk premium then lies within a range of 3.5% to 5.0%.

There are other models to estimate the cost of capital (Arbitrage Pricing Theory—APT, bond premium, dividend discount model—DDM, etc.), but most practitioners use the CAPM.

In practice, most valuers use the weighted average cost of capital (WACC) method, which is based on CAPM and also takes account of the tax shield on debt. This method, which is more complex to implement, is expressed by the following equation:

$$WACC = E \times k_E + (1 - t) \times D \times k_D, \tag{4}$$

where E = weight of equity in the capital structure;
k_E = cost of equity;

D = weight of debt in the capital structure;
k_D = pre-tax cost of debt;
t = tax rate.

WACC is the most widely used method to estimate the cost of capital. However, from an academic viewpoint, it is open to criticism. In particular, taking account of the individual risk to which each category of capital provider is exposed hides the fact that the overall risk of a business does not depend on how it is financed but only on the business itself. It is only the allocation of this risk among capital providers that varies according to the capital structure. The pre-tax cost of debt is lower than the cost of equity, because lenders are reimbursed ahead of shareholders. The default risk to which lenders are exposed is lower, so their risk is lower. If the total amount of debt increases, however, lenders are exposed to higher default risk, and the cost of debt will therefore increase. The only savings generated by higher debt is a tax savings, because interest paid is tax deductible, whilst dividends paid to shareholders are not. The WACC therefore only takes account of the positive effects of financial leverage (e.g., the debt tax shield) and ignores its negative impacts, such as loss of financial flexibility and monitoring costs.

In the end, it may be advisable to estimate the cost of capital using CAPM with an unlevered beta. This method has the dual advantage of being simpler and requiring fewer assumptions than the WACC model. From a theoretical point of view, it can be seen as more accurate. The equation to use is, therefore, the following:

$$k = r_f + \beta_A \times MRP, \tag{5}$$

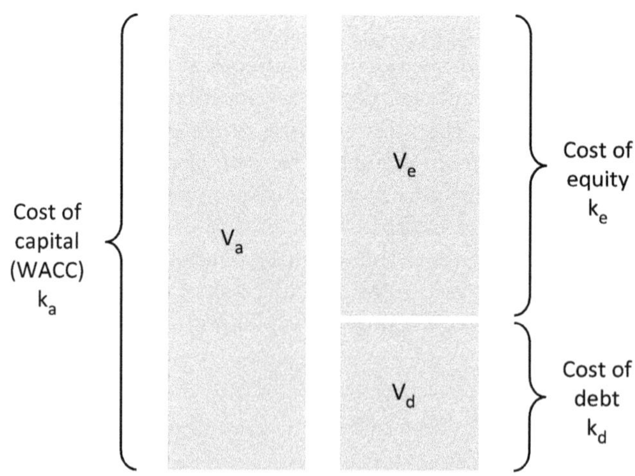

Figure A.1 Balance sheet and cost of capital.

where r_f = risk-free rate of return;
β_A = systematic risk of the business or sector;
MRP = market risk premium.

The only difficulty of this equation is to measure the business's beta. It is obtained by unlevering the beta of companies in the same sector by applying a formula such as equation (3bis) referred to earlier.

3. *Brand Cost of Capital*

Once the business's cost of capital has been estimated, the brand's cost of capital must be calculated. As discussed in Chapters 1 and 4, brands are thought by some to be inherently riskier than the overall business. On the other hand, others, and we tend to agree with them, consider that this distinction is meaningless and that a brand is only valuable because it is an asset intertwined with the other assets of the business (see Chapter 11).

In the end, the possible gap between the cost of capital of the business and that of the brand must be estimated on a case-by-case basis, depending on the brand (e.g., its age, its scope) and the context in which it is being valued.

4. *A Variety of Rates Which Should Not Be Confused*

In Chapter 2, we depicted a company balance sheet in its economic form (capital employed—capital invested). This presentation can also be used in terms of rates of return as shown in Figure A.1.

The different rates shown earlier respect the inequalities of equation (5). The risk-free rate of return is lower than the cost of debt, which is itself lower than the cost of equity. The weighted average cost of capital lies between the cost of debt and the cost of equity.

$$r_f < k_D < WACC < k_E, \tag{5}$$

where r_f = risk-free rate of return;
k_D = cost of debt;
$WACC$ = weighted average cost of capital;
k_E = cost of equity.

Appendix 2

Betas of the Main Industry Sectors

The beta of an investment measures the risk arising from exposure to general financial market movements (systematic risk). It is crucial because it has a direct impact on the cost of capital, which is used to discount the future cash flows generated by an asset such as a brand. The following table shows the levered and unlevered betas of major industry sectors given by the *Global Industry Classification Standard* developed by Morgan Stanley Capital International (MSCI) and Standard & Poor's (S&P).

Sectors with a beta (asset beta) lower than one have a lower exposure to systematic risk (e.g., consumer staples, telecoms, utilities) than those with a beta greater than one (e.g., information technology, capital goods, automobiles and components, and pharmaceuticals). The latter sectors are highly correlated with the market.

Table A.1 Median beta by industry sector (GICS)

Code	*Sector*	*Subcode*	*Industry Groups*	*Median Share Beta*	*Median Asset Beta*
10	Energy	1010	Energy	1.33	0.91
15	Materials	1510	Materials	0.96	0.91
		2010	Capital Goods	1.15	1.14
		2020	Commercial and Professional Services	0.84	0.76
20	Industrials	2030	Transportation	1.05	0.76
		2510	Automobiles and Components	1.25	1.16
		2520	Consumer Durables and Apparel	0.86	0.86
25		2530	Consumer Services	0.95	0.75
	Consumer Discretionary	2540	Media	0.97	0.63
		2550	Retailing	1.03	0.99

Code	*Sector*	*Subcode*	*Industry Groups*	*Median Share Beta*	*Median Asset Beta*
		3010	Food and Staples Retailing	0.75	0.61
		3020	Food, Beverage, and Tobacco	0.73	0.67
30	Consumer Staples	3030	Household and Personal Products	0.83	0.70
		3510	Health Care Equipment and Services	0.80	0.80
35	Health Care	3520	Pharmaceuticals, Biotechnology, and Life Sciences	0.94	1.02
		4010	Banks	0.54	ns
		4020	Diversified Financials	0.93	ns
		4030	Insurance	0.64	ns
40	Financials	4040	Real Estate	0.58	0.32
		4510	Software and Services	0.94	1.01
		4520	Technology Hardware and Equipment	0.99	1.07
45	Information Technology	4530	Semiconductors and Semiconductor Equipment	1.22	1.32
50	Telecommunications	5010	Telecommunication Services	0.92	0.63
55	Utilities	5510	Utilities	0.54	0.50

Sources: Compustat, CRSP. Median of annual betas calculated between 2008 and 2013 from 10,796 observations. Hamada's formula (1972) described earlier was used to calculate asset betas from share betas using year-end net debt and market capitalisation.

Appendix 3

Cost of Capital of the Main Industry Sectors

Based on the data in Appendix 2, the cost of capital of the main industry sectors is shown in Table A.2 for illustrative purposes.

Table A.2 Median cost of capital by industry sector (GICS)

Code	*Sector*	*Sub-code*	*Industry Groups*	*Risk-Free Rate*	*Asset Beta*	*MRP*	*Cost of Capital*
10	Energy	1010	Energy	3.5%	0.91	4.5%	**7.6%**
15	Materials	1510	Materials	3.5%	0.91	4.5%	**7.6%**
20	Industrials	2010	Capital Goods	3.5%	1.14	4.5%	**8.6%**
		2020	Commercial and Professional Services	3.5%	0.76	4.5%	**6.9%**
		2030	Transportation	3.5%	0.76	4.5%	**6.9%**
25	Consumer Discretionary	2510	Automobiles and Components	3.5%	1.16	4.5%	**8.7%**
		2520	Consumer Durables and Apparel	3.5%	0.86	4.5%	**7.4%**
		2530	Consumer Services	3.5%	0.75	4.5%	**6.9%**
		2540	Media	3.5%	0.63	4.5%	**6.3%**
		2550	Retailing	3.5%	0.99	4.5%	**8.0%**
30	Consumer Staples	3010	Food and Staples Retailing	3.5%	0.61	4.5%	**6.2%**
		3020	Food, Beverage, and Tobacco	3.5%	0.67	4.5%	**6.5%**
		3030	Household and Personal Products	3.5%	0.70	4.5%	**6.6%**

Code	*Sector*	*Sub-code*	*Industry Groups*	*Risk-Free Rate*	*Asset Beta*	*MRP*	*Cost of Capital*
35	Health Care	3510	Health Care Equipment and Services	3.5%	0.80	4.5%	**7.1%**
		3520	Pharmaceuticals, Biotechnology, and Life Sciences	3.5%	1.02	4.5%	**8.1%**
40	Financials	4010	Banks	3.5%	ns	4.5%	**ns**
		4020	Diversified Financials	3.5%	ns	4.5%	**ns**
		4030	Insurance	3.5%	ns	4.5%	**ns**
		4040	Real Estate	3.5%	0.32	4.5%	**5.0%**
45	Information Technology	4510	Software and Services	3.5%	1.01	4.5%	**8.0%**
		4520	Technology Hardware and Equipment	3.5%	1.07	4.5%	**8.3%**
		4530	Semiconductors and Semiconductor Equipment	3.5%	1.32	4.5%	**9.4%**
50	Telecommunications	5010	Telecommunication Services	3.5%	0.63	4.5%	**6.3%**
55	Utilities	5510	Utilities	3.5%	0.50	4.5%	**5.8%**

Sources: *Compustat, CRSP.*

Appendix 4

Taxation and Asset Revaluation: The Tax Amortisation Benefit

1. *What Is the Tax Amortisation Benefit?*

Valuation methods derived from the discounted cash flow approach focus on future cash flows earned by operating an asset. In practice, the owner of an asset can, in addition to these cash flows, benefit from a tax savings due to the tax deductibility of future amortisation charges of the asset. The valuation of the asset should then take account of this "Tax Amortisation Benefit" (TAB).

This idea originated in the United States where the FASB requires that the deductibility of amortisation charges of intangible assets revalued during a business combination be accounted for. TAB should only be accounted for when using a cash flow valuation method, because comparables methods already take into account all future expected earnings, including tax savings. Taking account of the TAB assumes that the amortisation of intangible assets is tax deductible. In practice, it is necessary to check that local tax legislation allows this deductibility.

The TAB can have a significant impact on the final valuation and can make up between 20% and 30% of the asset's pre-TAB value, depending upon the tax rate.

2. *Method of Calculation*

The post-TAB value (V_{POST}) of asset, which can be amortised for tax purposes over n years at a rate t, with a discount rate r and a pre-TAB value of V_{PRE}, is equal to:

$$V_{POST} = V_{PRE} + \text{TAB}, \tag{1}$$

where $TAB = t \times NPV$ (amortisation).

The annual amortisation charge is calculated as a linear amount: V_{POST}/n.

By discounting the tax savings at discount rate *r* over *n* years, we obtain for the post-TAB value of the asset:

$$V_{POST} = V_{PRE} + \sum_{t=1}^{n} \frac{V_{POST}}{n} \times t \times (1+r)^{-t}. \tag{2}$$

This equation is equivalent to equation (3),

$$V_{POST} = V_{PRE} + t \times \frac{V_{POST}}{n} \times \sum_{t=1}^{n} (1+r)^{-t}, \tag{3}$$

by simplifying as follows:

$$\sum_{t=1}^{n} (1+r)^{-t} = \frac{(1+r)^n - 1}{(1+r)^n \times r}. \tag{4}$$

We thus obtain equation (5), which gives the value of the intangible asset, including the tax benefits derived from theoretical amortisation charges:

$$V_{POST} = \frac{V_{PRE}}{1 - \frac{t}{n} \times \frac{(1+r)^n - 1}{(1+r)^n \times r}}. \tag{5}$$

By defining the adjustment to the asset's value as a result of TAB as V_{POST}/V_{PRE}, we obtain a "step-up" coefficient for TAB:

$$Step - up = \frac{1}{1 - \frac{t}{n} \times \frac{(1+r)^n - 1}{(1+r)^n \times r}}. \tag{6}$$

This step-up can be applied directly to the pre-TAB value obtained by the discounted cash flow method. As an illustration, for an asset amortised for tax over five years, owned by a company subject to a 30% tax rate, and using a discount rate of 10%, the step-up is 1.29.

References

Dimson E. Marsh P. and Staunton M. (2002), *Triumph of the Optimists: 101 Years of Global Investment Returns*, Princeton University Press, Princeton, New Jersey.

Hamada R.S. (1972), "The Effect of the Firm's Capital Structure on the Systematic Risk of Common Stocks" *The Journal of Finance*, Vol. 27, pp. 435–452.

Index

For Product Safety Concerns and Information please contact our EU
representative GPSR@taylorandfrancis.com
Taylor & Francis Verlag GmbH, Kaufingerstraße 24, 80331 München, Germany

www.ingramcontent.com/pod-product-compliance
Ingram Content Group UK Ltd.
Pitfield, Milton Keynes, MK11 3LW, UK
UKHW021959180926
475701UK00003B/99
9781138616899